MANAGEMENT DYNAMICS

CONCEPTS ON MANAGEMENT FOR A NEW CENTURY

SECOND EDITION

JANE R. FLAGELLO

SIMON & SCHUSTER CUSTOM PUBLISHING

Cover art: "Untitled," by Jan Lhomer.

Printed in the United States of America

10 9 8 7 6 5 4 3 2 1

Please visit our website at www.sscp.com

ISBN 0-536-01027-7
BA 97673

SIMON & SCHUSTER CUSTOM PUBLISHING
160 Gould Street/Needham Heights, MA 02194
Simon & Schuster Education Group

TABLE OF CONTENTS

Copyright Acknowledgments

Grateful acknowledgment is made to the following sources for permission to reprint material copyrighted or controlled by them:

"If I were the leader of a work group..." by J.W. Pfeiffer, reprinted from *What Kind of Leader Are You? Handbook of Structured Experiences*, Vol. 1, Jossey-Bass, Inc.

"The Evolutionary Vision of Dee Hock: From Chaos to Chaords," by Bonnie Durrance, reprinted with permission from *Training & Development*, April 1997, American Society for Training and Development. All rights reserved.

"The Unplanned Organization," by Margaret Wheatley, reprinted from *Noetic Sciences Review*, Spring 1996. Reprinted with permission of the publisher. All rights reserved.

"The Soul of the Hog," by Bob Filipczak, reprinted with permission from *Training*, February 1996. Copyright © 1996 by Lakewood Publications, Minneapolis, MN. All rights reserved. Not for resale.

"The Missing Piece in Reengineering," by Nicholas F. Horney and Richard Koonce, reprinted with permission from *Training & Development*, December 1995, American Society for Training and Development. All rights reserved.

"Group Genius," by Paul Roberts, reprinted from *Fast Company*, October/November 1997.

"The Citibank Private Bank's Portfolio Balancing Act," by William A. Brindley and Michael J. Bear, reprinted from *Journal of Business Strategy*, July-August 1997, Faulkner & Gray, Inc.

"Performance Appraisal: Can We 'Manage' Away the Curse?" by Chris Lee, reprinted with permission from *Training*, May 1996. Copyright © 1996 by Lakewood Publications, Minneapolis, MN. All rights reserved. Not for resale.

"Future Vision," by Michael A. Verespej, reprinted with permission from *Industry Week*, February 17, 1997. Copyright by Penton Publishing, Inc., Cleveland, Ohio.

"Parables of Leadership," by W. Chan Kim and Renee A. Mauborgne, reprinted with permission from *Harvard Business Review*, July-August 1992. Copyright © 1992 by President and Fellows of Harvard College. All rights reserved. Further copying without permission of Harvard Business School Publishing is prohibited.

TOMORROW'S WORLD

The challenge before all of us is great. The events of today will be realized tomorrow in a world of changed traditions in the national, political, social and economic arenas. Technological boundaries are altered daily and real-time communication networks bring all of us closer together as our differences compete to keep us apart. Tomorrow belongs to all of us, to each of you. Tomorrow will open opportunities to all who are ready, willing, and able to accept them.

The workforce needed to compete effectively tomorrow requires different skills and abilities than those required from a past generation. This statement does not only refer to new, increasingly sophisticated technical skills, but more important, to the softer skills associated with management, leadership, human relations, teamwork, and power. The future will belong to those organizations who can "engage the full efforts and capabilities of their employees" (Lawler, 1992). It follows from this statement that the future will belong to those individuals who are capable of continuous personal learning and development, who are self-motivated, self-led, and self-managed, and finally, to individuals who see themselves as full contributing partners in an ongoing drama called work—called life.

WHERE ARE WE NOW?

Management fads seem to come and go as quickly as many of the fashions of today's world. Books about management line the shelves of retailers and sell by the thousands. Open any one of these and you become hard pressed to tell one from the other.

Yet, when you talk to the people involved—the executives, the managers and the workers—the frustration within the workplace continues to grow. With all the words written to date about how to manage, why haven't we seen more real change in the behavior of the vast majority of organizations and the subsequent behaviors of the employees of those organizations? Where is corporate loyalty and, if it is truly dead, what replaces it? Where is the balance between work life and personal life? Why are so many young people increasingly cynical about their future prospects? What will employees need to do to earn their daily bread in the global village?

Management by Objective

Theory X/Theory Y/Theory Z

Participative Management

Total Quality Management

Learning Organizations

Reengineering

Chaos Theory

Co-Opetition

THE FUTURE OF MANAGEMENT

Future managers will no longer be people who "watch other people work," but rather people who create, coach and enable others as well as themselves to work to their optimum potential. As Matejka and Dunsing (1995) clearly emphasize, ". . . well-developed, strong, centered and capable individual managers who can deftly move among projects, groups, and organizations are critical to our global future" (p. 184). The goal of Management Dynamics is to have learners recognize that, although they may not have a formal title designation as a "manager," they need to effectively utilize managerial skills in order to be successful today and tomorrow. The challenge is to discuss management from a future-based, more proactive perspective, hoping to enable learners to begin to incorporate new skills and techniques into their current daily routines. It becomes important for all people who work to become active students of management; to continually learn about and incorporate new processes to improve their individual performance and their contribution to their respective organizations.

LEARNER ROLES AND GOALS

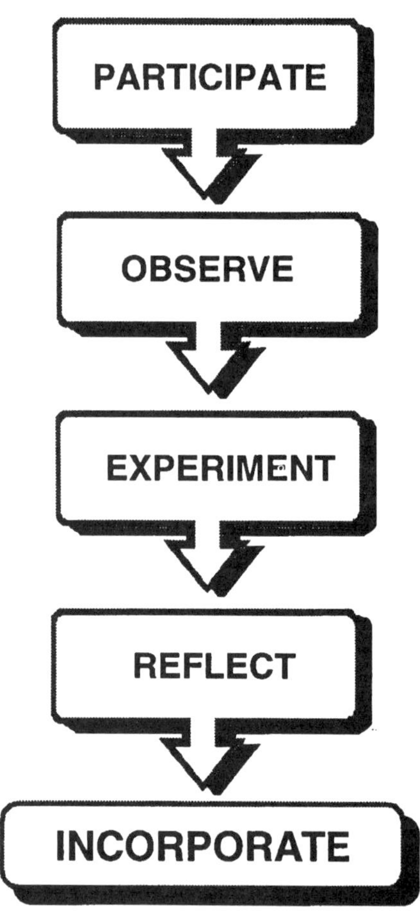

Participation asks the student to be "present" during class. A large percentage of learning in this course takes place in the classroom. This is an activity-based learning program.

Observer becomes the second critical role that the student must play. The learner must watch what is happening to others as the activities take place. Look for patterns of behavior and a variety of different attitudes to emerge and see how these impact the activity.

Learners should also experiment with new roles and behaviors to see how they fit and feel. Try to lead during one activity and take a follower role in another. Act like a disgruntled employee might during a third activity to see the reaction from the group and how well the group performs and achieves the activity outcome.

Learners are asked to think about and reflect on class activities and the readings in this book to better understand how each one relates to the business setting.

The hard part is changing behaviors. Hopefully, this process will lead to learners incorporating new behaviors and actions into their daily routines.

FOCUS ON THE PEOPLE . . . & THE PROFITS WILL FOLLOW !

Unlike many management courses that offer more quantitative methods and linear, rational, step-by-step processes and approaches to organizational management, this course will focus on the people side of the organization. A good (bad?) manager can make the "numbers" do and say almost anything he or she wants them to say. A full appreciation for the importance of the numbers is critical and it would be foolish to push the idea that they are meaningless.

> If you feel that you add value, contribute something meaningful or bring a unique skill or talent to the group, then your desire (motivation) to continue to work hard for this group will be high.

The numbers, however, cannot fix what is broken in today's workplace—the spirits, the hearts, the souls of the people involved. Everything begins and ends with the people directly involved. In any operation, company, family, or community organization, the results achieved will be directly (hard to prove this by the numbers) related to how each individual perceives himself/herself as a member of that operation, company, family or community. If you feel that you add value, contribute something meaningful or bring a unique skill or talent to the group, then your desire (motivation), to continue will be high. If you feel or realize no benefit from your efforts, (both tangible and non-tangible), those efforts will be diminished.

The human side, with all its idiosyncrasies and foibles, drives everything else. Many organizations now easily spout the cliché that "people are our most important asset." This is probably becoming one of the most overused phrases of the nineties. Unfortunately, actions speak louder than words (another old cliché) and there are still too many organizations whose actions simply do not square with the idea of people as important assets. Besides, as defined by the *American Heritage Dictionary,* an asset is "a valuable item that is owned." Many employees probably have a problem swallowing the idea of being "owned" by their organizations, regardless of the status of their bills and personal debt!

On a more serious note, most if not all of the programs designed to improve quality, competitiveness, productivity, and profits (the numbers!) start with the people who do the work. If their hearts and souls are not fully engaged in the tasks at hand, the required levels of competitiveness, productivity, quality and profits will not be achieved on a continual and long-term basis.

Yes, you can "motivate" (this will be argued later) people through carrot-and-stick incentive programs for the short haul, but not to the extent needed to produce world-class organizational success. Treat the people *right* (read fairly, honestly, with trust and integrity) and the numbers will follow.

PARADIGMS OF MANAGEMENT

New Views of Workplace 2000

Managerial Skills

Evolution of Management Theories

Change Management

LEARNING OBJECTIVES

After completing the course work in the *Paradigms of Management* module, the student should be able to:

- define management and its importance in any organization,
- analyze the key managerial skills that employees need to be effective managers in complex settings,
- diagram and discuss the historical development of management thought,
- debate the changing nature of the management process as it continues to meet the needs of a dynamic global reality,
- demonstrate through individual actions the integration of empowerment principles into daily work activities with the goal of developing effective employer/employee partnership work habits.

NEW VIEWS OF WORKPLACE 2000

There is no such thing as "business as usual" and, with the passing of that phrase, went the death of the control-based organization. Today and tomorrow will be times of uncertainty, of problems without precedent, requiring adaption, flexibility, and individual responsibility. The business community is moving forward in its integration of the historic values of individualism, innovation, teamwork, democracy, and competition that founded this country and made it great.

Those organizations that are creating structures that encourage their employees to empower themselves, create exciting, continuous learning environments, remove blame and other defensive behaviors, and encourage individual and organizational responsibility, are the organizations that will be the survivors and the news makers of the next century.

Even with ever-improving technology, the average worker spends more than 40 hours per week on the job. Overtime, sometimes required, and commuting bring the total of job-related activities to more than 45 hours per week.

Over 40% of workers have experienced downsizing and close to 1 in 5 fear they too will be fired or laid off.

Workers who have changed employers within the last 5 years reported that environment, communication, and the quality of management were key factors in their decision process.

More than 50% of workers reported success at work as being directly related to the personal satisfaction they gain in doing a good job.

Over 40% of workers feel "used up" by the end of a workday.

Over 25% of workers have seen cutbacks in managerial positions in the past year.

National Study of the Changing Workforce (1993).

THE MASKS OF COMMAND

For over one hundred years now, scholars and academicians have been trying to define, describe, evaluate, and control those activities that people do when they initiate processes that truly result in desired outcomes. Profiles of companies who successfully accomplish their goals fill the pages of business periodicals. Companies currently on a list of "successfuls" include General Electric, Herman Miller, 3M, Hewlett Packard, Motorola, Microsoft, W. L. Gore, Nordstrom, and Southwest Airlines, but who knows what will happen tomorrow? The key players who now lead and have led these "successful" organizations are interviewed repeatedly, but the formula or description of what specifics constitute the total range of parameters that make these organizations successful continues to be an elusive rascal.

"It" has been described as an organic system, an open system, as flexible and adaptive, participative, involved, customer-oriented, value-added, projectized, quality-centered, reengineered, and empowered to enumerate many of the descriptive terms that get tossed about. What becomes clear when you read about or examine many of these companies is that there is no one **"it."** There is no one best approach to effective management, but a myriad of right things that get done consistently, and over time, produce incredible, enviable results.

Management is a unique phenomenon in all of its permutations. As employees, we know **"it"** when we see and experience **"it"** being done well and we appreciate **"it"** in this permutation. Alas, we also know **"it"** when we see and experience **"it"** being done poorly and in this permutation **"it"** zaps motivation, productivity and energy from all involved.

Fortune magazine (Dumaine, May, 1995) recently identified a set of key principles that should enable any organization to achieve its goals. These included acknowledging management as a practice as Drucker defined it in the mid-1950s, recognizing people as resources not costs, seeing marketing and innovation as key functions, the ability of individuals to discover what they each do well, and finally, the principle that quality pays for itself.

And in a telling story about the workplace today, a recent survey of professional men and women found that 89% felt stressed in their jobs and related that stress directly to their bosses. Clearly, the study of management and learning how to effectively manage is a critical need in the workplace.

OLD VIEW >>>>>> LOYALTY = SECURITY

NEW VIEW >>>>>> SECURITY = EMPLOYABILITY

PERSONAL REFLECTION

What will your role, your place, be in the companies of tomorrow?

Are you really preparing to become an employee of the future or are your outdated perceptions of a work world now nonexistent holding you prisoner?

Have you developed the self-management skills and goal-setting techniques necessary to enable you to be a strong, contributing member of a twenty-first century organization or do you still require another person to watch you, monitor your activities, and tell you what to do?

Are your expectations of your future based on solid plans that you are actively achieving and fulfilling or are you dreaming of unearned riches that will never be?

Organizations

"An organization is a human group, composed of specialists, working on a common task. Organizations do. The function of organizations is to make knowledge productive."

Peter Drucker,
Post-Capitalist Society, page 49

"We are beginning to recognize organizations as systems; . . . conscious entities, possessing many of the properties of living systems.

Margaret Wheatley
Leadership and the New Science, page 13

". . . stable patterns of social interaction . . . to accomplish one or another set of shared purposes."

John W. Gardner
On Leadership, page 60

"An organization is not a mob. It may be nicely participative, but not democratic. It is hierarchical by necessity, but everything else is by choice, chance, indifference, or neglect."

Theodore Levitt
Thinking about Management, page 42

Management

"is the process of planning, organizing, leading, and controlling the work of others toward achieving organizational goals"

traditional management textbooks

"is the art of getting things done through other people."

Mary Parker Follett

"is manipulation carried to the point that subordinates are not supposed to be aware of the fact that they are being manipulated."

Abraham Zaleznik
referring to another's ideas

"was rank and power."

Peter Drucker, circa 1945

"the application of knowledge to knowledge."

Peter Drucker, 1993

Managers

"are individuals in organizations who get work done through other people."

traditional management textbook

"think about the purposes of the organization and the directions in which it must be led; foster and manage change; and conducive operations so that the organization and its people function effectively and efficiently."

Theodore Levitt

"one who is responsible for the application and performance of knowledge."

Peter Drucker

MANAGERIAL SKILLS

Managers utilize a full repertoire of skills in a variety of settings. These skills develop over time through a unique combination of knowledge or information, practice, and evaluation which leads to increased knowledge, more information, more practice, and continuing evaluation.

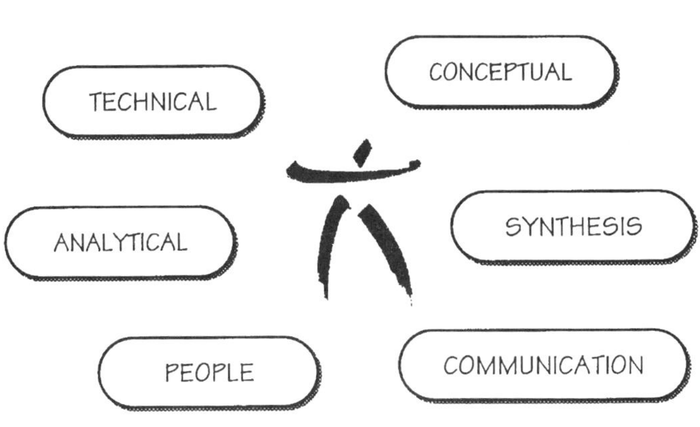

Some people may be tempted to "pass" on the relevance of management skill development, seeing it as "common sense." This thinking cannot be further from the truth. Management is something that each person participates in every day, whether it be managing time, managing schedules, managing relationships, or managing money.

See if you can match the type of managerial skill shown above with its meaning.

_______________ Ability to interact and relate effectively with a variety of other people.

_______________ Ability to perform a specific task or grouping of tasks; an area of expertise.

_______________ Ability to visualize or "see" the whole, understand basic theories or ideas, or the ability to bring ideas to mind; mentally bringing parts into focus as a whole or complete understanding.

_______________ Ability to break concepts into discrete elements for study.

_______________ Ability to convey and exchange ideas and thoughts in a coherent manner through a variety of mediums (oral, written, nonverbal).

_______________ Ability to bring elements together to form a whole.

PERSONAL REFLECTION

Where are *you?* Your ability to assess the current status of your skills in these key managerial skill areas will be important to your success. Ask yourself if your skills are values to be offered to an employer or weaknesses that you need to work on during your schooling.

PARADIGM CHANGE

The word paradigm seems to be another one of these new words that are being tossed around lately. What actually is a paradigm?

The word comes to us from the scientific community. Thomas Kuhn (1962) wrote that a *paradigm* is a term that denotes "models from which spring particular coherent traditions of scientific research" (p.10). In this group he included such theories as Aristotelian dynamics, Newtonian dynamics, Ptolemaic astronomy. All of these were models of scientific research that provided the framework or model for future research.

We all have paradigms about how we live our lives. Think about the traditions or rules that surround holiday celebrations at your home. Who sits where? Who carves the turkey? What foods get served when? Spring means baseball to many people and fall starts the "new" year because children start a new year at school.

School itself is a paradigm. Think about how knowledge is passed in school. This is a paradigm of the highest order. As school choice, voucher systems, and other innovative educational strategies become more prevalent, and prove more successful, the struggle to reframe the paradigm of what it means to provide education to a generation of children heats an emotional debate with no end in sight.

Our topic is management and management too has its paradigms: models of how things have always been done in the past and, therefore, should be done for ever more. Today, many people in business recognize that the old methods are no longer bringing the desired results and new models are being fervently sought to fill the void. Alas, the management community moves into "flavor of the month management." Whatever the latest buzzword or fad, managers hungry for answers to complexities beyond their wildest imaginations, and longing for the good old days of stability and security, jump on board.

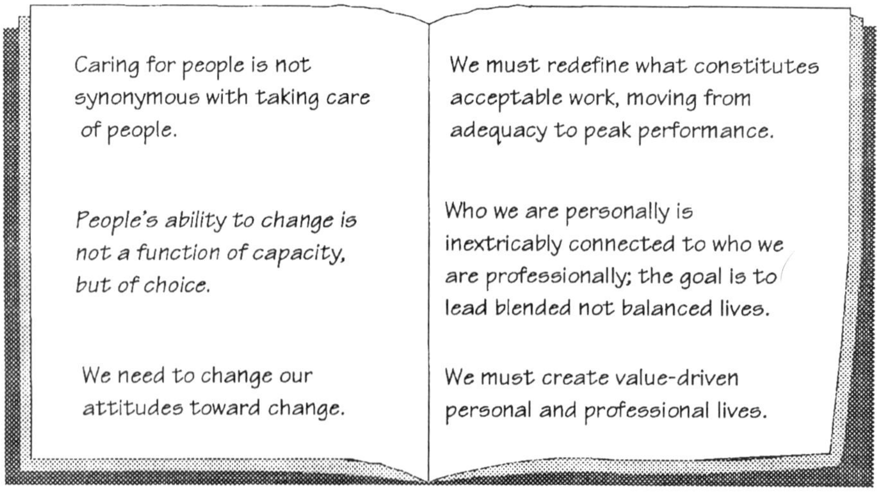

Shectman, *Working Without a Net,* 1994

The two paradigm changes that are presented next dramatically show the dimensions of the issues at hand. They do not simply refer to new work rules or policies that can be easily implemented, but rather to changes required at the very core (heart?) of a person's belief and value system about work and the role that work plays in one's life outside of work.

PARADIGM SHIFT #1

The first paradigm change that must be understood is that between a partnership model of work and a power or command and control model of work.

PARTNERSHIP MODEL

The new workplace will be one of partnership between employers and employees. The new workplace will be an empowered workplace for all involved. But in order for the new workplace to become an empowered workplace, and in order for employees and employers to create dynamic partnerships, several changes must take place. New levels of personal vision, power, responsibility, accountability, and trust will be required of everyone. Management must move from a hierarchical position slot to a personal action. To prepare for these changed levels of commitment will require many adults to rethink work and its role in their lives.

COMMAND & CONTROL MODEL

For years, companies have created divisions of power and control in the name of efficiency. In the workplace one finds divided "houses" of workers, managers, and senior managers, with different goals and different agendas that seem to be in constant conflict. The contract between the employer and employee was a paternalistic illusion built on a premise that the company would "take care of" the employee if the employee worked hard, kept his/her nose clean and followed the rules. Health benefits, a job for life, vacation time, promotion possibilities, steady pay increases, and sick pay were some of the trappings that lured employees into states of silent compliance. Work was nine to five, Monday to Friday and weekends were life. Work interrupted weekends. Work interrupted life.

There is clear evidence today that companies cannot fill the role of the eternal parent, taking care of employees' needs. As an example, one need only remember the wave of recent corporate restructuring that left many employees without needed health insurance. The expectation of the company always being there, of the company *acting as parent* and providing these benefits fell apart. Employees had acquiesced on responsibilities that they implicitly knew were their responsibilities. The comfort of the promise of being taken care of was too powerful a lure for many to deny.

These roles and divisions can no longer contain the spirit of an emerging employee prototype nor are they accurate depictions of dynamic organizations meeting the challenges of a changing work world. Depending on where one sits on the economic ladder, the following statement may be hard to accept, but research has continually shown that many people are looking for more from work than just a paycheck. Yankelovich noted a shift from an "instrumental" view of work as a means to an end, to a view that links work with a person's higher aspirations (Senge, 1990, p. 5). Once past the subsistence level, today's employees want challenging work, meaningful tasks.

Where initially people might take a job for a salary (money to pay those bills), job security or advancement opportunities (both illusions), as these needs are satisfied (and, with planning, they do get satisfied) people are realizing that a job, a career, a life must be more, provide more. There have been several articles about Generation X, the generation following the baby boomers, that have highlighted the desire of this group to have more balance in their lives, be in more control of their comings and goings, as a generation not tied to the corporate apron strings. Rather than linking individual identity to the company one might work for, employees are finding meaning in the actual work that they do.

This changes the control and power relationship of an organization *over* its employees. It is time to bring these groups together. There must be a unification within the workplace. It must become a place of shared commitment, shared responsibility, and shared rewards. Peter Block wrote about this in his recent book, *Stewardship*, and other management and business leaders have taken up the task of changing the mental model that employees and employers have about their relationship and their responsibilities to one another.

PERSONAL REFLECTION

Take a few minutes to reflect on the two different models of employer/employee interaction that were described above—the partnership model and the command/control model.

On the following page, create a "balance sheet" diagram. Write down what you see as the advantages/positives and the disadvantages/negatives of each management model of work.

Which model does your current employer practice? What specific norms, behaviors, or actions do you experience or do you observe that support your opinion?

Which model do you prefer? ______________________________

Give 2 reasons why this model is your preference. ______________________________

____

Do you have the skills that this model would require? Which skills do you need to work on developing to be successful in the model you chose?

PARTNERSHIP MODEL VERSUS COMMAND & CONTROL MODEL

Advantages/Positives

Advantages/Positives

Disadvantages/Negatives

Disadvantages/Negative

Putting the "POWER" in Partnership

Most people have not been taught to think in "partnership" terms. To many, partnerships are formal, contractual agreements that spell out every detail of the business arrangement, lest anything be left to chance that might come back to haunt one at a later time.

To really begin to understand the power that being in partnership with another person can offer, and to reap the quantum benefits that a solid partnership can bring to the relationship, perhaps it is time to broaden your understanding of partnership and learn what you have to begin to change about how you think and operate in order to become an effective partner.

P*ersonal* This is about *you*—who you are—your investment in the development of your own character (trust, integrity). Your commitment to be a certain type of person, to act from a certain conviction and to choose like-minded associates creates the foundation of your personal power. From a solid foundation here, all else becomes possible.

O*pen* Being open enables a two-way information flow. It defuses defensive routines that inhibit open action. If you always must first protect yourself, it is difficult to grow and to make things happen. Openness is about respect, first self-respect, then other-respect. It sometimes necessitates acknowledging that information exists that must remain unshared. To be open is to be vulnerable and in that vulnerability there lies incredible strength.

W*in–Win* Winning is more than achieving a desired outcome. It is about what goes on during the process of the interaction. The real "win" in a partnership only comes when the continuation of the relationship is paramount. Thinking win–win requires creativity. The ability to find new solutions so that everyone gets what they want is at the heart of the win–win mind set.

E*nergy* The energy of "more than one" creates the sum that is stronger in unity than any of its parts. It is the synchronicity of the individual force united, that raises the partnership to heights impossible to achieve alone, no matter how great the individual accomplishment may appear to be.

R*elationship* Everything is about relationship. Nothing really exists in isolation. The power of the partnership comes from the bonds of the relationship that endures, evolves, and strengthens in the face of triumph and defeat.

THE GREAT COW HUNT!

Before organizations are able to make any real changes in their operations, they must go on a sacred cow hunt. Sacred cows, as defined by Robert Kriegel, in a book called *Sacred Cows Make the Best Burgers*, are "all those hallowed practices, unnecessary rules, and outdated policies that don't work anymore" (Kriegel and Brant, 1996).

The idea that things must continue to be done the way they have always been done does not work in today's fast paced world. Management knows this at some intellectual level, but often has trouble really acting on this knowledge—getting rid of the sacred cows is difficult. Often it is the sacred cows that are getting in the way of real change initiatives and real progress.

Examine the organization where you work. How many of these sacred cows can you find alive and well and in need of extermination?

THE PAPER COW

Although technology enhances operations, many companies still require a vast amount of paper documentation and reports. Often these go unread!

TECHNO-COW

Technology was supposed to free up time, make companies and their employees more efficient. Does your company get caught up in technology and leave the customer out in the cold?

OTHER SACRED COWS TO HUNT—

The Downsizing Cow
The Low-Price Cow
The No-Mistakes Cow
The Speed Cow
The Cash Cow
The Competitive Cow

THE MEETING COW

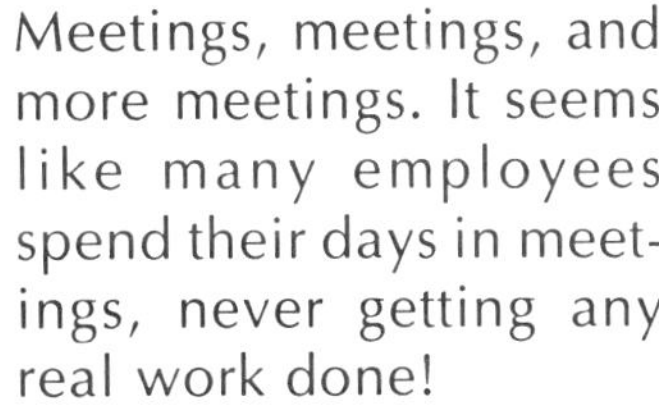

Meetings, meetings, and more meetings. It seems like many employees spend their days in meetings, never getting any real work done!

CUSTOMER SATISFACTION COW

Don't merely satisfy your customers—delight them—surprise them—make them your personal word-of-mouth advertising agency!

EVOLUTION OF MANAGEMENT THEORIES

> Those who cannot remember the past are condemned to repeat it.
>
> George Santayana

You may be wondering at this point in our discussion of management how organizations got to where they are today. We know that everything has an evolutionary path. Organizations are no different. The times, the circumstances, the challenges of the day have always led the way. Before moving on to the second major paradigm shift, let's take a side trip, a brief excursion down memory lane of management theory. For it is in our past successes and mistakes that we discover our future possibilities.

To begin this adventure into the past one must understand that although work had been "organized" or managed to some degree throughout time, with some people doing one task and other people doing other tasks, it was not until the Industrial Revolution that processes were sought to make workers efficient and effective. As people flocked to the cities to work in factories, the owners of these factories began to realize that these "human" resources would have to be put to work in extremely efficient settings to provide for the needs of an expanding industrialized society.

Some of these managers were harsh and brutal taskmasters which led to the exploitation of children, immigrants, and women in these factories. This then led to the formation of unions and the beginnings of many of the protective labor laws that we now take for granted. Other owners recognized that the people that labored in their factories were key resources needed to create the products and services they offered, and these owners tried to provide a more humane environment for these workers.

In a rational world there are rules, processes, procedures, and policies that, when applied and diligently followed, ensure predetermined successful outcomes in a host of different management situations. The 1950s and 1960s in America appeared to many people as just such a rational world. Corporate America was humming after World War II ended and there was a hunger for new products and services, single family homes, and more education that seemed like it would never end. Efficiency, coordination, each person to a specialized job worked in these "predictable" days just as these concepts had worked throughout the Industrial Revolution. There was no reason to suggest that perhaps the times were not what they appeared to be. The world was viewed as America's marketplace and the profits earned by American corporations were the clear evidence that everything was working fine.

> Enter management not only as theory and as science, but as art and as illusion.

Alas, every bubble has its bursting point as did this one. We see these bubbles bursting all around us, every day, as corporations see through the illusions and myths of success they thought would last forever, and come to terms with a fundamental truth. The world is not rational. It is that simple. Our attempts to manage our organizations (ranging from a business to the local church to the family) with a logical, rational, and consistent game plan appear to be falling short.

Today, companies run the full range from taskmasters to benevolent dictators to partners. What tomorrow will bring in the form of managerial approaches will depend on the innovative and creative talents of employees and employers, and how each group sees its role in the creation of wealth for an individual, an organization, a community, a society, a world.

To present the progression of management thought effectively, two diagrams have been provided. First, a chart has been designed to help students visualize the movement from the quest for pure scientific efficiency through the awakening realization that this needed to be blended with more humanistic components. These two elements exist at opposite ends of a work continuum.

The mechanistic end of the work continuum represents an environment that is rigid, highly structured and formal. It is not adaptive to the changing needs of customers, products or services, and/or employees. This structure promotes efficiency first. There is little interaction between levels of employees, decisions are made at the top, and employees are very dependent on their supervisors.

The organic organization emphasizes flexibility and is highly adaptive to the dynamic work environment that exists today. Interaction and communication are ongoing and employees are involved and responsible throughout the organization. Decision making is encouraged at all levels. The organic organization is able to change and be more responsive to the fast changes in the marketplace.

TIME LINE OF MANAGEMENT THEORY EVOLUTION

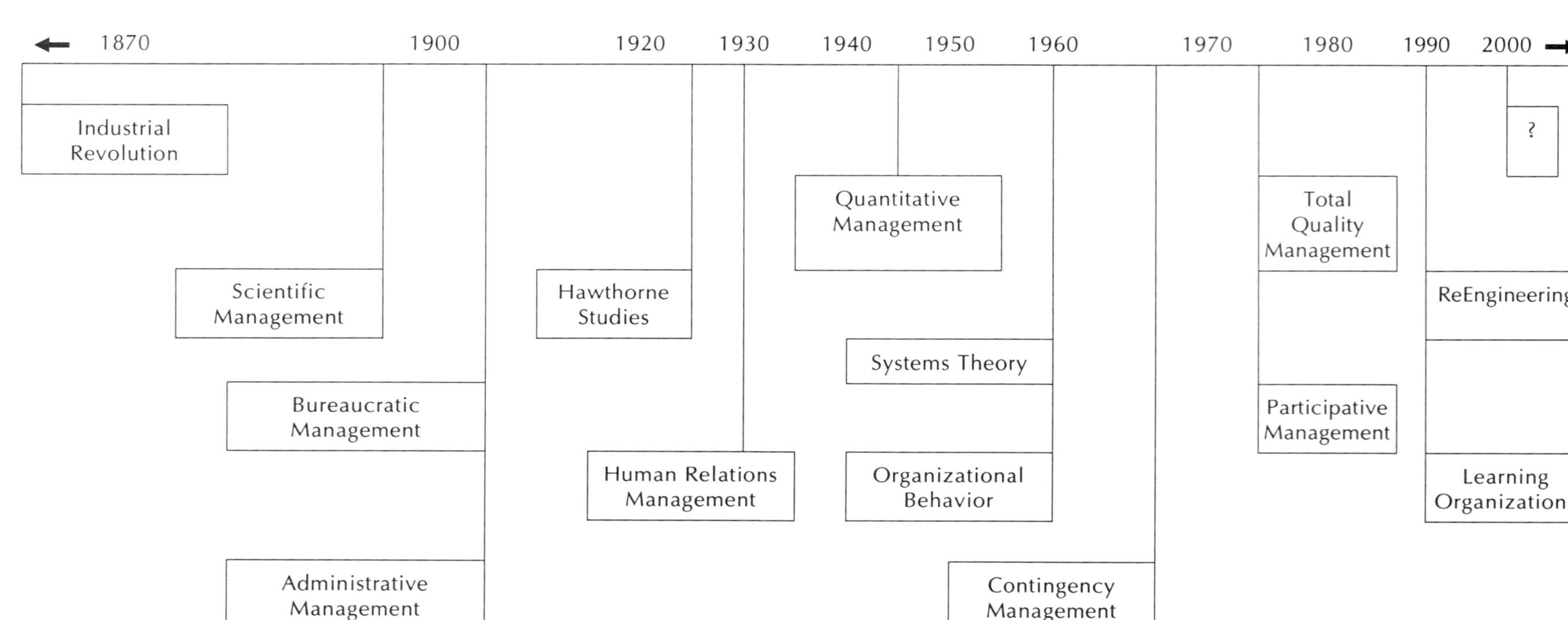

APPROACH	MAJOR THEORIES	KEY PEOPLE	BASIC TENETS	■ CONTRIBUTIONS ❑ LIMITATIONS
Classical	Scientific Management	Frederick W. Taylor	➤ Focused on management of the work itself ➤ Efficiency was key; performed time and motion studies ➤ Apply "scientific principles" to work to increase productivity ➤ Specialization; find out "best" way to do job ➤ Incentive pay; piece work pay	■ Developed many of the current ideas about scheduling and production processes ■ Ideas about incentive pay still being used today ■ Many organizations still use bureaucratic approaches very effectively ■ Described management as planning, organizing, directing, and controlling ❑ Did not pay attention to human/people issues ❑ Did not understand psychological and social factors of motivation as important aspects of the work environment ❑ Better when environment is stable and predictable ❑ Seen as too simplistic today and not responsive to dynamically changing marketplace
	Bureaucratic Management	Max Weber	➤ Concentrated on the structure of the company ➤ Specific authority hierarchy ➤ Very formal rules, procedures, and policies ➤ Specialization of labor	
	Administrative Management	Henri Fayol	➤ Concentration on division of work into planning, organizing, directing, and controlling ➤ Management was a profession that could be taught ➤ Emphasized senior management's role in establishing organization's purpose, hiring, and maintaining communications	
Behavioral	Human Relations	Mary Parker Follett Chester Barnard	➤ Focused on individuals working in group settings ➤ Organizations are groups of people who have interacting social relationships ➤ Coordination of group achieved real control, not power over people	■ Encourages managers to take human and people issues into consideration ■ Shows that employees are motivated by more than economic factors ■ Exposed workplace as a social system with formal and informal patterns of authority and communication ■ Brought balance to Classical theories with recognition of human element ❑ Manipulation became an influencing technique ❑ Can lead to oversimplified views of managing and motivating employees
	Behavioral Sciences	Elton Mayo	➤ Hawthorne Studies ➤ Led to examination of social relationships and the work group ➤ Uncovered informal norm-based rules of behavior	
	Acceptance Theory of Authority	Chester Barnard	➤ Focused on building cooperative systems where individuals worked for the good of the organization ➤ Authority only comes from the willingness of subordinates to accept it and respond to it.	

Contemporary	Quantitative Operations Research Management Science	Herbert Simon Robert McNamara	➤ Evolved after World War II ➤ Focus on problem solving and decision making using mathematical models and statistics ➤ Rational orientation ➤ Computer simulations and optimization models showed how to increase efficiency	■ Made for efficient use of resources ■ Contributed to the development of a more sophisticated decision making process ■ Used a wide variety of tools for problem solving ❑ Not good with non-routine or unpredictable situations ❑ Neglects unquantifiable information ❑ Human issues hard to quantify
	Systems Theory	Ludwig Von Bertalanfly Kenneth Boulding	➤ Organization is a system of interrelated and interdependent parts; a very holistic view ➤ Open System is dynamic and responds to its environment ➤ Closed System is not influenced by and does not interact with its environment ➤ Balance of efficiency with effectiveness	■ Stresses importance of seeing organizations as entities that do interact with outside forces ■ Actions in one place may have consequences elsewhere ■ Concept of synergy ❑ No specific guidelines on duties of managers
	Organizational Behavior	Douglas McGregor Chris Argyris	➤ Continuation and extension of Human Relations school ➤ More than satisfaction of social system needs ➤ Must understand individual, group, and organization to effectively achieve goals	■ Increased participation of all employees ■ Built on Theory Y assumptions ■ Importance of individual development to enhance organization as a whole ❑ Can get too caught up in individual aspects
	Situational/ Contingency	Fred Fiedler	➤ Situation variables must be assessed and then appropriate actions chosen that "fit" those variables ➤ There is NO one best way to manage	■ Provides needed flexibility and adaptability ■ Encourages individual analysis of issues as they occur ❑ Used as an excuse for not developing a depth of knowledge about management ❑ Can't possibly provide contingencies for all situations
	Total Quality Management	W. Edwards Deming	➤ Promotes high quality work all of the time ➤ Looks to systems and processes for causes of errors ➤ Continuous improvement	■ More cost effective in the long run ■ Promotes management and employees working together ❑ Definitions of quality differ ❑ Still evolving with many ideas competing for space
	ReEngineering	Michael Hammer James Champy	➤ Start with a clean field and ask how company would look ➤ Not incremental, quantum	■ Many companies have made tremendous progress ■ Improves key efficiencies ❑ Forgot about the people part resulting in low morale, downsizing, and lay-offs

WHAT NOW ?????

Hopefully, the charts you have just studied have given you a sense of where management has been and why it is so important to understand this bit of history. What should be evident is that effective management is a delicate balance between effectiveness and efficiency, between people and processes, between management and leadership. Every time management has skewed its efforts too much in the direction of increased productivity at the expense of the employee relationship, or focused on the employee without the requisite attention to results, the balance above falls apart. The outcomes have proven to be less than what was desired.

Management today constitutes the effective implementation of many concepts that integrate an increased awareness and recognition of the importance of blending productivity with building strong employee relationships. This is where understanding concepts and realities about partnership become truly significant. Partners work together to achieve common, desired outcomes. The partnership model exists when there is balance between efforts to become as productive as possible with efforts to develop a "humane" environment. The ideas inherent in total quality management, empowerment, participative management, Theory Y, Theory Z, and reengineering all require a committed cadre of employees working together to achieve mutually desired results.

This is the organization of the future, the one Tom Peters (1994) calls "the organization of businesspeople-entrepreneurs." This is where all members of the workforce today must target their energies—learning how to become an individually collaborative and contributing member of an integrated conglomerate of other individually collaborative and contributing members. Much of the focus of this management course will be to assist students in assessing their current skill level to become an individually collaborative contributor and then to present opportunities to develop and enhance those needed skills.

PERSONAL REFLECTION

When students begin to read about the different theories of management they often start to recognize these theories played out on the stage they call their company.

Which of the theories is used by your manager? What specifics can you identify that support your choice?

How about your organization as a whole? Which of the theories are at work in the ongoing functioning of the company where you work?

If you owned a business, which of the theories just presented would you choose to use? Why? If you decide on more than one, which would you use in what types of circumstances?

ON TO EMPOWERMENT!

Empowerment is the new "E" word. Overused and not understood, the concept has suffered greatly and is in need of quick attention before it too joins the ranks of buzzwords too soon forgotten.

PARADIGM SHIFT #2

Empowerment is the second major paradigm shift that must take place. Organizations are looking for a few good employees: employees who do not need to be supervised, who can think and solve problems, who take risks and accept responsibility, who do more than "just enough to get by," and who are looking for environments in which to become active, contributing members of an exciting enterprise. The birth of the knowledge century is at hand. For those who are mentally ready and educationally prepared to play a role, there will be high-involvement: enthusiastically committed business communities where the hard work and success of members will be recognized and rewarded. For those not prepared, there will be bitterness, blame, envy, and despair.

Real empowerment requires a **fundamental** change and herein lies its biggest problem. The fundamentals that need to be changed are the underlying values, beliefs, skills, and habits that have become second nature to most people, management and employees. To change these requires serious, conscious surgery and continuous, focused effort.

Empowered individuals believe that their actions have significance and meaning. Empowered people have discretion, but also obligations. They live in a culture of respect where they actually can do things without getting permission from some organizational parent figure. Empowered organizations are characterized by trust and system-wide communications (Bennis, 1994, p. 109).

No one can empower another person. When a company's management initiates an empowerment program, what it really needs to do is initiate fundamental changes in the actions and behaviors that it utilizes when dealing with its employees. Speeches and lunches won't do it. Management and employees must learn how to behave differently in everything they do. Behaviors must change and this takes time. This is serious work.

As an example to help clarify this further, think about all the information a company does share with its employees and then all the information that it does not share with its employees. Empowerment is about taking responsibility for one's actions, making decisions about what course of action to follow, initiating that action and then evaluating and being responsible for outcomes of that action. Empowerment requires information so that these decisions are informed decisions. Yet, how many organizations are truly willing to open the books, to allow that level of access, so that employees can really make informed decisions?

This puts the spotlight on the trust issue. The benevolent parent employer is worried (perhaps rightly so) that employees can't be trusted, won't understand, won't be able to handle confidential information. The employee is angry that management doesn't trust him/her with key information, and perhaps implicitly decides that without that level of trust, this is "just a job" that pays the bills, and important, meaningful work must be found elsewhere or not at all. It is a vicious cycle that plays itself out every day in company after company.

Sharing important (all?) information is mandatory if an organization wants to establish an environment where employees act as partners, accept responsibility, and do more than just enough to get by. Without it, decisions are at best guesses. If the organization, cannot trust employees with key information maybe it has hired the wrong employees and the recruitment process needs to examined. If the employees are not trustworthy, a key human value, perhaps that aspect of human development needs to be examined. Regardless, empowerment is an internal process that only flourishes in mutually trusting environments.

It can be clearly seen from the brief scenario above that empowerment is an uphill climb. It is simplistic to think that by changing who has power or by "giving" employees power that an empowered work force will emerge.

Empowerment is more than power moving from one person to another. It is about shared commitments, shared goals, shared information, and shared rewards. When a person feels empowered, the inner energy and motivation created by that feeling flows into every aspect of his or her job. No one can give you this feeling—it must come from inside you and it is there, lying dormant, waiting to be called into service right now! Trust me, the view from the top of the hill is worth the effort!

STRATEGIES TO BECOME EMPOWERED

Be Positive, not Pollyana, but POSITIVE—ALWAYS—no matter what!
Keep Your Word—your integrity is everything!
Build a support network for yourself.
Under promise, Over deliver (everything always takes longer!)
Get Information that you need to do it right the first time!
Ask For Help.
Do Complete Work that you are PROUD to put your name on.
Support Others—be genuinely happy for them!
Stop being a victim—ever!

So, what will it take? How can organizations move in the direction of an empowered, committed partnership? This is where the excitement of work, the passion for the job becomes the enabler. Empowered organizations have a keen sense (vision) of their future. They hire carefully to ensure that vision, share information to protect that vision, and share the rewards of their successes. Empowered people take responsibility for their own actions. They are accountable. There are no excuses, no scapegoats, no victims.

Max DePree (1989), in his classic book *Leadership is an Art* called for a change in the relationship between management and employees from contractual, one based on "such things as expectations, objectives, compensation, working conditions, benefits, incentive opportunities, constraints, timetables, etc." to one that is covenantal (p. 25). "A covenantal relationship rests on shared commitments to ideas, to issues, to values, to goals, and to management processes . . . are open to influence . . . fill deep needs and they enable work to have meaning and be fulfilling . . . tolerate risk and forgive errors . . . they reflect unity, grace and poise" (p. 51).

PERSONAL REFLECTION

No one can empower another person. You empower yourself by virtue of your own acceptance of being responsible for your actions and then holding yourself accountable to that responsibility. Think of one project or activity that you are currently working on and examine it from a new perspective of *you* being totally responsible and accountable for its success.

What two specific things do you need to begin to do differently in order to empower yourself with respect to this project?

Where do you see your contribution in this project?

What do you need to do differently, think differently, in order to have this project finished at a standard better than that which you normally do your work?

CHANGE MANAGEMENT

Faced with the choice of changing one's mind or proving that there is no need to do so, almost everybody gets busy on the proof.

John Kenneth Galbraith

You can see the forces of change knocking on the doors of corporate America and on the egos and imaginations of employees who expect to participate in this dynamic future. Preparation will be the key to success for all of the players involved, and in this game, one is either a player or on the sidelines getting splinters!

The workplace is changing. *Ugh!* Change, like many of the other management buzzwords, has taken on a life of its own and (for me) congers up the same shivers as fingernails scratching a blackboard! Peters (1994) denounced the word "change" and called for "abandonment or revolution." He began to hint at the depth of the destruction that will be required in organizations, and in the people who work in these organizations, to meet the requirements of a dynamic, global, fast-paced business environment.

Change is a complex and difficult process because it affects many people at perceived critical survival points. Think about your own change paradigms and some of the personal habits you may have perhaps tried to change in your life. Simple things like deciding to eat healthier, dieting, quitting smoking, trying more effective study habits, starting an exercise routine—all those New Year's resolutions that barely survive January 1! Human behavior is a hard act to change!

People fear so much in the change process, the loss of one's job, one's social group or status, family networks, security. The negative aspects or possible losses as a result of change are all too often the focus, rather than the positive, the possibilities! Change is growth. Change is opportunity. Change increases potential.

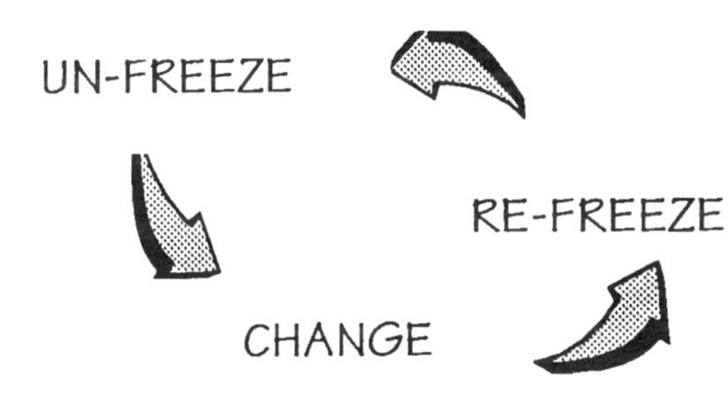

There have been several theoretical foundations upon which current change strategies are based. Kurt Lewin offered two for consideration. First, he described the process of change in three stages: *unfreezing, change* or *moving,* and *refreezing.* During the *unfreezing* stage, set or old routines are relinquished. In the *moving* or *change* stage, new behaviors, processes, systems, beliefs, and values are tried out, tested, experimented with, and the outcomes are assessed against expectations and perceived benefits. Finally, in the *refreezing* stage, those new behaviors which proved to provide value and positive benefit are incorporated into one's repertoire of activities (Robbins, 1991).

Another concept that Lewin proposed is called a *Force Field Analysis.* This is a process of understanding competing forces that push as organization or an individual in a pro-change direction against those forces that are anti-change and restrain the change process.

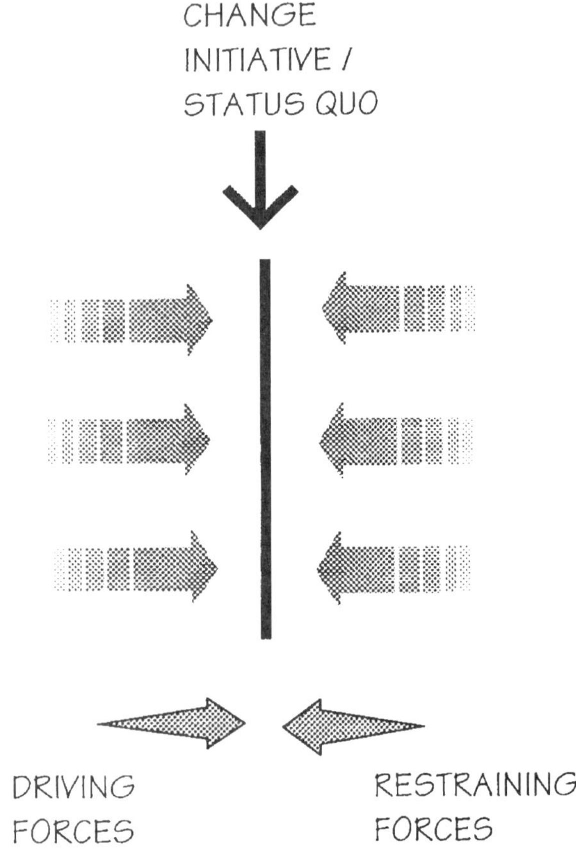

Any change that results is based on the interaction of these powerful forces. In the final analysis, Lewin found that decreasing restraining forces proved to be more effective in implementing the change process rather than increasing the power of the driving forces (Spier, 1973).

The question, then, to ask as managers initiating change is, "What would hold people back from changing?" Rather than focusing on the outcome of the changed event and telling employees how great it will be, a manager must first really understand the fears associated with letting go of old behaviors, routines, ways of doing things.

This is a major shift for most people. William Bridges (1991) calls the letting go process the *transition* phase of change. He states clearly that it isn't the change that stops people. That is a situational event. It is the transition to the new event that is the psychological part of the process and the part that causes the greatest stress. It is the internal nature of the transition where problems with change arise. To facilitate the change event, a smart manager should focus on the endings and losses, the letting go of the old situation. This will bring about the best results and is the part of the change process that so many organizations seem to forget.

Regardless of what type of change the company seeks—structural, philosophical, technological, strategic, cultural—the underlying element in all of these is that it is the internal person who must change, at an inner awareness or consciousness level, in order for the change initiative to be successful. While for convenience, change may be labeled by desired outcomes, whether those outcomes are developmental, meaning specific, incremental skill enhancement, or transformational; where beliefs about fundamental issues are totally reconceptualized, it is always about letting go first. It is only through compassion at this end of the change process that new beginnings will become a reality.

The bottom line here is that change can't really be managed. According to the dictionary *manage* means, *"to direct or control the use of; handle; to make submissive to one's authority, discipline or persuasion . . ."* Which part of this definition can be applied to the abstract concept of change? NONE—NADA.

> Change generates an opportunity for invention, creativity, and imagination.

Once this is accepted as fact, that change cannot be "managed," the whole idea of change management takes on a new perspective. The paradigm shifts away from the idea of managing change to one of effectively incorporating the dynamics of a changing environment into the daily life process.

These concepts—invention, creativity, imagination—are the critical competencies for personal and organizational success. They should be cultivated, developed, and nourished in all members of the work community. The process of how to accomplish this, how to nourish the imagination, is the question to be addressed, not how to manage change.

As the pace of changes in people's lives continues to accelerate, each person must become the creator of his or her own destiny in conjunction with organizations that must seek not only short term profits but long term prosperity. If, in the broadest sense, management is defined as "the optimization of resources" (Russell and Evans, 1992), then each person is and always will be a manager. He or she must commit to learning to utilize the tools and techniques of management to serve personal, organizational and community needs, to increase the capabilities of the individual and the whole.

THE "COMMON SENSE" CAVEAT

How often these words have been uttered by students in response to taking the time to learn and acquire a deeper appreciation for the finer details of managing in today's business environment is just too numerous to count. Alas, none of this is common sense. If it was, the organizations that were once paragons of success in America would not be in such trouble, the employer/employee relationship would be sound and strong, and none of us would ever work for a manager or a company with the people skills of a toad—my apologies to the toad!

What does make sense is that there are tremendous pressures on people today to move in a variety of competing directions. While some of these pressures are external, many are pressures that each individual puts on himself/herself. There are no actions without consequences. There are no "free" lunches.

There is also a great wealth of opportunity out there. Many of these opportunities are disguised as insurmountable problems with a thousand variables and reasons why each proposed solution won't work. What is clear is that each one begins and ends with the people involved and the strength of the relationships created between these people. It is here that the promise for tomorrow begins.

It is the job of every member of society—to enable the change and growth capabilities of each person in that society. It is the responsibility of each student to become a "forever student," a lifelong learner, so that individual invention, creativity, and imagination are continually challenged. Organizations must become "learning organizations, organizations where people continually expand their capacity to create the results they truly desire, where new and expansive patterns of thinking are nurtured, where collective aspiration is set free, and where people are continually learning how to learn together" (Senge,1990, p.3).

In the final analysis, it ALL begins and ends with you!

PARADIGMS OF MANAGEMENT

PERSONAL DEVELOPMENT EXERCISES

THE PARADOX OF LETTING GO

When I let go of what I am, I become what I might be. When I let go of what I have, I receive what I need.

These are the feminine or *Yin* paradoxes:

By yielding, I endure.
The empty space is filled.
When I give of myself, I become more.
When I feel most destroyed, I am about to grow.
When I desire nothing, a great deal comes to me.

Have you ever struggled to get work or love and finally given up and found both love and work were suddenly there?

Do you want to be free and independent? Conform to God's law; that is how everything happens anyway.

When I give up trying to impress the group, I become very impressive. But when I am just trying to make myself look good, the group knows that and does not like it.

My best work is done when I forget my own point of view; the less I make of myself, the more I am.

When I yield to the wishes of the person working, I encounter no resistance.

This is the wisdom of the feminine: let go in order to achieve. The wise leader demonstrates this.

The Tao of Leadership

MANAGERIAL SKILLS AUDIT

Here is a private opportunity for you to assess your current managerial skill development and develop specific plans for improvement. Think of a specific work related situation where these skills have been required. Assess how successful you have been in achieving your desired results and outcomes.

Below you will find the key managerial skill competencies listed with a scale where you are to indicate your perceived level of skill development. Choose the number 5 if you think your skill development is high in the particular area. Choose the number 1 if you feel that your skill is severely underdeveloped in that skill category. Be honest with yourself. The point here is to assess your current skill level so that you can **plan change**.

Because technical skills are specific there are three lines provided for you to personalize this instrument to your areas of technical expertise. For example, if you were a computer information student, programming might be considered a technical skill area, as would flow charting, systems analysis, debugging, etc. An electronics student might have circuit planning, fiber optic systems, and troubleshooting as technical skill areas.

	low				high
Technical	1	2	3	4	5
a) ______________________	1	2	3	4	5
b) ______________________	1	2	3	4	5
c) ______________________	1	2	3	4	5
Conceptual	1	2	3	4	5
Analytical	1	2	3	4	5
Synthesis	1	2	3	4	5
Communication	1	2	3	4	5
People	1	2	3	4	5

Which skill areas are your strongest?

Which skills are your weakest?

Choose one skill area to focus on this term. What classroom or work activities can you participate in that will build and develop this skill? List these on the following sheet. Your plan begins!

MANAGERIAL SKILL AUDIT WORKSHEET

Managerial Skill Focus Area: ____________________

How will I be able to tell when this area changes/ What will be different about me?

____

____

____

What specifically must I stop doing right now in order to grow this managerial skill area?

____

____

____

Class Centered Activities that will help me grow this managerial skill area:

____

____

____

____

Work Centered Activities that will help me grow this managerial skill area:

____

____

____

____

Who can I ask for help and support during this change process?

____

____

____

FORCE FIELD ANALYSIS

Change is difficult for many people. Often diagraming the dimensions of the change decision being contemplated proves helpful. Below you will find a technique created by Kurt Lewin called a **Force Field Analysis** that you read about in this module. While this is not a "required" assignment and its contents should remain confidential, please feel free to contact this instructor should you wish to discuss your completed analysis.

Part 1—Description

Think about a situation going on right now that is significant in your personal or professional life. For example, starting a semester at school is a significant event, especially if you have been out of school for a period of time. Respond to each item below as completely as possible.

The situation/event that I am focusing on is . . .

The following people are involved in the situation.

PERSON	RELATION TO ME	ROLE IN SITUATION

Other factors relevant to this situation are . . .

I would choose the following aspect of the situation to be changed if it were in my power to do so (choose only one aspect):

go on to the next page

Source: University Associates, 1974, *Handbook of Structured Experiences for Human Relations Training*, Vol. II, 79–84.

Part 2—Driving/Restraining Forces

If I consider the present status of the situation as a temporary balance of opposing forces, the following would be on my list of forces ***driving*** toward change. Fill in the spaces to the right of the letters below. Leave the smaller spaces to the left open at this time.

__________ a. ____

__________ b. ____

__________ c. ____

__________ d. ____

__________ e. ____

__________ f. ____

__________ g. ____

__________ h. ____

The following would be on my list of forces ***restraining*** or forces preventing the change:

__________ a. ____

__________ b. ____

__________ c. ____

__________ d. ____

__________ e. ____

__________ f. ____

__________ g. ____

__________ h. ____

In the spaces to the left of each set above rate the ***driving*** and ***restraining*** forces using this 1 to 5 scale.

1. It has almost nothing to do with the drive toward change in the situation.
2. It has relatively little to do with the drive toward change in the situation.
3. It is of moderate importance in the drive toward change in the situation.
4. It is an important factor in the drive toward change in the situation.
5. It is a major factor in the drive toward change in the situation.

go on to the next page

Part 3—Diagraming the Forces

On the following chart, diagram the forces driving toward change and the restraining change forces that you just rated. First, next to the "a through h" letters on the sides of the chart, write several key words to identify each of the forces (a through h) from part 2. Then draw an arrow from the corresponding numerical "degree" of force to the status quo line according to your ranking.

For example, if you considered the first item on your list of driving forces [letter a] to have a rating of 3, then your arrow under the "a" column would go from the 3 line across to the status quo line.

Driving Forces → ← Restraining Forces

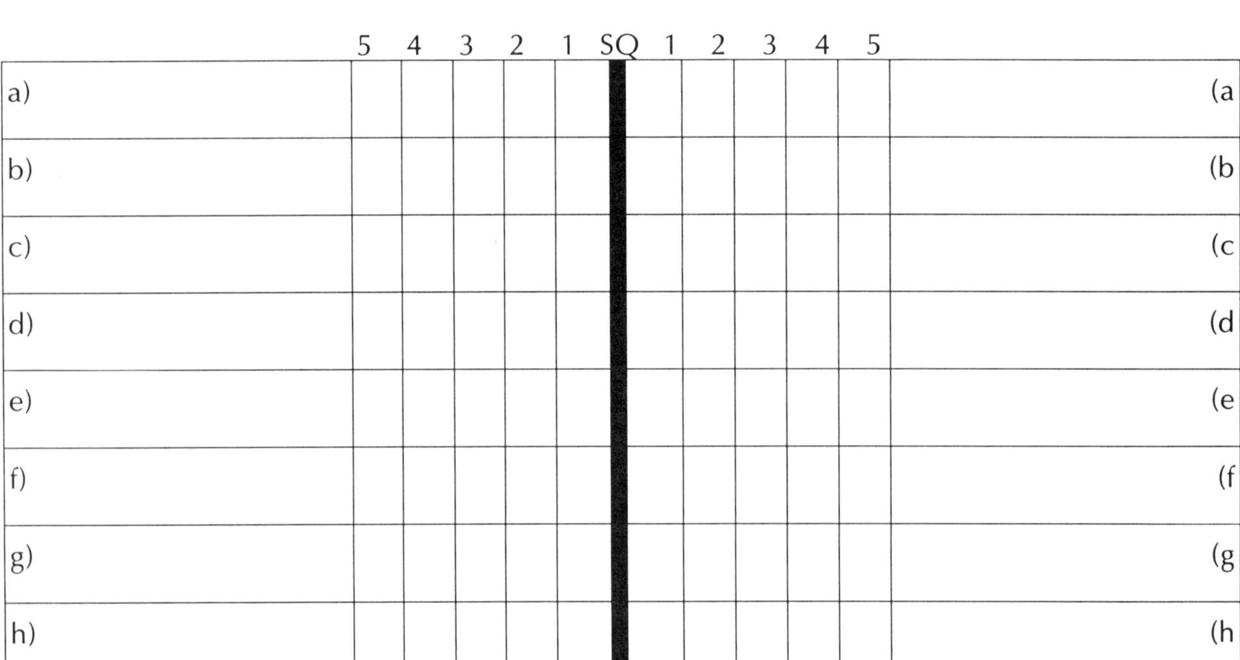

	5	4	3	2	1	SQ	1	2	3	4	5	
a)												(a
b)												(b
c)												(c
d)												(d
e)												(e
f)												(f
g)												(g
h)												(h

go on to the next page

Part 4—New Beginnings

Implementing the change now begins in earnest. Remember from your reading that it is decreasing the power of the restraining forces that facilitates change the best.

Select one or two restraining forces from your diagram as the initial targets for your change efforts. For each one, outline a specific strategy for reducing their potency. Use the following key questions to help you focus your planning.

S— Specificity	Exactly what are you trying to accomplish?
P— Performance	What behavior(s) is(are) implied?
I— Involvement	Who is going to do it? (You and who else?)
R— Realism	Can it be done?
M—Measurability	How will you be able to measure your results?
O—Observability	Can others see the behavior?

Restraining Force #1: ____________________

Strategy

S ____________________

P ____________________

I ____________________

R ____________________

M ____________________

O ____________________

Restraining Force #2: ____________________

Strategy

S ____________________

P ____________________

I ____________________

R ____________________

M ____________________

O ____________________

PURPOSEFUL MANAGEMENT

Strategic Management

Vision Mission

Goals/Objectives

Strategies/Tactics

Environmental Forces & SWOT Analysis

Organizational Structure

Organizational Culture

Organizational Transformation, Ethics & Social Responsibility

Diversity

LEARNING OBJECTIVES

After completing the course work in the *Purposeful Management* module, the student should be able to:

- define the relationship between vision, mission, goals, objectives and the strategies and tactics organizations implement to accomplish business purposes,
- analyze the changing nature of an organization's environment and the forces that impact organizational decisions,
- create a SWOT analysis for an organization under investigation in order to guide organizational strategic decisions,
- compare and contrast the relationship between organizational strategies, organizational culture, and the possible organizational structures available to carry out these strategies within the business setting,
- evaluate the key components of social responsibility and ethics for organizations today.

IN THE NAME OF PROFITS

What does it mean to undertake purposeful activity of any type? If we do something with purpose or intention we have taken the time to plan what we will be doing, to consider the alternative courses of action, to consider the variables that will impact the action and the possible scenarios and consequences of that action. When we do something with purpose or intention, we are focused on that event or action and working through a process or journey to arrive at a goal outcome or objective. Barriers are handled, sacrifices are made, objections are overcome; all in the name of achieving the desired end result. Clearly, the end result must be important to the people involved for all of this to work!

Purposeful action in management is no different. It is about "beginning with the end in mind" to quote a Stephen Covey phrase. Purposeful action in management is about "seeing" where you want to be at the end of the activity, and then planning the journey or route to accomplish that desired outcome. Purposeful action in management is about strategy.

Strategy—is it just the tactics, the list of steps, required to "take that hill" or accomplish a goal? Or, as many of the business elite are now saying, is strategy more than progressing through predetermined elements in the quest of an outcome? An interesting question!

The word ***strategy*** comes from the Greek word ***"strategos."*** This can be translated to mean "the art of the general" and it was originally used in a military context to describe the grand design behind a battle or a war. Today, we use strategy processes to plan all sorts of events from the military logistics of the Gulf War to the celebration party for the Chicago Bulls' fifth NBA championship.

This module will discuss the concept of strategy—business strategy—with all of the fundamental components, environmental considerations, organizational issues, and the social and ethical questions that must be addressed when strategic decisions are made. Hopefully, as a personal development application, students will be able to begin to more clearly develop their own personal and professional strategy which will act as the foundation of their career management plan.

PERSONAL REFLECTION

To make this module as relevant for you as possible, take a few moments now to think about yourself and answer this question.

What will it take to create what I really want for my future? Jot down some thoughts in this space.

DEFINITIONS • DISTINCTIONS

Strategic Management

a dynamic process of planning a firm's long-term future, managing its full complement of resources, and fulfilling its mission within the parameters of its internal and external environments

Strategic Planning

a specific series of procedures focused on achieving the desired goals/objectives of the organization, clearly spelled out as to action elements, targets, and decision variables

Strategic Thinking

a conceptual process to qualitatively frame and/or define the future state of an organization so that employees can have a shared vision and common understanding of the organization's direction and use it as a guide to their actions

Vision

a conceptual and inspiring statement or idea about what you want your organization to be

Mission

defined business scope/purpose of the company and operations arena that has an external focus on its customers, the markets served, and the products/services offered; it's more than a statement about making money—it gives a reason why the company is in business

Goals/Objectives

refined and specific steps to follow to achieve the organization's mission that provide focus on markets, customers, productivity, and performance issues with time parameters and measurement targets

Strategies/Tactics

specific targets with specific plans to achieve the desired goals/objectives, clearly spelled out as to action elements

Environmental Scan

an examination of factors and variables in both the internal and external environment of an organization that have the potential to impact decisions made by that organization

SWOT Analysis

an examination of strengths and weaknesses (skill deficiencies) that are internal to the organization, situation, or person, and the opportunities and threats that are external to the organization, situation, or person under analysis

STRATEGIC THINKING

Strategic thinking is focused on the future—on what the organization wants to accomplish, on where it wants to be, and on what it wants to stand for. The organization's strengths and weaknesses are articulated and assessed, and the marketplace is analyzed in light of the company's ability to compete effectively.

The benefit of strategic thinking in an organization is that it provides a common understanding for all members of the organization to follow. Decisions can be filtered through that common understanding about company direction so that they "fit" within the established agenda for the company. One of the best outcomes of strategic thinking is that it enhances communication within the organization. Everyone knows and is working toward the same results and, therefore, their combined efforts are stronger.

STRATEGIC PLANNING

Strategic planning is the process of moving from point A to point B and so on, in order to accomplish the goals of the organization. The plan becomes the road map or blue print on which departments, product and services decisions, and operational plans are made.

Strategic planning takes place after the strategic thinking process has established the common direction for the organization and members throughout the organization have a role to play in creating the strategic plan. To plan before the thinking process would be like putting the cart before the horse.

By the time the organization gets to the planning phase, all employees have a solid understanding of the internal workings of the company, about what makes it tick, about its ability to be competitive and in what markets, with which products and services.

STRATEGIC MANAGEMENT

Strategic Management is the ongoing process of planning a firm's long-term course of action, managing its full complement of resources, and fulfilling its mission within the parameters of its internal and external environments. It incorporates the development of a mission statement into operational goals and objectives that can be specifically targeted and achieved by members of the organization and sets the strategies and resources that are to be channeled to accomplish these tasks.

The ultimate aim of strategic management is to help organizations increase performance through improved effectiveness, efficiency, and flexibility. It requires a holistic view of the organization; one that acknowledges the accelerating rate of environmental change, turbulence, and complexity; the growing competition for ever scarcer resources; and the increasing demands from a growing number of special interest groups and individuals.

STRATEGIC QUESTIONS

WHERE ARE WE NOW?
WHERE DO WE WANT TO GO?
HOW WILL WE GET THERE?

Peter Drucker, an expert in the field of management, said that, "Every organization has to prepare for the abandonment of everything it does." In today's fast paced business climate, this statement rings true. Products are obsolete faster than they can hit the shelves of our favorite stores. New technologies make work easier, faster, cleaner and provide more time to create new products. Innovation becomes the battle cry that leads companies into the competitive arena.

The primary purpose of strategic planning is not to strategically plan for the future . . . it is primarily to develop a strategic management mind-set in each and every individual in the organization. It is to produce a plan that will be owned and understood by the people who have to execute it

Jim Belasco and Ralph Stayer
Flight of the Buffalo

Everyone must change. The change will go deeper than technique. It touches not merely what managers do, but who they are. Not just their sense of the task, but their sense of themselves. Not just what they know, but how they think

James Champy
Reengineering Management

These two quotes have been placed side by side because they highlight the essence of the change that is going to be needed by management, and really by all employees, in order to DO strategy—to strategically create the tomorrows they want to have.

Belasco and Stayer (Stayer is the CEO of Johnsonville Foods—you know, the sausage people!) go on to ask a series of strategic thinking questions in order to guide the reader through a thought process which will illuminate key strategic issues and areas of personal responsibility.

1. What do we really want to create for our customers?
2. What will it take to create what we want?
3. What obstacles prevent us from creating this "want" and who owns those obstacles?
4. What actions will the owners need to take to remove them?

"Ideals are like stars; you will not succeed in touching them with your hands. But like the seafaring man on the desert of waters, you choose them as your guides, and following them, you will reach your destiny."

Carl Schurz

There is nothing mystical about the strategic management process. It is simply developing the ability to take an idea from its conception through a structured and thoughtful process to its ultimate conclusion. It begins with values and a vision, moves through the articulation of that vision as a mission which guides the development of goals/objectives which lead to strategies, tactics, and evaluation of results.

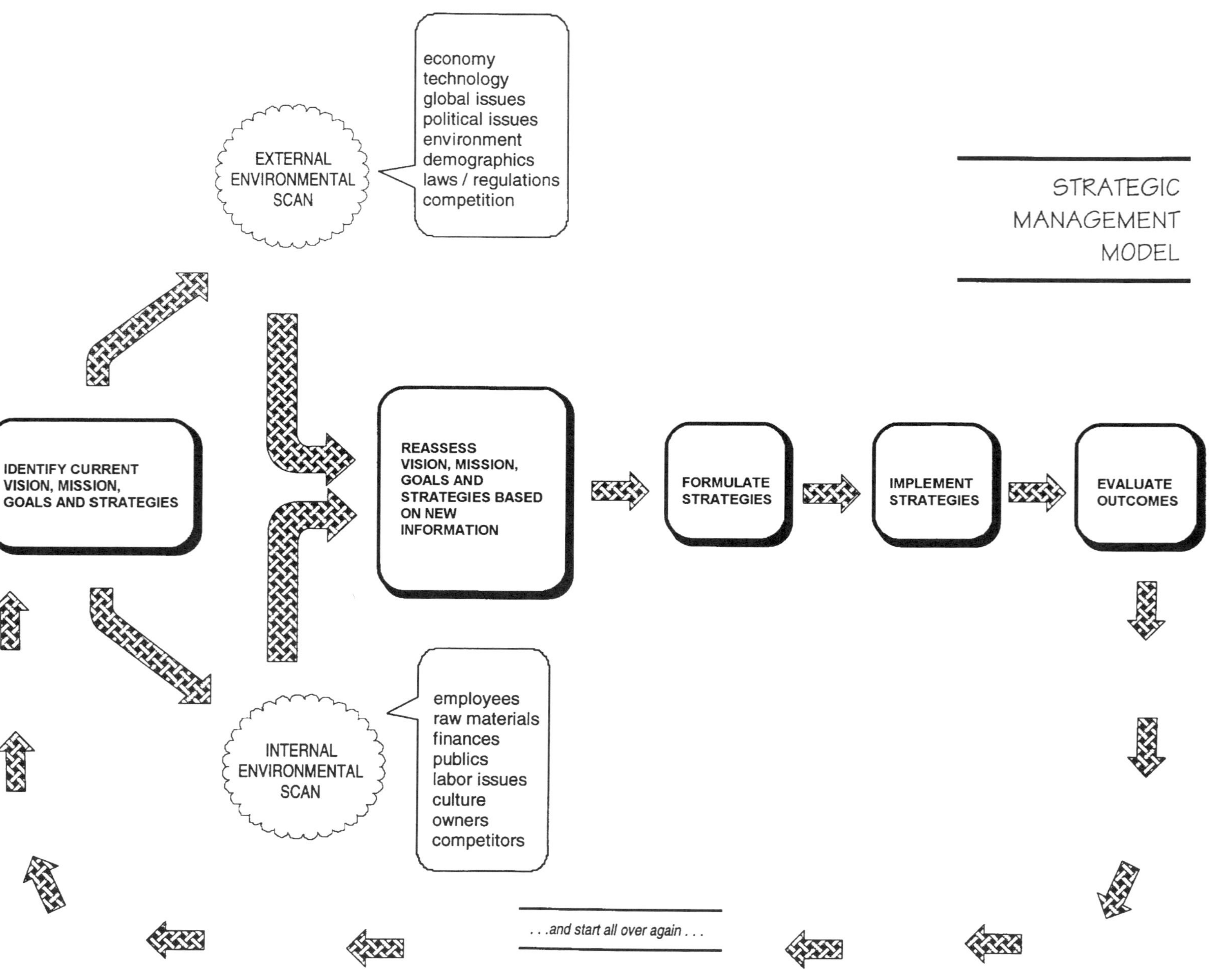
STRATEGIC
MANAGEMENT
MODEL
IDENTIFY CURRENT VISION, MISSION, GOALS AND STRATEGIES
EXTERNAL ENVIRONMENTAL SCAN
economy
technology
global issues
political issues
environment
demographics
laws / regulations
competition
INTERNAL ENVIRONMENTAL SCAN
employees
raw materials
finances
publics
labor issues
culture
owners
competitors
REASSESS VISION, MISSION, GOALS AND STRATEGIES BASED ON NEW INFORMATION
FORMULATE STRATEGIES
IMPLEMENT STRATEGIES
EVALUATE OUTCOMES
. . .and start all over again . . .

CORE COMPETENCIES

If one accepts the idea that everyone is not great at everything, then it becomes *strategically* important to analyze and assess one's competencies. A core competency is something that a company does better than any of its competitors.

Core competencies can exist in many different categories. A core competency can be achieved in many different areas of an organization. For example, an inventory control and replenishment process that is better in comparison than any other company is a core competency. Or, a core competency could be the level of customer service that a company provides. It could be a company's ability to research the marketplace and predict trends better than anyone else.

Once core competencies are known to a company they can be the focus of establishing competitive advantage. The idea is to accentuate the positives, the strengths while attempting to minimize the negatives, the weaknesses. As if this weren't enough to do, one must be constantly learning new skills and increasing one's competencies in diverse areas so as not to be broadsided when the environment changes!

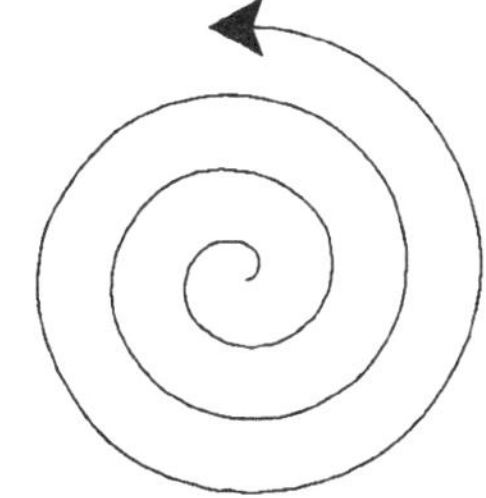

COMPETITIVE ADVANTAGE

Several years ago, Michael Porter, a strategic management expert, suggested three generic competitive strategies that organizations should consider in order to compete successfully in the marketplace.

First, Porter identified the strategy of *cost leadership*. With this strategy the company focuses on continuously improving process efficiencies in order to produce products and services more efficiently than its competitors. This would enable the company to offer comparable products/services at lower costs while still earning a profit.

The second competitive strategy identified by Porter is called *differentiation*. When a company chooses to focus on this strategy, it would look for the unique characteristics, qualities, and benefits of its products/services that make them different or distinguish them from other competitors. Although finding the key features that make your product or company different than its competition may be difficult and require a certain degree of creativity, it can have enormous payoffs! Customers will often become quite loyal to companies that are unique and will pay more for products/services that they perceive to add value to their purchase.

The final strategy is that of *focus*. Concentration of efforts is the key to this strategy. Companies that find and service a particular market niche, regional area or concentrate their resources on a more narrowly defined market segment, find that these energies help them fine-tune their efforts and reap generous rewards.

ENVIRONMENTAL SCAN & SWOT

An organization can "create" its future by setting a future path and effectively analyzing environmental forces in conjunction with the organization's SWOT (strengths, weaknesses, opportunities, threats) in order to make that future happen.

Think of an organization as an organism living within an environment. There are certain elements of that environment that the organism/organization can control, some elements that can be partially controlled or at least monitored, and finally, some elements of that environment that are totally outside of the organism's/organization's control. These outside elements may, however, exert a great deal of pressure or impact on the organism/organization.

Businesses exist within their external and internal environments. The external environment consists of a myriad of forces, most, if not all, of which are outside the direct control of the organization. These forces include such areas as the political climate, the legal/governmental area, economics, demographics, natural forces, and socio-cultural forces. Clearly, all of these forces will impact decisions that companies make about products and services, location, the population as labor supply and as customers, natural resources, advancements in technology, and a host of other issues.

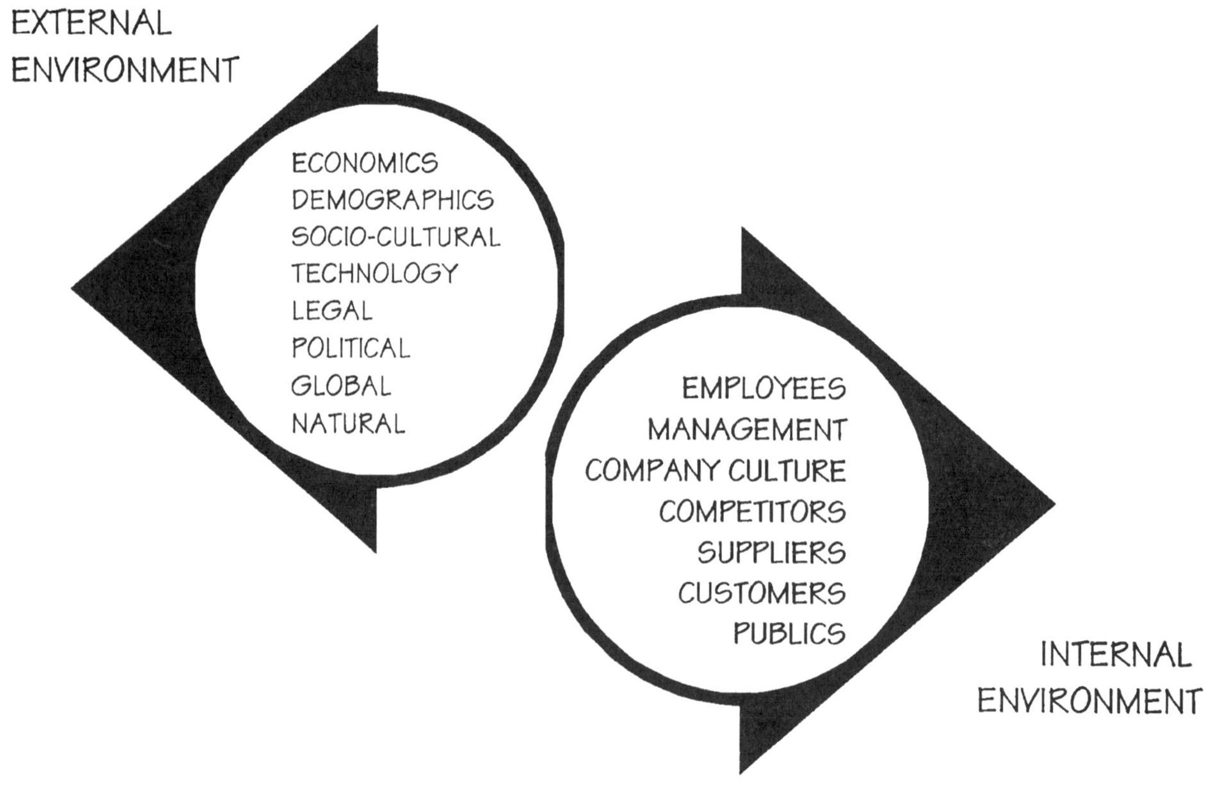

An organization "scans" its environment and formulates assumptions about these elements.

The internal environment also impacts the business decisions an organization makes. Some areas in the internal environment might be the company's employees, sources of new employees, suppliers and vendor resources, raw materials, the competition, the owners and stockholders, management and the operation of the company, its culture, rules, regulations and policies. In general, an organization has more control over its internal environment than it does over its external environment.

The organization then proceeds to create a *SWOT Analysis* based on what it learns as it "scans" its environment. The *SWOT* allows the organization to look at itself against the forces it is up against and, hopefully, make good decisions, or at least better decisions, about its future than it would have if it advanced blindly into the future.

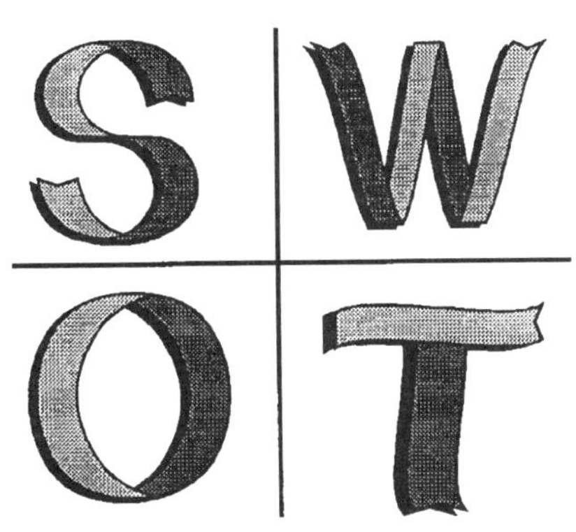

STRENGTHS AND WEAKNESS [Skill Deficiencies]
Every organization has areas where it is strong and areas where it is weak, or where the skill or competency in question is not fully developed. The S/W part of the SWOT Analysis is internal to the organization.

OPPORTUNITIES AND THREATS
These exist in the external environment and are areas where the company has the potential to create business or areas where something in the marketplace threatens the success of a business venture, new product, or service.

THEORY OF BUSINESS

It is important that an organization develop a realistic understanding of the environmental factors as it prepares its theory of business. Drucker defined a theory of business as the underlying assumptions that an organization makes that shape its behavior in the marketplace (Drucker, 1994). According to Drucker, a theory of business contains three parts including the organization's assumptions about the environment in which the company operates. Many of the elements of these assumptions have already been presented here. Next is the organization's assumption about its mission, or why it is in business. Finally, there are assumptions about the organization's core competencies.

When the assumptions made are accurate, a company's theory of business enables it to put forth a clear, consistent message about who the company is, what business the company is in and why, the company's values, behaviors, and customers and what the company is really good at doing. This is a powerful process. However, often the theory of business a company is working under is not valid or realistic for the current state of affairs in the world. The company's theory of business may have become obsolete, failing to change with the times. Then, we witness a once powerful organization suffering from its own failure to change and stay on top of the realities of a dynamic marketplace. Think about the struggles of IBM, GM, Kodak, or other companies that once led the way and were the epitome of American manufacturing power.

an example to show the way .. .. ..

ABC Company

Values the company lives by . . .	**Service**	**Quality**	**Integrity**	**People**
Mission Statement	The mission of ABC Company is to be the world leader in state-of-the-art telecommunications technology, providing customers with premier product selection and service, and working with our employees to create a team-centered and meaningful work environment within which we all can achieve our personal and professional goals.			
Goals	**Growth**	**Quality**	**People Power**	**Profits**
	• Increase market share by 10% per quarter	• Reduce product defects by 10% • Enhance delivery times by 5% • Improve overall quality of all systems	• Build learning organization • Encourage employee initiatives	• Target xx% profit • Increase stock value by 5% in 1998
Strategies to Achieve Goals	a) Add 2 account managers in Europe b) Prepare full scale marketing campaign for Product A c) Phase in new customer service positions in all US regions	a) Implement SPC in all plants b) Create task force to study delivery issues and create solutions c) Benchmark all order intake systems with pilot project at Houston plant d) Create cross functional quality review panel e) Pilot weekly shift meetings at Akron	a) Add % of savings award program in all mfg. plants b) Create training center at Houston facility by June 98 c) Create training center in Akron by Dec 98 d) Create employee idea gain-sharing program e) Initiate company wide newsletter	a) Increase ESOP by 5% in 1998 b) Communicate with shareholders about success of company c) Create profit monitor meetings with employees

This chart is an example of how an organization might fit the pieces together to create a solid road map for everyone to "see" where the business is headed. Employees looking at this chart should be able to understand how their actions "fit" into the company's plans. They will know where to target their activities to move the organization forward. They can see what the organization considers important. They can "see" how they fit into the organization now and in the future. If everyone lives up to the expectations of the company, then in the example above all should benefit.

Take some time to investigate the organization where you are now employed. If you do not work right now, either use a former employer or investigate the college you are attending. Set up interviews with the human resource people, your manager, and any other company executives who you feel might be ready, willing, and able to help you better understand their particular business. See how many spaces you can fill in about your employer.

Environmental Scan

External Forces	Internal Forces

SWOT Analysis

Values	
Mission	
Goals	
Action Plans	

What type of structure will best serve our customers?

What type of structure will facilitate communication between our employees?

Which structure allows for growth?

Which structure is most cost effective?

Which structure—

Which structure—

Which structure????????

While many companies have certainly experienced their share of restructuring in the name of getting rid of the hierarchy, there really is no one BEST way to organize or structure a business. Each company must look at its operations, products/services, and people and determine which of a variety of possibilities would work best under the current business climate. For some a hierarchy might in fact be the best way to structure, while for others a network, cluster, or team format might serve its constituency better.

Key issues that must be addressed when deciding how to structure or organize the flow of work center on the following areas:

specialization/ division of labor	the uniqueness of the tasks to be done and specialized skills needed to do them effectively
coordination/ integration	the flow of the work itself and how the divergent pieces come together to make a finished product or service via collaborative efforts across department lines and authority relationships
authority/ span of control	reporting relationships
centralized/ decentralized	decisions about whether all sites will act under the control of one central location or will be autonomous profit/loss units acting independently

HIERARCHY

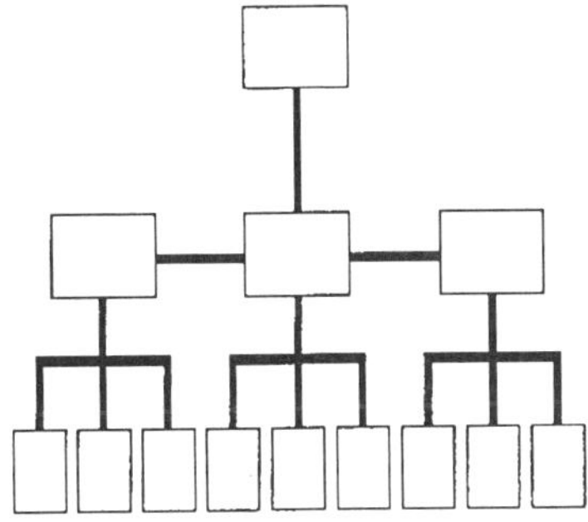

This is the classic pyramid organizational structure. A CEO/owner figure sits at the top followed by a stratified command structure down to the workers at the bottom. Authority and power flow from the top and are the glue that hold the structure together.

A hierarchy can be *tall,* with many levels of management, or *flat,* with only a few layers to the structure. Today, as organizations push decision-making responsibilities down to lower levels, organizations are flattening the pyramid structures. The hierarchy concept still remains, just with fewer levels. Many middle managers have had to reengineer their careers due to the flattening of the hierarchy.

Inverted Hierarchy

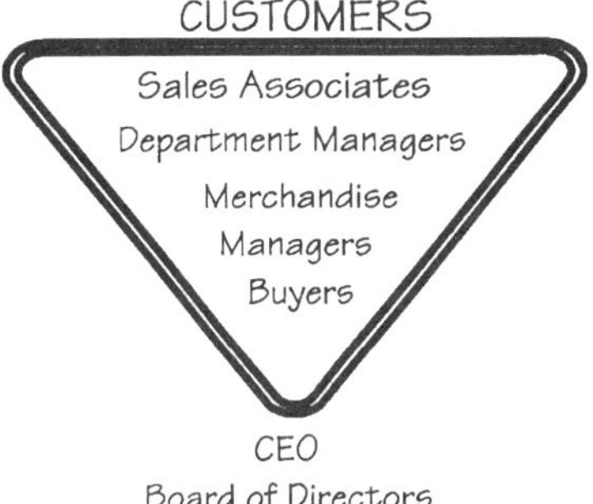

Some organizations have inverted the traditional pyramid. The most famous of these is Nordstrom. It placed the customers at the top level of an inverted pyramid shape because it saw the customer as the most important part of its business. All subsequent levels are there to serve the customer.

Matrix

The matrix structure combines the hierarchy with a project team or group component. Employees have a functional reporting relationship as well as a project reporting relationship. In effect, they have two bosses and often have two areas of responsibility to maintain.

This structure was very popular in the 1970s. As more organizations move to project teams, the matrix structure is experiencing a rebirth. Today's matrix structures are more about a "way to get things done" rather than formal reporting relationships. With increased pressures to hold down costs, get new products to market faster, communicate in realtime, and compete in a global setting, the matrix is revitalized because it enables these requirements to take place efficiently and effectively.

Shamrock

Charles Handy coined the name Shamrock organization to describe a structure that consists of three components: a core group of key players who create the business and plan and build it, a group of technical specialists contracted for specific projects on an as-needed basis, and a clerical or administrative group to support the ongoing activities of the company.

This type of structure, whether it is called "shamrock" or not, provides a great deal of flexibility for a company because people outside of the core can be hired as required by the business. As new projects are created, people with just the right mix of skills are brought together. When the project is completed, the specialized group disbands.

Today, many companies are opting to create "shamrock" style organizations. A new generation of workers also finds this structure pleasing. As specialists (consultants), they focus their energies on specific technical problems and don't get caught up in the ongoing operation of the entire enterprise. Whether it be software development, electronics, or other high-tech specialties, this new breed of employee wants the freedom to work in the nontraditional setting offered by this structure.

The problem that this style must contend with is that each "leaf" of the shamrock has different goals and it is difficult to build long-term commitment and loyalty from all three leaves. The core group wants the business to prosper. The specialists are focused on their tasks so that they can get rehired for the next project or recommended to another company by the core group when the current project is over. The support group is there for support. They are the 9 to 5 workers, who want to do what they are told, and seek the security of a work relationship that seems to be slowly disappearing.

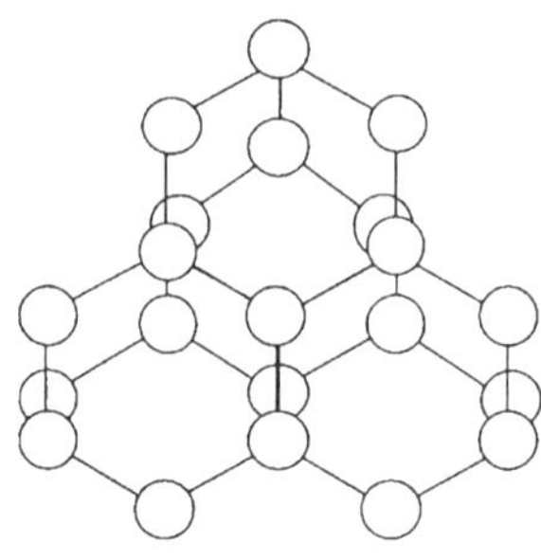

Cluster/Network/Lattice

Think grapes—think connection—think powerful communication! This is the cluster, the network, or the lattice form of organizational structure. It is a highly flexible structure where people are in constant contact with each other, where information is openly shared and free flowing, and where the dynamic changes of the marketplace are easily integrated into the working and reporting relationships so that the company can respond quickly and compete effectively.

Project Team

Creating project teams seems to be the way many organizations are going. Specific groups of people, each with a specialty needed on the project, are assigned as a need arises. When the project is over the team disbands. Hopefully, the team will have new assignments to develop.

Effective project teams require members who understand the dynamics of what makes a group of people with a set of skills into a high performance team. These skills and this developmental process will be addressed in great detail in the people/team building section in module #4.

PERSONAL REFLECTION

Take a few minutes to examine the company where you are employed. What structure is in place? Is it the same for all departments?

What do you think are some of the problems managers face as they experiment with new organizational structures?

Within which structure do you think you would be most comfortable? Why?

ORGANIZATIONAL CULTURE

Culture can be thought of as the socially transmitted values, beliefs, and patterns of behaviors that a group of people share and follow. It's the "way we do things around here." The culture of an organization provides the boundaries or framework so that the people in the organization "know" how to act, what is acceptable behavior, and what is not acceptable behavior.

For example, GE operates with a "business casual" dress code. Regardless of where they are or who they are meeting, all members of the GE community, from Jack Welch the CEO on down, are not required to don the traditional corporate attire. Mr. Welch has initiated other ways of being at GE. He is famous for the GE "workouts" which are meetings to brainstorm and shake out new ideas and new thinking structures. Many of Mr. Welch's ideas have been shown to be highly effective and have led GE to a position of prominence in the business community.

Herb Kelleher started Southwest Airlines with three key values:

#1—Work should be fun . . . it can be play . . . enjoy it.
#2—Work is important . . . don't spoil it with seriousness.
#3—People are important . . . each one makes a difference.

Halloween is the most celebrated holiday at Southwest. This airline has created a culture of fun and it works. Its symbol on the stock exchange is "LUV"! It is one of the most profitable airlines in the industry today. Turnover at Southwest is almost nonexistent. Southwest takes time to hire well and make sure people will "fit" into the corporate culture.

Almost every organization can be listed here, not necessarily with the same culture as that found at Southwest Airlines, but simply because a culture does exist within it. Clearly some organizational cultures are more conducive to certain outcomes, while other corporate culture styles bring about other outcomes. The key here is for the organization to realize the "goal" and then work to develop the culture that will enable the organization to best achieve that goal.

This is more difficult than it sounds. Once a culture becomes ingrained in an organization it takes a great deal of time, energy, and trust to change it. This is especially true when a company is moving from a fear based culture to a more humanistic or people centered one. Culture is *more than* a dress code. Creating, building, or changing a corporation's culture requires more than "saying" it is changing. Actions, consistency, and follow through are critical here. Leadership becomes the key to any change of culture and to the keeping of the culture.

COMPONENTS OF ORGANIZATIONAL CULTURE	Myths and stories about company heros and the people Terminology, language, basic assumptions and beliefs, official documents of stated values, daily actions Ceremonies, rituals, and celebrations

Think about some of the other companies that you have heard about—Mary Kay Cosmetics, Federal Express, Nordstrom, Disney, Hewlett Packard, the Marines—many of these have distinctive language, actions/behaviors, beliefs, ways of belonging, and rewards that are known world wide. How many can you think of? Seen any pink Cadillacs (Mary Kay) lately?

PERSONAL REFLECTION

Do a culture audit of the company where you now work. What are the shared beliefs, assumptions of this company? What is it like to work there? Who are its heros? What stories and legends circulate about the company's past?

ORGANIZATIONAL TRANSFORMATION, ETHICS AND SOCIAL RESPONSIBILITY

A great deal of research is being conducted on the attributes of what makes an effective corporate culture and how to go about transforming the company's current culture into something else. No one is totally clear on what that "something else" should be, but the concept of a learning organization continues to surface as the type of culture that would be the best for organizations in the new millennium.

The key question that any organization must ask is:

What kind of culture will help us accomplish our goals and be successful, both as individuals and as a company?

There is no one best answer for this question—companies must come to terms with all of the complexities of their own operations, products, services, ways of doing business and create a culture that will be conducive to that particular organization.

Research has been conducted that suggests that an organization's readiness to go through the cultural transformation process will be a factor of its ability to correlate its own survival coping mechanisms with its adaption to a constantly changing external environment. This is not an easy process. The shared beliefs and assumptions about how to survive as an organization may not be as deeply "shared" in today's workplace with its diverse work force and competing (and often unexpressed) needs and values.

The challenge remains. Companies need to reward energies focused on innovation; learning, product quality, high levels of customer service, and creating work that brings a sense of meaning and contribution to its employees. Employees need to think of companies not as surrogate parents, but rather as environments where that employee can make a significant and meaningful contribution and receive a fair compensation in return for that contribution.

CORPORATE ETHICS

There are many out there who would call corporate ethics an oxymoron, like "jumbo shrimp" or "plastic silverware." However, as business moves to a global status, ethical behavior becomes critical to success in a diverse marketplace. To understand corporate ethics is to understand the values that guide the actions of the members of that corporation. How do companies balance legal behaviors with ethical behaviors?

SOCIAL RESPONSIBILITY

Some organizations consider it part of their mission to have a positive impact on society. They see it as their obligation and have programs designed to contribute to society in a variety of ways. Most people are familiar with Ronald McDonald House and the good work that it does for families with critically ill children. The Shriners is another example of an organization whose *raison d'etre* is helping sick children. There are many more.

> It is truly enough said that a corporation has no conscience; but a corporation of conscientious men is a corporation with a conscience.
>
> Henry David Thoreau

Discussions about business ethics and corporate social responsibility are usually found together. It is almost as if there is a correlation between a company doing business in an ethical manner and that same company behaving in a socially responsible way as well. This may or may not be true.

It could be argued that once a person reaches adulthood it is difficult to teach ethics. Ethics have their foundation in a person's values, religion, and belief structures. Key concepts usually associated with ethics might include honesty, trustworthiness, and integrity. These are usually taught at home or in conjunction with a person's religious upbringing. Some people argue for something called situational ethics. In this frame of mind, each situation must be considered separately and there are no solid, bottom line guidelines that must not be breached. Once out in the working world, it is hoped that the foundational understandings about how to be an ethical person and why this is important will provide the guidance so needed in today's enticing world.

PERSONAL REFLECTION

What are the values that you hold dear? Where would you draw your "line in the sand" concerning issues of theft, lying, cheating?

Under what circumstances would you report a co-worker who was violating your ethical principles?

DEFINITIONS • DISTINCTIONS

Ethics

The rules and principles that define right and wrong within a society; the moral choices that an individual makes in relationship with others

Codes of Ethics

The written rules, policies, and procedures that address and establish how a company will operate within its environment. Codes of Ethics facilitate consistent decision making at all levels of the company

Corporate Social Responsibility

The extent to which a company believes it has a responsibility to a social public beyond that of providing goods and services to make a profit for stockholders

Social Audit

An analysis of the activities that an organization engages in with respect to its community, its environment, and other areas of social responsibility

Today's organizations fall somewhere on a continuum between those companies who feel a great deal of responsibility to society and are committed to actions that enhance the greater good, and those companies that feel this is not their role. There are many companies and stockholders who would argue that a company is only in business to make a profit for its owners and that societal issues are best handled elsewhere.

Milton Friedman, a world renown economist, argues this point and promotes a narrow view of corporate social responsibility. His *profit concept* states that the purpose of business is to make money within the rules of business. Society, outside of the business entity, should take care of society.

The *stakeholder concept* states that the organization must look at the impact of its decisions on all of its stakeholders, not just stockholders who will profit, but also other publics who might be impacted. The interests and needs of all of these groups must be considered in order to be socially responsible.

There is also a *social power* concept which implies that because of the enormous power that corporations have over their environment, they then become responsible by the very nature of that power. In other words, power requires responsibility.

How management makes ethical decisions can also be examined from a utilitarian perspective or an individual rights perspective. The *utilitarian perspective* states that decisions are to be made based on the outcomes that reflect the greatest good for the greatest number of people. The *individual rights perspective* states that decisions are focused around protecting individual rights, liberties, and privileges such as privacy, speech, due process, etc.

Johnson & Johnson's Code of Ethics

We believe our first responsibility is to the doctors, nurses, and patients, to mothers and all others who use our products and services. In meeting their needs everything we do must be of high quality. We must constantly strive to reduce our costs in order to maintain reasonable prices. Customers' orders must be serviced promptly and accurately. Our suppliers and distributors must have an opportunity to make a fair profit.

We are responsible to our employees: the men and women who work with us throughout the world. Everyone must be considered as an individual. We must respect their dignity and recognize their merit. They must have a sense of security in their jobs. Compensation must be fair and adequate, and working conditions clean, orderly, and safe. Employees must feel free to make suggestions and complaints. There must be equal opportunity for employment, development, and advancement for those qualified. We must provide competent management, and their actions must be just and ethical.

We are responsible to the communities in which we live and work and to the world community as well. We must be good citizens—support good works and charities and bear our fair share of taxes. We must encourage civic improvements, and better health and education. We must maintain in good order the property we are privileged to use, protecting the environment and natural resources.

Our final responsibility is to our stockholders. Business must make a sound profit. We must experiment with new ideas. Research must be carried on, innovative programs developed, and mistakes paid for. New equipment must be purchased, new facilities provided, and new products launched. Reserves must be created to provide for adverse times.

When we operate according to these principles, the stockholders should realize a fair return.

SOCIAL AUDIT

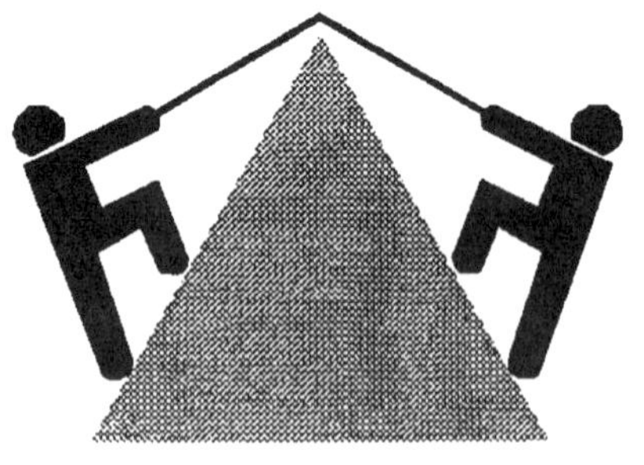

Conducting a social audit is a technique that an organization can use to measure how well it is doing in the area of social responsibility. Of course, this requires that the organization accept some measure of itself as a primary actor in the social community. Goals set during planning can be evaluated during a social audit to determine how well the organization is doing. And remember, the social community consists of a vast array of stakeholders including employees, suppliers and vendors, customers, and stockholders as well as the general public.

It should be clear by now that ethical actions are one of the major challenges facing organizations today. It is easy to apply situational ethics. It is easy to bend the rules, see many shades of gray. The pressures of managers, employees, and companies to perform and turn in record profits is intense. It is much harder and hopefully more rewarding to act in a consistently ethical manner, with everyone in the organization committed to the same high standards of ethics and moral conduct.

PERSONAL REFLECTION

What is your position with respect to corporate social responsibility? What role do you think business should play in society?

DIVERSITY

The changing workforce in the United States is making diversity a critical organizational issue. Reaping the benefits from a population with different backgrounds, beliefs, capabilities, experiences, languages, and cultures is at the heart of the meaning of diversity. Diversity is not about hiring minorities and women; it is not a quota program. Diversity brings together people with different ways of looking at events, different ways of being in this world, and celebrates these differences in order to create opportunities for growth and profitability within a business that recognizes its power.

The challenges that go with honoring and then managing diversity in the workplace can seem staggering. Companies have to adjust their communications to accommodate many languages and the nuances of language. In addition to communication, ethnocentric attitudes must be visible through dialogue so that understanding can grow where once there might have been only fear of someone different than oneself.

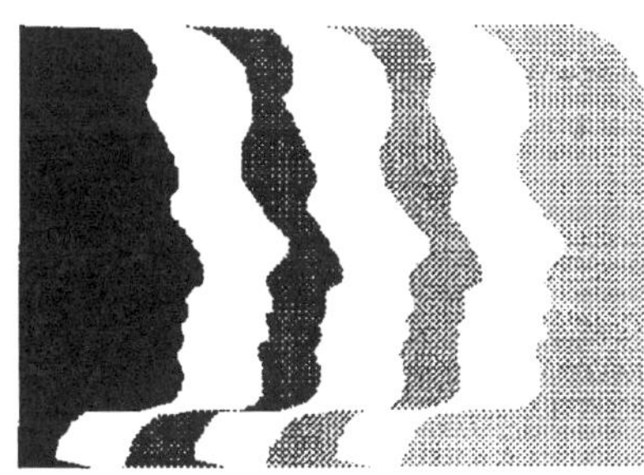

Mentors and role models need to be found so that all groups can see themselves as potentially capable of great achievements. Training and development programs must be offered on a full range of technical and, most important, interpersonal skills and relationship building. Through this type of training, tensions are reduced, trust develops, and the cohesiveness required to create productive work environments can be fully realized.

Organizations can truly become multicultural environments. In these types of companies, the diversity of the workforce is valued and seen as a competitive advantage. To get to this point requires doing a few things, and doing them right. Like everything else, multiculturalism starts with a sincere commitment from top management. After that, it becomes an exercise in doing things right—assessing the current strengths of the employees, solid recruiting and orientation programs to integrate new employees into a multicultural environment, and creating programs so that employees can develop to their fullest potential and, therefore, be retained by the organization.

THE COLD WITHIN

Six humans trapped by happenstance
In black and bitter cold
Each one possessed a stick of wood,
Or so the story's told.

Their dying fire in need of logs,
the first woman held hers back
For the faces around the fire,
she noticed one of them was black.

The next man looking cross the way
saw one not of his church,
and couldn't bring himself to give
the first his stick of birch.

The third one sat in tattered clothes
he gave his coat a hitch.
Why should his log be put to use
to warm the idle rich?

The rich man just sat back and thought,
of the wealth he had in store.
And how to keep what he had earned
from the lazy, shiftless poor.

The black man's face bespoke revenge
as the fire passed from sight.
For all he saw in his stick of wood
was a chance to spite the white.

And the last man of this forlorn group
did naught except for gain.
Giving only to those who gave
was how he played the game.

The logs held tight in death's still hands
was proof of human sin.
They didn't die from the cold without,
they died from the cold within.

Anonymous

PURPOSEFUL MANAGEMENT

PERSONAL DEVELOPMENT EXERCISES

THE RIPPLE EFFECT

Do you want to be a positive influence in the world?

First, get your own life in order. Ground yourself in the single principle so that your behavior is wholesome and effective. If you do that, you will earn respect and be a powerful influence.

Your behavior influences others through *a* ripple effect. A ripple effect works because everyone influences everyone else. Powerful people are powerful influences.

> If your life works, you influence your family.
> If your family works, your family influences the community.
> If your community works, your community influences the nation.
> If your nation works, your nation influences the world.
> If your world works, the ripple effect spreads throughout the cosmos.

Remember that your influence begins with you and ripples outward. So be sure that your influence is both potent and wholesome.

How do I know that this works?

All growth spreads outward from a fertile and potent nucleus. You are a nucleus.

The Tao of Leadership

PERSONAL THEORY OF BUSINESS

What is your personal "theory of business"?

Taking the Drucker concept of a theory of business to a personal level, one might say each person operates within the context of a personal theory of business. We all make assumptions about our worlds and then make decisions based on those assumptions. There is a saying that goes, "If you continue to do what you have always done, you will continue to reap the same payoffs."

Are these the rewards/results you desire?

Do you walk your talk or do you say you want one thing but conduct yourself in a way that gets you other results?

Do you evaluate and then reevaluate your actions and behaviors based on the results you achieve as compared to the results that you say you want and then change course accordingly?

If you want to bring something different—new opportunities—into your life, you must change what you are doing. This can only be done if and when you change your assumptions about how things are out there.

> It is the height of absurdity to sow little but weeds in the first half of one's lifetime and expect to harvest a valuable crop in the second half.
>
> Percy H. Johnston

The time has come to begin to think about where you fit with respect to your goals and objectives and how you operate in terms of getting where you are going. As a personal development activity, you may begin to think about your "mission" and how it fits into today's environment. You may also want to consider what your core competencies are now and what competencies need to be developed to create the future that you really want to be living.

Here is a planning page to help you begin to focus your attention and your personal energies in order to realize your full potential. Do not aim to complete this overnight. Give each of these personal life elements the same thoughtful attention you would give to any other important and life altering decisions you make in your life.

You may also begin to think about the purpose behind your life. What do you want to stand for? What do you value and consider as nonnegotiable—your bottom line? How will you get there?

THE PRODUCT IS ME!

nonnegotiable Values ________ ________ ________

________ ________ ________

Needs ________ ________ ________

________ ________ ________

Purpose ________________________________

Life Mission ________________________________

____

Core ________ ________ ________

Competencies ________ ________ ________

Skill ________ ________ ________

Deficiencies ________ ________ ________

Type of Work I really want to do ________________________________

____

Type of Work I DON'T ever want to do ________________________________

____

3 events taking place in the marketplace that will HELP me achieve my goals	1) ______________________________
	2) ______________________________
	3) ______________________________
3 events in the marketplace that will act as BARRIERS to me achieving my goals	1) ______________________________
	2) ______________________________
	3) ______________________________
3 new habits I must begin today	1) ______________________________
	2) ______________________________
	3) ______________________________

PROCESSES OF MANAGEMENT

Performance Management

Basic Planning

Decision Making

Managing Performance

Employee Performance & Evaluation

Business Process Reengineering

Total Quality Management

Benchmarking

LEARNING OBJECTIVES

After completing the course work in the *Process of Management* module, the student should be able to:

- define the sequence of steps required during the planning, decision making, and problem solving processes,
- define business process reengineering, total quality management, and benchmarking,
- create an integrated solution to a business problem applying reengineering concepts and/or benchmarking,
- debate the importance of integrating a total quality management mind set with a total quality management process,
- define performance management,
- design a performance management process for a specific task.

A SIGN OF THE TIMES

It's a sign of the times that ideas like reengineering, quality, continuous process improvement, performance management, and benchmarking are beginning to tarnish for some companies under the harsh reality of how difficult these good ideas are to implement and maintain in today's fast-paced business environment. Millions of dollars have already been spent training employees in all facets of these "fad" ideas and yet many companies are not reaping the related gains in actual performance outcomes.

Are these new ideas really fads or did management simply miss the boat in its understanding of the real complexity of these ideas?

The question above is yours to consider in more depth as you learn, experiment, and read about various approaches to these process concepts in the pages that follow. There is a personal side to these concepts as well.

Is your personal process a quality process?
How can you make it so?
What would it really take to live your life and to do your work with quality as a priority?
Do you give excuses why you did not execute the task in a quality fashion rather than concentrating on **"DOING IT RIGHT THE FIRST TIME"**?

PERFORMANCE MANAGEMENT

All of the concepts we will be examining fall under the umbrella heading of *performance management*. It's the *"how"*—how we do whatever it is that we are doing. According to Philip Crosby, "All work is a process, a series of actions that produces a result" (Crosby, 1991, p.17). The process of understanding how we plan the work that needs to be done, how we each manage our individual performance, the way we choose to do our work and assigned tasks, and then merge, balance, or blend these processes within a larger organization's performance holds the key to being successful. The tools we utilize to do these intricate details are the process tools of management.

And remember that an organization need not be a company per se; it could also be a family, a community, a church. Any time people come together to do work, the process of how to accomplish a specific task comes under scrutiny. Understanding how work is completed, from both an efficiency and effectiveness perspective, is critical to any continuous improvement process and performance management program.

DEFINITIONS • DISTINCTIONS

Organization

A number of persons or groups having specific responsibilities and united for some purpose or work; something comprising elements with varied functions that contribute to the whole and to collective functions (*American Heritage Dictionary*, 1979, p. 926).

Reengineering

Fundamental rethinking and radical redesign of businesses to achieve dramatic improvements in critical, contemporary measures of performance, such as cost, quality, service, and speed (Hammer and Champy, 1993).

Benchmarking

A systematic and rigorous examination of an organization's products, services, and/or work processes against those organizations that are recognized as the best, in order to produce changes and improvements in the company's enterprise (Ettorre, 1993).

Total Quality Management

A process improvement program where everyone in the organization is committed to incremental and continuous improvements in the services, products, and outcomes of the organization.

Plans

A specific set of action steps proposed and then followed in order to achieve a desired outcome. Plans are usually aimed at specific levels within organizations, are focused in scope, and have a time parameter.

Control Processes and Tools

Any processes or set of tools used to target performance efforts toward desired outcomes and then used to measure the progress toward achieving the specific outcome against planned outcomes. Control processes contain corrective action measures to implement when performance results are not in line with planned objectives.

Logistics

The movement of materials from one point to another. Also known as distribution, the key criteria is to move the right products in the right amount to the right location at the right time.

Memes

Units of information in the mind whose existence influences events such that the events are copied and reproduced and perpetuated.

BASIC PLANNING

> Plan your work
>
> Work your plan

Planning is the foundation of all that we do in order to accomplish goals. There are many different planning models at work today, and it should be recognized that effective planning is a very systematic process. Planning enables effective decision making. Plans lead to decisions that produce desired outcomes at some future point. It is a very dynamic process involving many variables that are often outside of a company's control.

There are several different types of plans and purposes for developing plans. Depending on one's position within the organization, different plans are utilized. A senior management person is more involved with *strategic planning* whereas a middle manager or a supervisor may work with *tactical* or *operational plans*. These are the day-to-day plans for the organization's ongoing operation.

Plans allow for the efforts of the work force to be more efficiently and effectively coordinated. Everyone should know what the plan is so that each employee can contribute his or her best to the plan's success.

Plans also help people recognize and respond to changing internal and external factors. Plans provide focus and direction, reduce uncertainty, and minimize waste.

Benefit ☛

Plans define the performance standards that are expected and required by the company and help with the allocation of key resources. Measurements of success are established within plans so organizations can know when they are on and/or off track.

The usual criticisms of planning—that planning stifles innovation and creativity, plans are too rigid and unresponsive to a changing environment or marketplace, and plans are not forward thinking—clearly exist. However, researchers have found that it is not planning per se, but ineffective planning that gives these criticisms their perceived truth. When planning is done correctly—with a quality mind set, with clearly articulated goal and targets, with consideration toward the environment, and with solid communication throughout the organization—significant positive results are achieved. Perhaps it is not the concept of planning, but the planners' skills that should be examined more closely whenever these criticisms surface.

PERSONAL REFLECTION

On the following page create a specific plan for your next 3 months of activity. Set 2 goals that you want to accomplish within 90 days and plan the steps and activities that you will commit to doing in order to "work your plan."

GOALS PLAN

In the next 90 days I plan to accomplish the following two goals. Goals must be:

S—specific
M—measurable
A—action oriented
R—realistic
T—time bounded

GOAL #1	Action Steps	Time Segment
	a) b) c) d)	

GOAL #2	Action Steps	Time Segment
	a) b) c) d)	

DECISION MAKING

Sometimes the decision process involves very routine items. These may be considered structured or programmed decisions. They are usually far less risky than nonstructured decisions which usually lack predictability and an experience base. Nonprogrammed or nonstructured decisions involve more risk, often create conflict and require more creative thinking techniques.

Like other techniques and tools that are being presented, effective decision making is a process and a series of steps can be followed to ensure the best possible outcomes.

Problem Definition

Defining the problem, situation, issue, or goal is a critical step in any decision making process. Often, decisions are made around the evident symptoms of a situation and the real source of the problem is not touched. These types of decision often don't create the desired end result and the problem resurfaces.

Possible Solution Generation

It is important to brainstorm a list of possible alternative solutions. Too often, people solve new problems with old solutions that don't produce the same results in today's environment. Generating many possible alternatives to solving the problem or achieving the goal creates flexibility and encourages innovation.

Evaluate Alternatives

In this step each alternative solution is evaluated separately and completely. Costs and other factors associated with using each alternative are considered. Alternatives are compared with one another as to feasibility. Long and short term goals and impacts are also considered.

Choose & Implement

Making a choice and implementing that choice is a difficult step as well. Once one chooses a path to follow, other paths are put aside. All must support the choice with their actions and their words. There are many companies that are great planners and poor implementers. Choosing also brings risk. Risk can be minimized only to the extent that information has been openly presented and communication has allowed all voices to speak their piece honestly.

Evaluate Results

Evaluation, monitoring progress, and reviewing outcomes make up the final step in any decision making process. Many times evaluation can be difficult because the results were not what was desired. However, honest evaluation enables real progress.

Each of these steps can act as hurdles to leap. Often it is difficult to focus on exactly what the problem situation really is. Many times key issues surrounding the problem are deeply imbedded in the organization's culture or hidden from view.

This can also be a power issue. It is difficult to tell someone, especially your boss, bad news. Previous history in the company might reveal that the bearers of bad news have suffered consequences (loss of job, demotion) not warranted by their openness. Organizational trust has been diminished as a result of employees feeling they must cover their tracks rather than come forward in a safe atmosphere.

Many companies skirt around issues with extreme levels of conflict, hoping by staying on the fringes of the main issue that it might simply, magically, go away. For example, a manager who does not want to confront an employee about lateness or not completing his/her share of the work may center the "problem" discussion on other issues like productivity, machinery, supplier deliveries. This manager might feel these areas are "safer" than confronting one employee about behavior and then possibly having to take corrective action.

Or an organization that has a salary compression problem, where new staff members are making less money, may address it by revamping the merit increase pool to compensate newer employees more than employees who have been there longer. The idea of being compensated for actual performance changes to being compensated for time served. The issue of salary compression still exists and is now compounded by feelings of mistrust generated by a merit system that was changed after the performance was completed. If salary compression is the issue, then adjustments to those staff salaries should be made. The problem was never clearly defined so the solution does not really fit. These examples are taken from today's workplace and show how organizations easily slip into actions that are safer but do not really address the real problem.

Generating alternatives is a difficult step because most people do not actively think about all the possible solutions to issues. They usually go with one or two alternatives and then pick from A or B. Brainstorming has been an effective technique that has helped companies and individuals to create a bigger list of alternatives to consider during the problem solving process. This is where creativity has its biggest opportunity. It is then followed by the third step, which is an evaluation of all the alternatives *before* deciding on a course of action.

Choosing and implementation come next, followed by a close monitoring and evaluation of the outcomes. If the outcomes are those that are desired the problem has been successfully handled. If not, the situation must be reviewed with any new variables that have been added to the mix as a result of problem solving efforts.

PERSONAL REFLECTION

Think about a decision that you recently made regarding an event at work. What was the process that you utilized to make the decision?

Now choose a current problem you are encountering and on the back of this page, work through the decision making process steps.

DECISIONS—DECISIONS—DECISIONS!!!!!

Problem Identification	________________________________ ________________________________ ________________________________

Alternatives	Evaluation FOR this Alternative	Evaluation AGAINST this Alternative
1) Do nothing		
2)		
3)		
4)		
5)		
6)		
7)		
8)		
9)		
10)		

Choice	
Evaluation of Results *What really happened*	
Reflection/Next Step	

CREATIVE CREATIVE CREATIVE
PROBLEM SOLVING

The nine dot exercise is the usual starting point for exercises designed to get people to think "out of the box," beyond their boundaries and preconceived notions, biases, or past experience. There is, however, so much more to creativity and creative problem solving. What is creativity? How is it expressed? How is it developed?

After studying creativity for many years, Mihalyi Csikszentmihalyi, from the University of Chicago, has premised that creativity results when three elements are present and then interact. These elements are "a culture that contains symbolic rules, a person who brings novelty into the symbolic domain, and a field of experts who recognize and validate the innovation" (Csikszentmihalyi, 1996, p. 6). Regardless of whether you are talking about an idea, a discovery or a new product/service, his research has shown that all three of these elements must be present. Csikszentmihalyi likens this to genetic changes, where mutations do not survive unless they, in fact, improve and enhance the overall survival of the species itself.

In our minds, there are units of information or thought and these have been named *memes*. In *Virus of the Mind*, Richard Brodie defines a meme as "a unit of information in a mind whose existence influences events such that more copies of itself get created in other minds" (p. 32). People use memes to describe their reality. Memes label things and help people organize and categorize thoughts and information so that they can be retrieved and used more easily. Memes are not truths, they express a person's point of view or way of seeing a particular item or event.

Creativity happens when a new thought or idea is expressed and challenges a current thought or idea. It is an accepted meme that is being challenged, and if and when enough other people see the challenge as an improvement over the old way of doing something or the old belief, that new idea or thought is accepted and becomes part of the new way to think and do and be.

> If you want to change the way someone thinks, don't tell them what to think, give them a tool.
>
> Buckminster Fuller

The tools of creative thought are the tools that enable a person to break through boundaries and frames that they have unconsciously set around their ideas or their own notions of their abilities. These are the "can't do it that way" expressions, the "it's not the way we do it here" expressions, the "I'm too busy to be creative" thoughts.

When organizations want to encourage more creative thinking processes, they need to get employees out of a "reaction" mode and into a "pro-active/creation" mode. Employees need to stop thinking in a linear "B" follows "A" mind set. Employees need to relinquish the need to be "right" and the fear associated with the notion that they might be "wrong" and play with other modes of operation. Creativity takes time. Creativity takes a child-like energy and naivete. Creativity requires unleashing the five-year-old hiding inside you.

Your Brain
=
Creativity's Tool Box

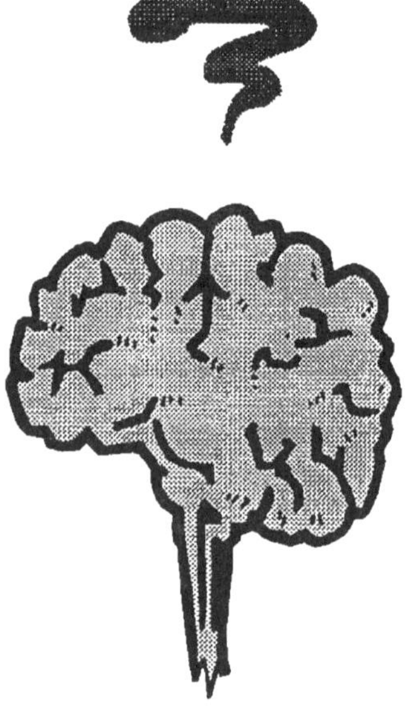

CREATIVITY GENERATORS

Try some of these tools the next time you have a problem that you want to solve in a more creative fashion. Remember, the more you practice with these tools, the better you become at using them naturally.

Reverse the Obvious
Separate into Parts
Re-Arrange and Re-Group
Concept Mapping
Word Association
What Else Can IT do?
What Else Can DO it?
Enlarge/Reduce
Adaption
New Links

PERSONAL REFLECTION

It is time to try your hand at more creative problem solving. Think of one situation that you are now facing and apply some of the tools from the list above. See if you can jump-start your creativity thinking engine and come up with 10 possible ways to deal with your issue. Do not evaluate your ideas. Simply list them and see where the list leads you. Take your time. Do this over the course of several days, at different times of day, in different locations. Try to figure out when you are at your creative best.

MANAGING PERFORMANCE

Performance needs to be managed or, perhaps more correctly, monitored over a full range of business issues. A target level or goal for performance is set and then the performance of the company's systems and resources are managed in order to reach or surpass the target. If the performance falls short of the target, an assessment needs to be done to ascertain why the performance target was not reached, and what changes need to be implemented to correct this situation.

This includes not only human performance, but also financial performance, sales performance and production performance. Clearly, there is a human element in most of these areas too. Methods to better evaluate the entire dynamic of performance and recognize the gap between desired performance and actual performance in all areas are very useful. Identifying the performance "gaps" provides opportunities for creative problem solving to accomplish a full range of performance improvements from a stance of pro-activity, rather than taking a reactive or crisis management posture as is now often the case.

12 ATTRIBUTES OF A QUALITY REVOLUTION
a la Tom Peters

1. Management is obsessed with quality.
2. There is a guiding system or ideology (passion)
3. Quality is measured.
4. Quality is rewarded.
5. Everyone is trained in technologies for assessing quality.
6. Teams involving multiple functions/systems are used.
7. Small is very beautiful.
8. There is constant stimulation.
9. There is a parallel organization structure devoted to quality improvement.
10. Everyone plays—suppliers, distributors, customers!
11. When quality goes up, costs go down.
12. Quality improvement is a never-ending journey.

The case might be made that one of the reasons companies today are in such states of upheaval is that their employees are not there for "common purposes" but rather for unique individual purposes. One employee might be there for the challenge and pleasure that the job itself presents. Another employee might be there because it is ten minutes from home, a third for the money, and a fourth because it was the only job he or she got offered.

The challenge for management is to unite this group of individuals and build successful outcomes for all involved. This unification process begins with the mission of the organization, which was the heart of the previous module. After the mission brings the organization into alignment, it must implement and utilize a variety of process tools and techniques to monitor its progress and ensure that it is on target.

These are the performance management systems that provide clear direction about how the company is doing or how the job is going when compared to pre-set standards or goals. Several process tools and techniques have been introduced over the years that accomplish this task. You may be familiar with some of these tools like goal-setting and performance appraisal.

Other tools that are presented may be new to you like benchmarking, total quality management, and business process reengineering. You may find some of them quite useful. Remember, performance management systems and techniques help the organization get the best from all of its resources, especially its "most valuable resource"—its people.

Some key questions that can help companies focus their performance management efforts can be found on the following list. As self-management skills are what more and more companies are looking for from their work force, you may want to consider asking yourself some of these questions about your own personal performance in a variety of areas.

What are the characteristics of an excellent performer in this area?

What is the performance of the typical employee in this area?

What is my performance like in this area?

How do these compare/contrast?

What specifically can I do to improve my performance in this area?

Many structured performance management systems have been developed with specific, step-by-step processes established so that companies can follow more of a cookbook formula. Here are some general steps that can be used to systematize the performance management process. Regardless of the system implemented, the entire process must be viewed as a partnership between employees and employers. It cannot be seen as something done *to* employees *by* employers.

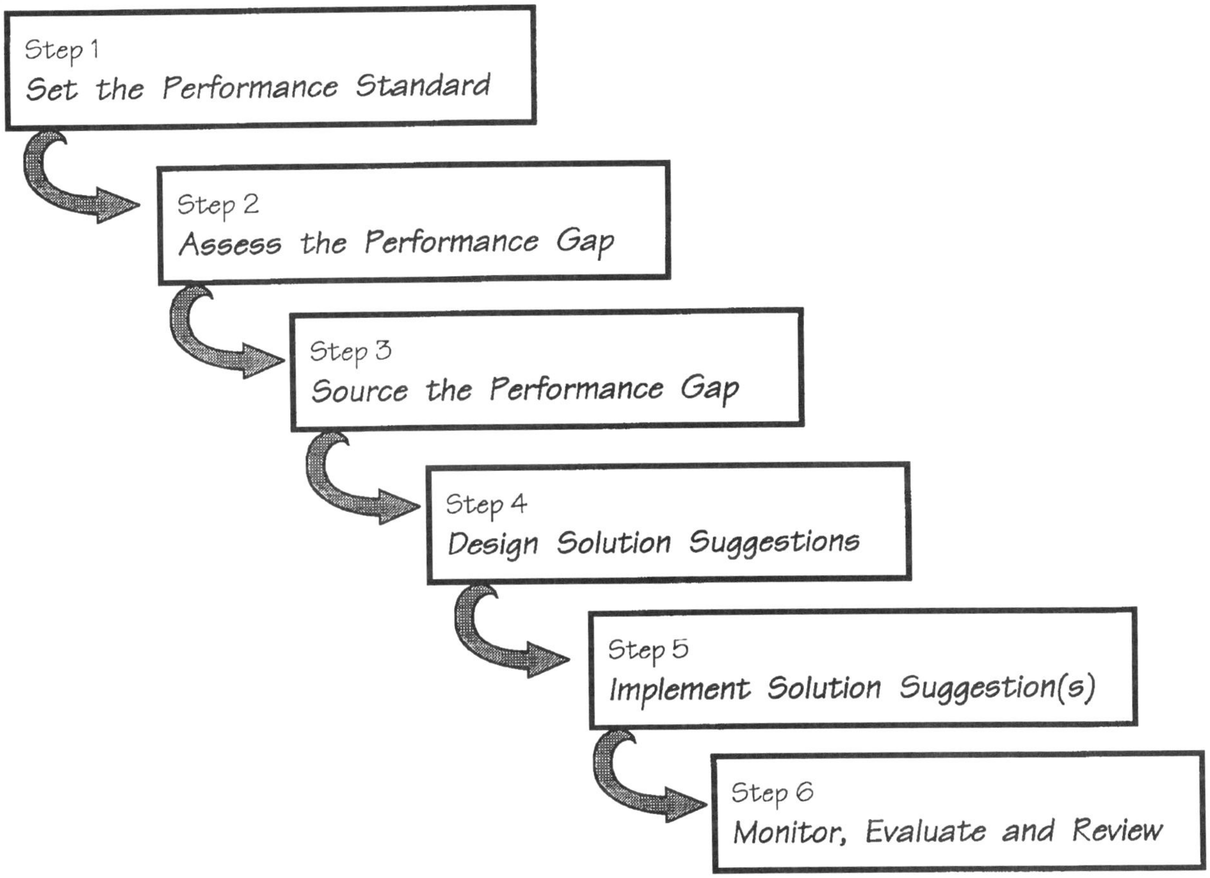

Step 1
Set the Performance Standard

Step 2
Assess the Performance Gap

Step 3
Source the Performance Gap

Step 4
Design Solution Suggestions

Step 5
Implement Solution Suggestion(s)

Step 6
Monitor, Evaluate and Review

It is often difficult for management to work through a process like this simply because the people involved have a "stake" in the outcomes. Managers don't want the performance "gap" to be in their department. No one wants to admit that his/her skills are not up to standard.

Each step outlined above requires the people involved to step out of the picture. You must detach the person from the performance standard in order to objectively evaluate the current process. The deficiency between the desired performance standard and the current actual performance must be clearly articulated. From this point, positive solution alternatives can be suggested, tried, and evaluated. Solutions that would change the environment, the work itself, and/or the process, must all be considered, as well as the costs associated with implementing changes to determine whether it is or is not worth it to implement them. Careful monitoring of the process is essential, as is the evaluation of the end results against the desired performance standards.

EMPLOYEE PERFORMANCE AND EVALUATION

The most difficult performance management issue to be discussed in this module is employee performance management. When we are talking about machines and inanimate equipment, decisions about replacement, repairs, and costs associated with fixing the machine so that it meets the required standards of performance become routine and common place. They are safe decisions, reactive at best. These decisions do get performance improvement results over the short-term. According to Bennis and Mische (1995), "most operational processes are transaction driven: Do more of the same, but do it faster and with greater control."

When one adds the human element to the performance management equation the stakes and potential results change dramatically. Unfortunately, many organizations struggle with improvements in their performance because they focus most of their efforts in the people direction, the direction with the highest level of resistance to change *with* the tools they use for processes. Wrong tools! People performance is an entirely different matter and improvements here must be integrated into a full range of organizational activities including operational planning, acquisition of resources, and distribution of rewards. This type of performance management is "transformational."

Most companies utilize some type of formal performance management system to document employee performance. This usually takes place as an appraisal of an employee's performance against some set standard. More often than not, formal appraisals are done yearly and because they are often emotional events, many managers do not give preparation for a performance meeting the attention it deserves or requires. Many managers have never had any training in how to do a performance appraisal. Controlling employees has been the primary reason for appraisal systems in the past, although other reasons have existed including enhancing motivation, legal compliance, reward and promotion issues, and staff planning. There are so many tangential issues that come into play when discussing employee performance.

A problem with performance management systems is that these systems usually have two different and often competing goals. The first goal is the appraisal of the performance itself which is usually then tied to some form of increased compensation. The second goal of many employee performance management systems is employee development. Research has repeatedly shown that it is difficult to utilize one instrument for both performance evaluation and performance development. Based on this research, it is suggested that these two goals of employee performance management be separated. Current trends in management suggest that the emphasis of employee performance management should be on developing the skills of all employees.

As organizations struggle with how to best handle the review process several new ideas have become quite popular including portfolio creation, self-evaluation, and peer reviews. Self-evaluations are becoming very popular. The employee prepares a self-review that documents from his/her perspective how well established goals were accomplished within the performance period. A meeting is then held and the manager and employee share their perspectives, arrive at some common understandings of the performance that has been witnessed to date, and then set new goals for the next performance period.

The key point is that nothing within the employee performance management process should be punitive. This cannot be stressed enough. For too long organizations have used performance appraisal as a weapon against employees and this has only strengthened the negative "us versus them" feelings.

The goal of the relationship being developed through effective performance management is one of trust, that of partners on a common quest. Goals and performance standards should be openly communicated and agreed to between all parties involved before any performance initiatives or changes are implemented. Remember, your goals cannot be forced on another person. They are your goals. Should agreement not be forthcoming, then there are other discussions which must be entertained and the direction and focus moves away from performance to other management issues.

BUSINESS PROCESS REENGINEERING

In order for any performance management system to help a company improve its competitiveness in the marketplace, the company must "examine the key processes that affect the way customers perceive quality and value" (Gale, 1995, p.37). This is a market orientation to the utilization of reengineering, benchmarking, and total quality management, tools in the Business Process Reengineering toolkit.

Gale (1995) states that "good reengineering and benchmarking focus on the effectiveness of your company's functional units to deliver a product your customers believe to be a good value. Bad reengineering and benchmarking focus solely on the efficiency of the processes of the functional units" (p. 37).

Reengineering has been used to describe so much of what organizations are doing right now including reducing staff, that the term seems to have taken on a life of its own. In its broadest sense, reengineering is about quantum improvement in the performance of an organization, not the incremental improvements usually associated with total quality management. Performance improvements may appear as reduced costs, increased speed, better quality, better service, improved accuracy. The results of real reengineering are dramatic as the definition states.

In 1995, during the introductory phase of the reengineering concept, Michael Hammer stated that he felt reengineering was about business processes and the processes were the only thing that could be reengineered. This thought was shown to be somewhat off the mark as companies' efforts to reengineer were continually thwarted by people in management positions.

We now know that in order for reengineering to be effective the full commitment of the company's leadership must be visible. Reengineering is a radical redesign of how an organization operates and does business within its current environment. All employees must move out of their old paradigms. They will only feel safe doing this if they feel the strength and commitment of the company's leadership behind the entire process. Reengineering is hard work. It is about change, about letting go, about real growth.

TOTAL QUALITY MANAGEMENT

Every job is a self-portrait of the person who did it. Autograph your work with excellence.

The movement that seems to have shaken up corporate America the most is the *Total Quality Management (TQM)* movement. Perhaps it was the defensive anger felt by many corporate chieftains who had previously ignored the work of W. Edwards Deming and Joseph Juran. Two decades ago their ideas came back to haunt corporate America with a vengeance. Japan, who welcomed the ideas of these men into their post-war reconstruction industries, became the home of preeminent manufacturers of high quality, high-tech products that were recognized, respected, and bought over American products by Americans.

Total Quality Management (TQM) is a process improvement program. It focuses on customers. It targets continuous incremental improvements in processes, often employing a structured problem-solving process to identify areas where the process may not be performing as well as it could. W. Edward Deming, Joseph Juran, and Philip Crosby have been three key players in the quality movement in the United States. There are others. The TQM process looks for statistically significant differences in output and makes corrections at the process level to aim for "zero defects," a concept in the words of Crosby.

TQM VERSUS THE TRADITIONAL WESTERN ECONOMIC MANAGEMENT MODEL

	TQM Model	**Economic Model**
Organizational Goals	Serving customer needs by supplying goods and services of highest possible quality	Maximizing profits (shareholder wealth)
Individual Goals	Individuals motivated by economic, social, and psychological goals relating to personal goals	Individual motivated only by economic goals; maximization of income and minimization of effort
Time Orientation	Dynamic: innovation and continuous improvement	Static optimization: maximizing the present value of net cash flow by maximizing revenue and minimizing cost
Coordination and Control	Employees are trustworthy and are experts in their jobs—hence emphasis on self-management. Employees are capable of coordinating on a voluntary basis.	Managers have the expertise to coordinate and direct subordinates. Agency problems necessitate monitoring of subordinates and applying incentives to align objectives.
Role of Information	Open and timely information flows are critical to self-management, horizontal coordination, and quest for continual improvement.	Information system matches hierarchical structure; key functions are to support managers' decision making and monitor subordinates.
Principles of Work Design	System-based optimization with emphasis on dynamic performance	Productivity maximization by specializing on the basis of comparative advantage
Firm Boundaries	Issues of supplier-customer relations, information flow, and dynamic coordination common to transactions within and between firms	Clear distinctions between markets and firms as governance mechanisms. Firm boundaries determined by transaction costs.

Source: *TQM's Challenge to Management Theory and Practice*, 1994.

The table just presented contrasts two underlying philosophies about how to run a business. It is not a question of right versus wrong, but simply a management decision about how a business will operate within a dynamic environment. One is based strictly on an economic model of making money, as much money as is possible without real regard to the long term implications of short term decisions. This model emphasizes cost efficiencies, contracts as the basis for relationships between individuals, and profit maximization.

The other philosophy flows from a foundation that emphasizes customer satisfaction over the long term as the way to increase a company's profitability. The TQM orientation recognizes that individuals are motivated by more than money; the need to create, the desire to contribute, to do good work that has meaning, are all important to people who work. The long term interests of employees, companies, customers, and shareholders can all be realized through the TQM model.

Harvey Mackay's Taxi Cab Story

This story is taken from *The Tom Peters Seminar* book, page 235.

"First, this driver gave me a paper that said, 'Hi, my name is Walter. I'm your driver. I'm going to get you there safely, on time, in a courteous fashion.' A mission statement from a cab driver!

"Then he holds up a *New York Times*, a *USA Today* and asks would I like them? So, I took them. We haven't even moved yet. He then offers a nice little fruit basket with snack foods. Next he asks, 'Would you prefer hard rock or classical music?' He has four channels."

Mackay goes on, listing more features, such as a cellular phone for his use. Then he concludes, "You know what? This man makes $12,000 to $14,000 extra a year in tips. You should have seen the tip I gave him. Incredible."

Quality becomes the operative word in TQM; the commitment to total quality and not just lip service! This also proves to be the stumbling block to real success for many companies who have attempted TQM programs and for many people. It is difficult to have a quality mind set one minute and then discard it the next. Let's see, I'll do this project with quality in mind and I'll just get this other project done. This split focus does not work well and is a major reason many quality initiatives have proven less than successful. Quality work is quality work, it is that simple. People who do high quality work do it in all aspects of their lives. The commitment to quality is an internal commitment that cannot be turned on and off like a water faucet. The commitment to quality—every day in every way—no ifs, ands, or buts!

How is your personal quality revolution going?
Are you winning your quality battle?

THE MEN BEHIND THE QUALITY MESSAGE

No conversation about quality is complete without acknowledging the men who championed its importance. Three of the most prominent are W. Edwards Deming, Joseph Juran, and Philip Crosby. The similarity of their message was the continuous commitment to quality; the approach to achieving this commitment established their differences.

W. Edwards Deming

After World War II when American industries were in their glory, W. Edwards Deming attempted to promote his ideas about utilizing *statistical process controls* (SPC) to improve the quality of the products being manufactured. He found his most receptive audience in Japan, because the reconstruction of their industrial base was of primary concern. Deming advocated ideas centering around the continuous improvement in design and manufacturing of products and incessantly called for top management to take the lead and accept the responsibility for all that went on in their facilities. An award is given in Japan to honor this man who introduced Japan to the quality techniques that would make its industries leaders in the modern world. In the 1970s American industries began playing catch-up, implementing Deming's ideas at a rapid pace in order to compete effectively in a developing global economy that demanded quality products and services at reasonable prices.

Deming's 14 Points

1. Create constancy of purpose.
2. Adopt the new philosophy.
3. Cease dependence on mass inspection to achieve quality.
4. End the practice of awarding business on the basis of price tag.
5. Improve constantly and forever systems of production and service.
6. Institute training and education.
7. Institute leadership.
8. Drive out fear.
9. Break down barriers between departments.
10. Eliminate slogans, exhortations, and targets for the work force.
11. Eliminate work standards that prescribe numerical quotas for the day.
12. Remove the barriers that rob all employees of the pride of workmanship.
13. Institute a vigorous program of education and retraining.
14. Put everybody in the company to work in teams to accomplish the transformation.

Joseph M. Juran

Another American who became a significant leader in the quality movement also had his start in Japan. Joseph M. Juran expanded the notion of "the customer" to be more than the person who buys a product, but rather the person who receives the work that you do. Your customer might be the person in the next department or the next stage of the production process. In Juran's view, every step in the process affected the next step. Quality required that every person in the production process be trained to determine cause and effect relationships in the workplace and then to work together to solve problems using a variety of group oriented strategies.

The *Juran Trilogy*, as it has come to be known, encompasses three areas: quality planning, quality control, and quality improvement. *Quality Planning* requires the identification of internal and external customers, the determination of customers' needs, the development of products and services to satisfy those needs, and finally, the development of processes to produce those products and services. *Quality Control* is the ongoing internal quality guide practiced by all employees while *Quality Improvement* speaks to the continuous analysis and remediation of problems.

Philip B. Crosby

The third in this series of "guru" status people in the quality movement is Philip B. Crosby. His approach is a nontechnical one and many organizations have found that it is more conducive to both technical, field, and administrative operations. Crosby's message focuses on behaviors of people and creates a common language and mission that can be quickly established. This creates awareness about quality. After this, other more statistical methods and nuts and bolts practices can be more easily incorporated and understood.

4 QUALITY ABSOLUTES
Philip Crosby

1. a definition of quality
2. a prevention (not appraisal) system of quality
3. a performance standard of quality
4. a measurement of quality

Crosby believed that companies had to act from a strong position of integrity, with solid internal communications, good systems, operations procedures, and policies in order to achieve any long lasting and significant progress in the quality arena. Like Deming, he had a 14-point list for achieving "zero defects," his slogan for rallying employees in the quality program.

PERSONAL REFLECTION

Observe the company where you now work. Do they have a quality program at work? What operations do they do with quality in mind? How do they measure quality? How do they encourage quality work consistently? How do they reward it?

When you are totally in charge of your performance, do you do a quality job or just enough to get by? When is your work of its highest quality? How do you know?

MALCOLM BALDRIGE Award Winner

QUALITY AWARDS AND CERTIFICATIONS

The Malcolm Baldrige award was established by Congress in 1987 and is given annually to companies recognizing their achievement in quality. The award is not given for specific products or services, but rather for implementing processes that enhance the competitiveness of American companies.

Since 1988, the first year it was awarded, over 28 companies have won the Malcolm Baldrige Award. There can be two winners in each of three categories: manufacturing, service, and small business. It is not a requirement of the program that each category have a winner each year.

SEVEN PROCESS AREAS EXAMINED

leadership
information and analysis
strategic quality planning
human resource development and management
management of process quality
quality and operational results
customer focus and satisfaction

ISO 9000

ISO 9000 is a certification process that is also becoming more important to American organizations. The purpose of ISO 9000 was to provide a quality system or business process that would provide a consistent method of doing things in a business. It was developed under the auspices of the International Organization for Standardization. Many international companies are demanding ISO 9000 certification before they will do business with an American company.

ISO 9000 Basic Requirements

Say What You Do	➡	Document
Do What You Say	➡	Daily Practice
Record What You Did	➡	Facts—Just the Facts
Check On The Results	➡	Review
Act On The Difference	➡	Corrective/ Preventive Action

ISO 9000 attests to the consistency of a quality system or a process, but does not certify the quality of the product or service itself. This can be very misleading. Originally designed for manufacturing, the standards can be readily applied to service sector operations.

BENCHMARKING

Benchmarking is a process tool that has probably been informally used since the beginning of time. When you look at the work of another person and compare it to what you have done, you are doing a form of benchmarking. Benchmarking is a measurement of work against other work that is perceived to be the best. It can be easily and effectively applied to techniques, processes, and service delivery.

An organization seeks out the "best-in-class" and then systematically and rigorously compares its processes to that best-in-class company. Companies do not necessarily have to be in the same industry to act as benchmarks for other companies. This is not industrial espionage; it is not about stealing product ideas or secrets. Processes are the focus of benchmarking. Some of the most common processes to benchmark include customer service, order fulfillment, inventory control and replenishment systems, facility management. The outcome of this type of comparison is information—both quantitative and qualitative information that can then be utilized to generate performance improvements, eliminate inefficiencies, reduce costs, and improve competitiveness.

Types of Benchmarking

Internal Operations
Specific Process(es)
Contract
Competitive

Benchmarking can be done internally, where one department of a company benchmarks its operations against another department within the same company. This often works well when a company has different locations and decentralized management. Specific processes or functions can also be the target of benchmarking efforts. The accounting operation, order entry process, employee selection and orientation process are all excellent candidates for benchmarking.

Lately, consulting style companies that sell benchmarking as their product/service offering have appeared in the marketplace. These third party operations do the benchmarking work and report back to the hiring company. Competitive benchmarking speaks for itself. A company examines its processes against that of its competitors.

BEST-IN-CLASS PLAYERS

Xerox	Braun	Motorola
3M	Wallace Co.	Florida Power & Light
GE	Levi Straus	IBM
AT&T	HP	Milikin
MCI	Disney	Dow Chemical

a small sampling of companies who have been targeted as best-in-class sources for other companies to facilitate the continuous process improvement effort

BENCHMARKING PROCESS

IDENTIFY FOCUS GOAL OF THE BENCHMARK PROJECT

IDENTIFY BEST-IN-CLASS OPERATION

IDENTIFY KEY PERFORMANCE VARIABLES FOR DATA COLLECTION

CHOOSE THE TEAM MEMBERS FOR THE BENCHMARKING VISIT

ANALYZE / COMPARE FINDINGS AND COMMUNICATE FINDINGS

DEVELOP ACTION PLANS AND IMPLEMENT CHANGES

ASSESS NEW RESULTS AGAINST TARGET GOALS

As with any process, benchmarking has its share of problems and traps to avoid. The biggest problem in benchmarking is a lack of focus on what to benchmark. This goes hand in hand with making sure that the process being benchmarked is part of the strategic plan. It must be critically important to the company's overall success in order to make the benchmarking activity worth the time and effort that it will take. Often, too many people are assigned to the benchmarking team and/or the wrong people are chosen to conduct the benchmarking site visit. Those doing the benchmarking should be intimately familiar with the process—namely, the actual employees who do the work every day. Timetables for implementation must be realistic and proper procedures and courtesies should be followed when contacting a company to use as a benchmark. *Remember, this is not industrial espionage!* It is not about copying—benchmarking is a learning tool that then applies the new learning in a different environment.

When used properly, benchmarking becomes a key resource tool for major process improvements. Several organizations have used this technique to successfully change inventory management programs, distribution services, customer service programs, and order entry systems to name but a few areas where benchmarking has proven itself to be a great tool.

PERSONAL REFLECTION

Choose one function that you do now and follow the steps in the benchmarking process to compare/contrast your process (your "how to do it") with that of someone you consider to be "best-in-class" with that function. You may choose a work process, a school related process, or something from your personal life.

Step 1	Focus/Goal *(what you're examining)*	
Step 2	Best-In-Class	
Step 3	Key Performance Variables *(what you're looking at and measuring)*	
Step 4	Team Members	
Step 5	Analysis & Comparison *(what you saw & experienced)*	
Step 6	Action Plans & Date Targets *(what you're going to change by when)*	
Step 7	Evaluation of Results *(what you learned)*	

CONCLUDING THOUGHTS

Ideas like business process reengineering, total quality management, and benchmarking fall under the performance management heading because these are tools and techniques used to improve performance of individuals, groups, and organizations as they work to achieve their overall strategic agenda. The power within these concepts comes from their total integration into how organizations and the people who make up the organization do everything they do. These concepts do not exist within a vacuum.

The process section of management deals with the "how." Monitoring, controlling and revising performance and steering it along a constantly changing course to accomplish the organization's mission is the bottom line of any continuous process improvement program. And yes, we all can always improve. It is death to think otherwise. Every job we do should provide us with new understandings of that job so that we can strive to do it better and better and better . . .

PROCESSES OF MANAGEMENT

PERSONAL DEVELOPMENT EXERCISES

UNFOLDING PROCESS

Group process evolves naturally. It is self-regulating. Do not interfere. It will work itself out.

Efforts to control process usually fail. Either they block process or make it chaotic.

Learn to trust what is happening. If there is silence, let it grow; something will emerge. If there is a storm, let it rage; it will resolve into calm.

Is the group discontented? You can't make it happy. Even if you could, your efforts might well deprive the group of a very creative struggle.

The wise leader knows how to facilitate the unfolding group process, because the leader is also a process. The group's process and the leader's process unfold in the same way; according to the same principle.

For example, facilitating what is happening is more potent than pushing for what you wish were happening. Demonstrating or modeling behaviors is more potent than imposing morality. Unbiased positions are stronger than prejudice. Radiance encourages people, but outshining everyone else inhibits them.

The Tao of Leadership

MENTAL FLEXIBILITY INVENTORY

Creativity does not just happen to many people. Some need a little prompting, a little practice juggling and manipulating their gray cells.

The inventory that follows does not measure your intelligence, your fluency with words, and certainly not your mathematical ability. It will, however, give you some gauge of your mental flexibility and perhaps even your creativity. See how many of the brain teasers below you can unravel in about 15 minutes. Do your own thing here. You may also want to "observe" how you approach this problem solving experience. Do you have any specific processes that you follow?

EXAMPLE: 16 O in a P = 16 Ounces in a Pound
60 S in a M = 60 Seconds in a Minute

26 L of the A

1001 A. N.

54 C in a D with the J's

88 P K

9 P in the S S

32 D F at which W F

90 D in a R A

3 B M (S H T R)

10 C

5 D in a Z C

29 D in F in a L Y

7 W of the W

57 H V

8 S on a S S

76 T

3 C in the F

6 F in a F

3 S and Y O

20 C in a P

99 B of B

13 S on the A F

18 H on a G C

200 D for P G in M

2 T D and a P in a P T

24 H in a D

11 P on a F T

64 S on a C B

12 S of the Z

4 Q in a G

7 B for 7 B

8 B in the S P

6 O in an I

20000 L U the S

2000 P in a T

PEOPLE AND MANAGEMENT

Motivation

Communication

Group Process & Team Effectiveness

Power

Leadership/Followership/Self-Leadership

Conflict!

LEARNING OBJECTIVES

After completing the course work in the *People & Management* module, the student should be able to:

- define the content and process theories of motivation and discuss the implications motivation has on achieving successful outcomes personally and professionally,
- assess the dynamics of communication as an integral component of human interactions and propose several techniques to enhance the student's personal communication effectiveness,
- identify the stages of the group formation process and measure the effectiveness of individual behavior within a specific group setting,
- evaluate various theories of leadership and assess their effectiveness,
- discuss the concept of followership in today's business environment as a necessary component toward the development of self-leadership capabilities,
- compare and contrast power styles and conflict resolution strategies enabling you to more effectively respond to an increasingly complex workplace.

> "Do the people part right and the profits (all kinds of profits) will surely follow."
>
> J. R. Flagello

We have now reached the heart of the matter—that point where all the plans, strategies, and processes ever devised by anyone in relation to managing a business are put to the acid test—the people part.

More words have been written and spoken about these illusive concepts—motivation—communication—leadership—teams—power—conflict—more time and energy spent in trying to understand the full depth of their meaning, than probably any other ideas in the history of modern times.

As you explore this next group of topics, the key point to remember is that you, as an individual, an employee, a spouse, a parent, a friend—all the roles that you play in your everyday life—are impacted by your capabilities in each of these areas. They are not separate from you—they are you! You are part and parcel of what motivates you, how you communicate, what you say, how well you really hear when listening, how you lead or are led, how you interact with a variety of "others." You cannot divorce yourself from the responsibilities of your actions although many people attempt to do this every day. The limelight is yours when you succeed. No one is to blame for your mistakes or any lack of success you may encounter, although many of our first instincts are to blame others when things don't go our way. Hopefully, you succeed far more often than you don't succeed. Learning about your intimate "self" can raise your success level tenfold.

> "The future will belong to those individuals who are capable of continuous personal learning and development, who are self-motivated, self-led, and self-managed, and finally to individuals who see themselves as full contributing partners in an ongoing drama called work, called life."
>
> J. R. Flagello

PERSONAL REFLECTION

As Shakespeare said, "To thine own self be true." Look deeply into yourself as you read and learn about motivation, communication, leadership, followership, power, and conflict. For some of you, this will be difficult to do. Coming to terms with our own behaviors, our frailties and fears, and balancing them with our hopes, dreams, and desires can prove to be overwhelming for even the hardiest soul.

Motivation

the forces both internal and external that energize, direct, and sustain a person's actions and activities

Group

two or more people who come together either on a formal or informal basis who may perform similar tasks, or work together to accomplish a task influencing one another in the process, or who consider themselves alike in some way; members influence each other and think of themselves as a group

Team

two or more people with complementary talents who come together with a focused goal to achieve through their combined efforts, commitment, and mutual accountability

Leadership

a process of focusing, directing, enabling, and engaging the skills and talents of others to accomplish a goal or objective

Power

the ability to influence other people

Authority

the right that comes with a particular position to give orders, expect those orders to be obeyed, to command, to determine, and to judge

> Don't aim at success—the more you aim at it and make it a target, the more you are going to miss it. For success, like happiness, cannot be pursued; it must ensue, and it only does so as the unintended side-effect of one's personal dedication to a cause greater than oneself, or as a by-product of one's surrender to a person other than oneself. Happiness must happen, and the same holds for success: you have to let it happen by not caring about it. I want you to listen to what your conscience commands you to do and go on to carry it out to the best of your knowledge. Then you will live to see that in the long run—success will follow you precisely because you had forgotten to think of it.
>
> Viktor R. Frankl
> *Man's Search for Meaning*

MOTIVATION

What makes anyone strive to perform, to be the best at something, whether it be sports, a job, a talent, as a parent, or as a person?

Research tells us that there are only two aspects of motivation that control us—pleasure and pain. The human being is either chasing pleasure (however or whatever a person perceives pleasure to be) or the human being is avoiding pain (again, however or whatever the person perceives to be painful). All behaviors center on these two ideas. Think about it. All that we do—*pleasure—pain—pleasure—pain*—how simple—how complex!

On the next two pages is a chart which covers several key motivation theories that have been used to try to explain human behavior. Theories of motivation can be classified as either *Content Theories* or as *Process Theories*. A content theory describes "what" motivates a person to act in a certain manner. The process theories attempt to show "how" to go about initiating the action, sustaining it, and eventually how to extinguish it. It stands to reason that both content and process theories must come into play. Together, they work to achieve desired outcomes.

The difficulty comes in connecting these theoretical abstractions to the workplace. From a bottom line orientation the question becomes "Can one person really motivate another?" Working strictly for the paycheck, from 9 to 5, with the job being seen as an inconvenient, but necessary interruption between weekends is no way to go through life. There is so much more available!

THE CARROT—THE STICK—OR WHAT?

Are you motivating or manipulating when you hold out something that someone else wants as an incentive to get that person to perform?

Manipulation of others with promises or out of fear does get people to do things, but this is not motivation. The "carrots" and the "sticks" must continue to get bigger in order for manipulation to work for the long-term.

Motivating others seems to be more about creating an environment where the behavior of another person will be influenced to the extent that he or she will be "motivated" to do something. It is about creating an environment where another human being will feel comfortable, safe, and secure enough to pursue his or her goals in order to realize a reward of some type.

This distinction may seem to be minor, but it is at the heart of the motivation discussion and the underlying reason why one person cannot motivate another person to do anything. Think about this. Have you ever been in a situation where you and another person were being treated the exact same way and you were motivated to do great things, but the other person was not? The rewards being placed before each of you were the same, and yet, one of you was not motivated to perform?

MOTIVATION THEORIES

Content—"WHAT"

THEORY	THEORIST	KEY POINTS	RATIONALE	APPLICATION
HIERARCHY OF NEEDS	Abraham Maslow	5 "need" levels physiological safety/security social esteem self-actualization	Assumption was made that lower level of need had to be adequately satisfied before the next higher level became a motivating force. Lower levels were seen as extrinsic where factors were initiated outside of the person; higher levels were intrinsic—the individual initiated and controlled these.	Awareness of where one is on Maslow's hierarchy can help focus motivation and target actions to be successful.
2 FACTOR THEORY	Frederick Herzberg	Hygiene Factors salary, security, status, supervision, policies, working conditions, work relationships Motivating Factors growth, achievement, recognition, responsibility, the work has meaning	Assumption that motivation is two separate factors—satisfiers and real motivators. Today's workers expect certain needs to be met and when they are, there is no subsequent motivation energy released—just a sense of satisfaction as opposed to dissatisfaction. Real motivators energize the person to perform at higher levels.	First step is to eliminate factors that create job dissatisfaction. This creates satisfaction with the job and can generate loyalty, build positive attitudes, and commitment. Management must then create an environment where employees' natural internal motivators can operate. This is more than job satisfaction.
3 NEEDS THEORY	David McClelland	Achievement Power Affiliation	Three key motives within the work environment. It is the relationships between these three factors that motivate work.	By understanding which need is important to each employee, management can create environment to focus on that motive.
EXISTENCE GROWTH RELATIONSHIPS	Clayton Aldefer	Reconceptualized Maslow's hierarchy with only 3 levels.	People can move between levels and lower levels do not have to be satisfied before higher levels are activated.	Similar to Maslow. Management can attempt to create environment where employees can satisfy needs.

MOTIVATION THEORIES

Process—"HOW"

THEORY	THEORIST	KEY POINTS	RATIONALE	APPLICATION
EQUITY THEORY	J. Stacey Adams	States of positive equity, equity, and negative equity exist. Comparison made against a referent person or group as to where one is in equity.	Individuals want their efforts and performance to be judged fairly relative to others. Person is motivated by the perceived fairness of the rewards received for a certain amount of effort as compared to relevant others.	Management must work to ensure a perception of "equity" throughout employee ranks. When an imbalance is perceived, employees will work to correct it through whatever means are available to them.
EXPECTANCY THEORY	Victor Vroom	E > P > O effort > performance > outcome	Individuals consider alternatives, weigh costs and benefits, and choose course of action with maximum utility. The perceived value of outcomes (results) plays a strong role for each person.	Outcomes or rewards must be valued by individual person. This requires different rewards to be offered for similar performance.
REINFORCEMENT THEORY	B. F. Skinner	Rewarding behaviors produces repetition of the behaviors. Environmentally based, not a source of internal motivation.	Control theory more than motivation theory. Positive reinforcement and negative reinforcement exist and can be used to control performance.	Management can use reinforcement schedule to control performance, giving rewards for acts they desire and punishing employees for acts they do not want repeated.
GOAL SETTING THEORY	Edwin Locke	Personally set goals motivate people to performance. Goals that others set are not as motivating.	Each person sets specific goals that have time parameters, are measurable, attainable, and realistic to that person. Once achieved, new goals must be set that require higher levels of energy and skill to obtain.	If goals are accepted by the employee, they will motivate performance. Management must work *with* employees to set mutually relevant goals and celebrate achievement.

In the final analysis, it must be clear that one can physically manipulate someone (perhaps) to do things, can even move them through physical means, but to motivate—ah, that is an inside job—an individual, inside job. Only I can motivate me. Only you can motivate you. So, how are you doing?

INTRINSIC

Intrinsic rewards are those elements of whatever we are doing that make us feel good about the action. They are derived from the job itself, from a person's inner sense of contribution and accomplishment. The more people can achieve a sense of self-worth from the work they do, the greater the motivation to continue with that work. Intrinsic motivation is the highest form of motivation because it is iterative, continual, ongoing.

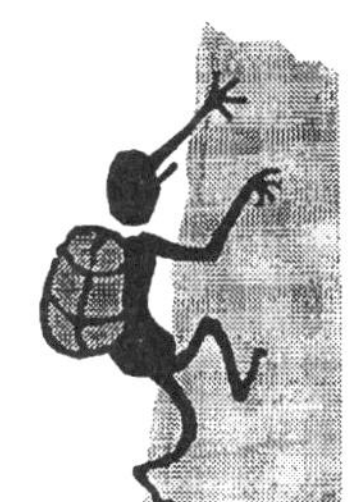

EXTRINSIC

Extrinsic rewards are those that are offered by the outside world. These may come from our bosses, our peer group, our family or fans. Extrinsic rewards include such things as salary, benefits, cheers, notoriety, and other tangible or material goods that we do not do to or for ourselves. These material items or recognitions often hold great power and can be easily used to manipulate a person's behavior.

We all have a desire to gain something for our efforts. The problem comes from the overuse of material reward and external validation for our work and the under use of inner reward, the reward we gain from the work itself. This brings us to the heart of the motivation question. What rewards do we seek and where do they come from? Do we value intrinsic rewards or must rewards be extrinsic to have any meaning for us?

The costs of extrinsic rewards keep getting more expensive. Companies are realizing that it is difficult to continue to provide these types of rewards because of their increased costs. Several of the options organizations have been using to control these escalating costs have led to decreased trust between management and employees and both of these groups are struggling as they try to find new ways to interact.

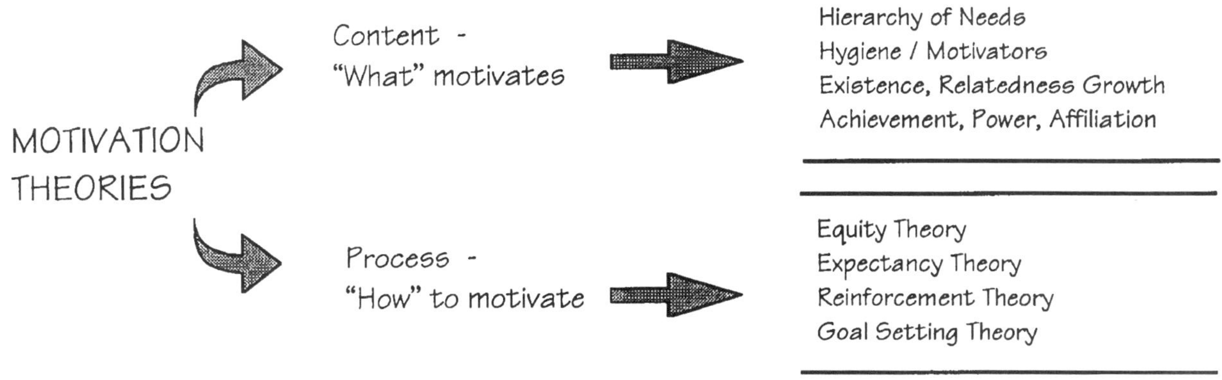

MATTERS MATTERS MATTERS

A classic motivation argument centers on money as the supreme motivator. Pay me and I'll do what you want.

> The person who takes a job in order to live—that is to say, for the money—has turned himself into a slave. Work begins when you don't like what you're doing.
>
> Joseph Campbell

As you examine the Motivation Theory charts you will recognize that, depending on the theory under discussion, money can be a motivator because it can help people acquire things they need and want. Money is clearly important in today's society and having money buys many of the external trappings that deem a person as successful from society's point of view. However, many of the other theories argue that true motivation must come from inside a person and that money is external and controlled by external factors. Further, there will come a time when there will not be enough money available to pay a person to perform a job that needs to be done so something else must then take over as the motivator. Theorists from this school of thought feel that true motivation is more than money, beyond money.

The decision about whether money motivates is an individual one and one that will change as a person's circumstances change. Clearly, there are many jobs that are critically important to society, but on the lower end of the pay scale. There are other jobs which earn good salaries, but offer less in the way of social value. People do both of these types of jobs and are satisfied and dissatisfied with both. There are many people earning good money who are unhappy with their lot in life. Go figure!

> WIIFM—
> What's in it for me?
>
> PMMFI—
> Please make me feel important.

I can find no reference as to who first coined these acronyms, but they seem to have merit as we pursue an exploration of motivation. They represent the cries of humanity. We all want to feel important, like we matter; we want to know that people care about us. In our throw away society, this has become very difficult. Commitments and vows made are often quickly tossed aside when the going gets rough. Many enter into agreements and contracts with a mind set that if it doesn't work out the way they expect, they will simply break the contract, walk away, quit. People have somehow become expendable commodities, not only in the workplace, but also in families and communities.

As organizations continue to experiment with programs to increase employee motivation, the phrases above should be at the center of their actions. All people interactions should be initiated as if we "see" these signs around each other's necks. It is the classic "do unto others as you would have others do unto you." People are motivated to perform when they feel they are being treated fairly and when they feel important or recognized for that performance. These should be ongoing activities, not special events.

COMMUNICATION

Managers spend most of their days in one of the basic communicative actions—reading, talking, listening. Then again, don't we all? How well we utilize each of these skills will have a dramatic effect on our ability to be successful in the workplace as well as in our personal lives.

Communication occurs when one person (the sender) chooses symbols and signals to convey a message that he/she wants to convey and then sends that message through a chosen medium to a receiving person. The receiver interprets the message based on his or her perceptions, understandings, culture, and experiences and then initiates some action to show that the message has been received. Those actions represent feedback to the sender. Depending on what the receiver does, the sender has a sense that the message was received as it was intended to be received, or else that the message was somehow miscommunicated. At that point the sender must re-send a new version of the message and again wait for feedback from the receiver.

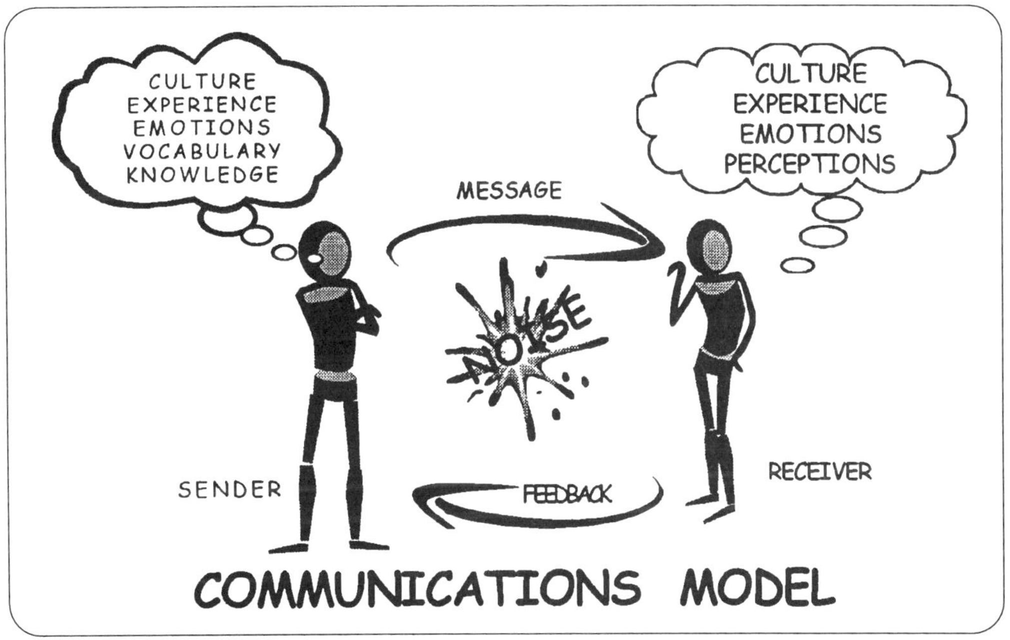

Considering all of the ways a message can get scrambled, this is no easy task. Think of how often you say something and it gets misunderstood. There are many barriers to effective communication including such things as culture, personal bias, language differences, medium chosen, distances, and internal and external distractions. When all of these are considered it is a wonder anything gets done at all!

Communicate unto the other guy that which you would want him to communicate unto you if your positions were reversed.

Aaron Goldman, CEO, The Macke Company
—sign given to all managers

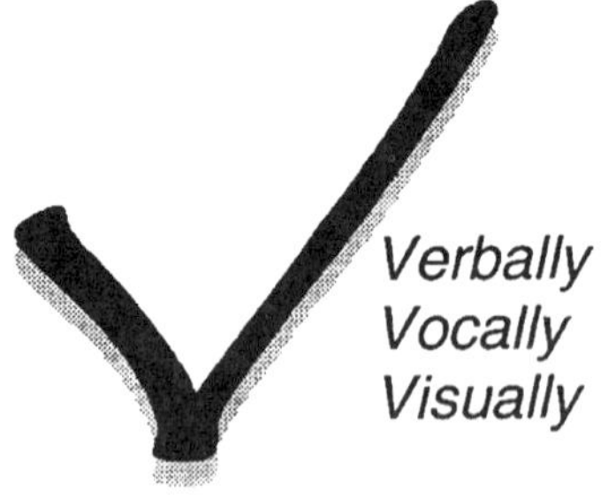

Add to this mix one other aspect of the communication process—the different ways people communicate—and the problems are intensified. This manner of communication has been called the three "V's"—verbal, vocal, and visual.

The *verbal* component has to do with the words we choose to use. We have a huge range of choices as to the words we use. We can use high powered technical language, street slang, and anything in between.

Vocal issues consider the tone, volume, and enunciation of those words. From a dull monotone to a loud roar, our tone can convey a considerable message on its own. Finally, the *visual* component of communication—how one looks when one participates in the communication process. You know that even when you are on the receiving or listening end of a communication, your body language can scream loud and clear about how you are receiving and feeling about the message being sent.

Another component of communication that must be considered in the communication process is whether the communication is supportive or destructive. As we come to recognize the importance of collaborative action in business and personal routines, the idea of utilizing communication that is "*supportive*" and makes others want to help and work with us becomes an important consideration.

SUPPORTIVE COMMUNICATION is:

problem-centered

descriptive

interactive

specific

Several of the key elements of supportive communication are shown above. Supportive communication focuses on the problem or issue at hand, not the person. Personal attacks and blame are not effective in this mode of operation. Communicating in a supportive fashion is descriptive, not judgmental or evaluative. The person communicating simply describes what is occurring without any finger pointing or assessment. This style of communication is interactive, meaning that the communication flows in two or more directions, not just one.

Supportive communication is specific about the issues under discussion and people involved in this type of process take responsibility for what they are saying. Other aspects to consider are a consistency between what is being said and the *verbal, vocal,* and *visual* display being observed. The discussion stays focused on one topic and comments made by those participating are targeted to that topic before other topics are considered. Finally, everyone in the discussion participates as an equal. There are no power plays, no inferior positions, no posturing. Everyone is seen as a valuable participant and is treated as such.

Two other aspects of communication that are important are your ability to listen and your ability to come from a place of respect in all of your communication activities. Both of these will probably require the development of some new skills. As a society, many people feel no need to really listen to what other people have to say, and we often discount other people, calling it teasing and flirting. These two behaviors have no place in a successful work environment, let alone any meaningful personal relationships.

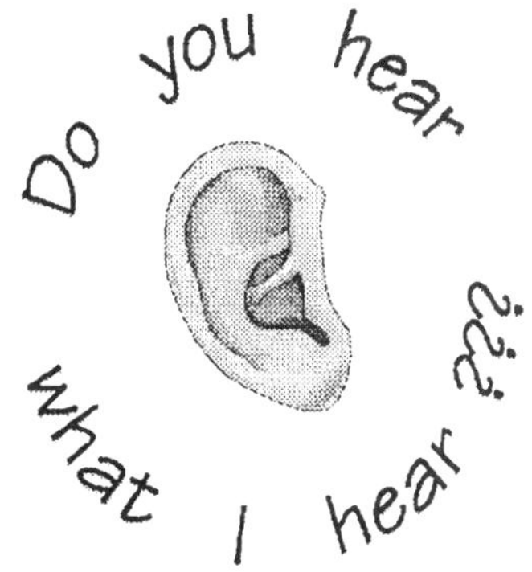

THE ART OF LISTENING

Although people do it all of the time, being able to really listen to what someone else is saying, and then carry that listening one step further, to really understanding the point being expressed, is an art unto itself. Too often people are only half listening, while the majority of their attention is focused on how they will make the speaker wrong, counter with a sassy comeback, attack or defend their positions or point of view. Hence, the lost art of listening!

When people listen effectively, they are engaging all of their senses and aiming all of those senses to the speaker. They must not only hear the words being said, but they must also listen for shades of meaning, observe the body movement of the speaker, reflect on a variety of behaviors, motivations, reasons for what the speaker is saying and why the speaker is saying it. It ain't easy! People spend over 45% of their day in some form of listening activity.

> I know that you believe you understand what you think I said, but I am not sure you realize that what you heard is not what I meant.
>
> Anonymous

There are habits that characterize good listeners and there are habits that people who are not good listeners seem to display. How many of the good listening habits can you honestly say that you exhibit consistently on a daily basis? See how well you do answering the following questions. Rate each question from 1 to 5, with 1 as a low ability and 5 as a high level of ability on each point.

1 2 3 4 5 Can you listen even if you think the subject is not interesting?

1 2 3 4 5 Do you often interrupt to get your point in?

1 2 3 4 5 Do you focus on and then criticize the speaker's delivery or can you get past delivery issues and focus on the content of the message?

1 2 3 4 5 Do you listen for facts only?

1 2 3 4 5 Do you need to be the center of attention or can you allow others to take center stage?

1 2 3 4 5 Do you need to be entertained in order to listen?

1 2 3 4 5 Do you lose control of your emotions or can you maintain your composure even while listening to ideas you may disagree with?

LANGUAGE IS POWER

When you speak, your words have a great deal of power—the power to do good and the power to destroy. Words can be affirming, neutral, or discounting.

+	~	–
affirming	neutral	discounting

When we affirm another person and their comments and ideas, we are creating a safe and collaborative environment. This is the type of environment where we all probably want to work, live, and play. It takes so little to make a person feel good when they are sharing their thoughts. Affirming does not mean automatic agreement with what is being said. Affirming is an important part of the process of communication. It requires participants to recognize and honor other people, listen without rushing to judgment, encouraging others to get involved and speak, and not tolerating actions that limit the group's problem solving process.

Discounting other people and/or their ideas is very costly. It stifles creative expression and often forces people to withdraw from participation. Many companies have lost important ideas and suffered reduced productivity and creativity simply because employees felt their ideas were not valued or welcome. They stopped contributing.

To become aware of discounting one need only to watch, look, and listen. When you hear phrases like, "Be serious, will you" or "That's a dumb idea" or "We don't do it that way here," you are hearing discounting. How often have you heard, "Get your facts straight" or "Wrong!" or "Not!"—all are examples of discounting. Teasing is another form of discounting that is most often used in the social environment. Feelings get hurt and people withdraw, all because one person had to make himself or herself feel important at the expense of another person.

PERSONAL REFLECTION

Spend the next 5 days observing your own listening skills and affirming/discounting behaviors and those of the people around you. What do you notice? Record your observations on the following page.

Actively work to incorporate good listening skills into your daily routine. Take active notes, be attentive to the speaker, focus on the content of the message, be curious about the topic, find a point that you can apply immediately.

On a separate sheet of paper make two columns, one for phrases you hear and the other for things you say. Record every "discounting" phrase you hear over the course of the next 5 days. Be observant to the body language exhibited by the person who is the target of the discounting. Record your findings.

LISTENING SCORE CARD

OBSERVATION RECORD

Day	Observation	Reflection
Monday		
Tuesday		
Wednesday		
Thursday		
Friday		
Saturday		
Sunday		

DISCOUNTING DIAGRAM

Discounting Phrases Heard	Discounting Phrases I Said

GROUP PROCESS AND TEAM EFFECTIVENESS

THE PARABLE OF THE SPOON

A holy man was having a conversation with the Lord one day and he said, "Lord, I would like to know what Heaven and Hell are like."

The Lord led the holy man to two doors. He opened one of the doors and the holy man looked in. In the middle of the room was a very large, round table. In the middle of the table was a large pot of stew, which smelled delicious and made the holy man's mouth water.

The people sitting around the table were thin and sickly. They appeared to be famished. They were holding spoons with very long handles and each person found that it was possible to reach the pot of stew to take a spoonful, but because the handle of the spoon was longer than the person's arm, one could not get the food back into one's mouth.

The holy man shuddered at the sight of their misery and suffering.

The Lord said, "You have seen Hell."

They went to the next room and opened the door. It was exactly as the first one. There was a big, round table and the same pot of delicious stew, which again made the holy man's mouth water. The people, as before, were equipped with the same long-handled spoons—but here the people were well nourished and plump, laughing and talking.

The holy man said, "I don't understand."

"It is simple," said the Lord. "It requires but one skill. You see, they have learned to feed each other."

Anonymous

GROUPS TO TEAMS

You drive past the theater and see people waiting to go in for the show. Are they a group or a team? They are all there for the same reason—to see the movie. They all have the same goal. Why is this mass just a group of people and not a team?

With this mental picture we begin the discussion of groups and how groups of people with similar goals are *not* really teams, but can learn and grow and become teams. As more organizations move to team-based approaches to accomplish work, it becomes critically important to understand the difference between a group of employees working on the same project and a real team. Although the first may evolve into the second, these two concepts are very different.

STAGES OF GROUP FORMATION

FORMING

Members come together. Roles of leadership and task assignments are unclear.

STORMING

Members interact and egos compete for control. Conflict and tension are often high. Roles and relationships begin to take shape.

NORMING

Group cohesiveness develops and members' expectations about behaviors are set. People accept their roles and work really begins.

PERFORMING

Members are functioning well together and energy is focused on accomplishing the task(s) of the group.

People join groups for a variety of reasons. Some feel that being a member of a group will offer them security, status, or power. Others just want to enjoy the social relationship that group membership offers. Joining some groups offers a boost to self-esteem and finally, people realize that groups can accomplish goals that are often difficult for an individual, working alone, to complete.

Groups move through several stages as the members learn how to work together. These have been given rhyming names: forming, storming, norming, and performing. As you read the descriptions, think about the various groups that you are in and try to assess where each one is in the formation process.

A group's ability to perform effectively is dependent on

a. its ongoing ability to complete its goals,
b. maintaining and enhancing the relationships among the members, and
c. continually adapting to dynamic conditions focused always on improving the performance of the group.

To accomplish these three tasks, members of a group often assume different roles when the group comes together. The easiest person to spot is the person(s) who takes charge and becomes the leader of the group. Within the follower ranks you may find a variety of different roles including a *summarizer*, an *energizer*, a *tension reliever*, a *comprehension checker*, a *supporter*, an *opinion giver*, an *opinion seeker* and so on (Johnson & Johnson, 1987).

There is also the role of the *noncontributor*, the *laggard*, the *leech*. This is the role that makes many people not want to participate in group types of projects at work. They resent that someone among them will not do his or her fair share of the work and yet will often receive the same rewards as the group members who did perform. What makes matters worse is that there is often a code of silence that prevents members from speaking out against these people, and noncontributors can exist for years in organizations. Everyone knows who they are, but no one addresses the problem.

This is where management must step in. Management has a responsibility to employees working in group environments to deal with noncontributors in a forthright and honest manner. This crucial management responsibility must not be ignored. Unfortunately, this is often one of the uncomfortable roles that a manager must perform. Many managers prefer to ignore this lack of performance, hoping the group will force the employee to perform, or that the offending employee will remain in the background.

PERSONAL REFLECTION

The question that now becomes important is what role do you play within a group? Are you a leader, a key contributor, a doer, or are you the person who is always late, is never prepared, does little if any real work, but is out in front when the accolades are handed out? What key skills do you offer groups in which you are involved? Do you facilitate the group's progress or hold it back? How can you improve your contribution to the success of the group?

Answer these questions honestly on the the following page. Would you choose *you* to be a member of your group if you knew the stakes were high? Why or why not?

HIGH PERFORMANCE TEAMS

Teamwork is being hailed as *"the"* organizational structure of the 21st century. Companies are jumping on the teamwork bandwagon, making teams for every task. There are clearly some tasks that lend themselves to the team concept while other tasks do not. Organizations must be careful not to exploit a powerful and exciting concept.

Groups evolve into teams—high performance teams—for a variety of reasons. Just because employees work in the same department or have the same goals, it does not necessarily follow that they will become a team. They may forever be a strong work group and this should be recognized and rewarded just as vigorously as the team approach.

> Groups become teams through *disciplined action.* They shape a common purpose, *agree* on performance goals, *define* a common working approach, *develop* high levels of complementary skills, and *hold* themselves mutually accountable for results.
>
> Katzenbach & Smith
> *The Wisdom of Teams*

The concept of true teamwork needs to be more clearly understood so that more organizations will reap the colossal benefits that can be achieved through team performance. There are several key components of effective teamwork that were identified by Katzenbach and Smith during their investigation of the concept.

GROUP ROLES & GOALS

Think about a group in which you are a member. It can be a work group or a school project group. Keep your focus on this group and answer the following questions. Be as honest with yourself as you can be. The value is in learning how you really act in a group in order to enable your growth.

What role(s) do you play in a group? (*Refer back to the reading if you do not remember the various roles.*)

____

____

What key skills/strengths do you bring to the group?

____

____

How do you specifically know that you are helping the group achieve its goals?

____

____

How can you improve your contribution to the group's success?

____

____

____

Would you chouse YOU to be a memeber of your group if you know the stakes were high? Why/why not?

____

____

____

What one specific thing can you begin to change about yourself to make you a better group member starting today—right now?

____

____

____

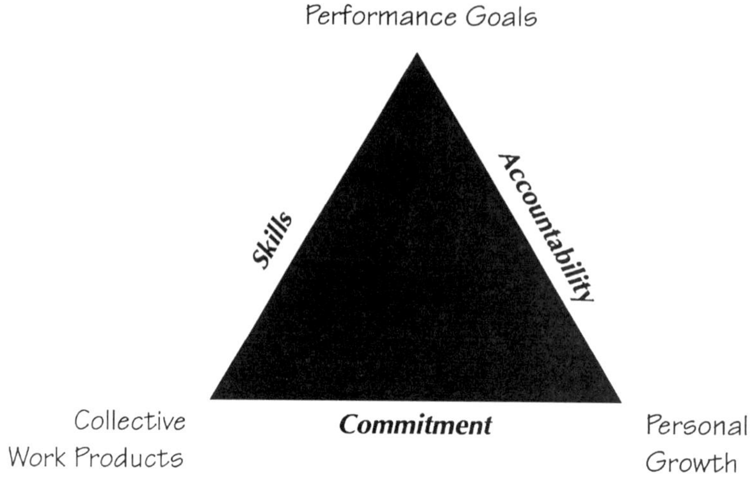

Performance Goals

Skills

Accountability

Collective Work Products

Commitment

Personal Growth

Source: The Wisdom of Teams

The three critical areas that must be present for a group to move to a high performance team are performance results, collective work products, and personal growth. High performance teams do not just do the job within a department. Most often, their assignments or projects are outside the traditional department's daily goals and tasks.

In the skills area, teams have complementary technical skills that create a stronger whole than each person as an individual. In addition, team members have strong interpersonal skills, good communication skills, and are highly creative problem solvers.

Their accountability is both individual and mutual. They do not let themselves down and readily work with one another feeling a strong bond. High performance teams do not require designated leaders. All share the leadership role. Their commitment is to a common goal that all feel is significant, worth accomplishing, and all have agreed to pursue.

Reading the definition above and examining the diagram gives one a sense of the deep level of commitment and drive that truly high performance teams require. These teams have clear and challenging goals that require a high performance commitment. They recognize the unique and complementary strengths of the individual team members, and they establish a recognition and reward system that rewards the entire team as a whole unit and its members as individuals. There is no "I" in this type of team and each member will come away from the team project stronger for having served on the team.

High performance teams are more than departments or people traveling along a similar path. Their tasks are within the framework of the organization's mission, but have starting and ending time parameters. In other words, high performance teams are the embodiment of collective and collaborative targeted performance. This creates a strong team "one" from a qualified "many." The emphasis is always clearly on the performance requirement. Teams come together to perform a specific assignment, not to exist forever.

Not all projects require a high performance team. Both high performing ongoing work groups and specialized teams should probably share the stage throughout the organization. Each has its unique talents and both are important to the successful functioning of the company. The trick for management will be learning which to use when, so that the talents of each are deployed correctly.

There's no "I" in team.

PERSONAL REFLECTION

Creating a clear understanding of what is expected on any project builds an atmosphere of shared expectations and facilitates the successful, high quality completion of any team's projects. Check the box after each element of effective teamwork has been discussed.

1. ❑ The team has met to set the ground rules for the team's interactions.
2. ❑ The project's purpose is understood. All members are committed to achieving this outcome.
3. ❑ A time line and budget are established to help the team move forward, stay focused and on budget.
4. ❑ Leadership is a shared responsibility.
5. ❑ Consensus has been designated as the primary means to achieve agreement.
6. ❑ A meeting plan and communication process is set up so team members stay connected.
7. ❑ All resources needed to complete the project are available and have been committed for the team's use.
8. ❑ We have agreed on a process to disagree and handle conflicts that arise immediately.
9. ❑ The team agrees to collaborate and work for win/win solutions. There is no "I" on this team.
10. ❑ There has been open discussion concerning the specific skills and strengths that each member brings to the team. Every member is fully competent and skilled. There are no weak links.

POWER

Before discussing leadership, let's turn our attention to a discussion of power. Power is about influence, and, if used correctly, it can have tremendous effects on all that it touches. If used incorrectly, it can do great harm. Power is about relationships. There are different types of power and different ways to apply them in order to achieve one's objectives. For the most part, they fall under two headings—*Positional Power* and *Personal Power.*

> Power in organizations is the capacity generated by relationships . . . power is energy; it needs to flow through organizations; it cannot be confined to functions or levels . . . What gives power its charge, positive or negative, is the quality of relationships. Those who relate through coercion, or from a disregard for the other person, create negative energy. Those who are open to others and who see others in their fullness create positive energy.
>
> Margaret Wheatley

POSITIONAL POWER

Legitimate
Reward
Coercive
Information

Positional power is that power that comes from the position that one holds within a company or any type of organization, even within the family. This type of power is considered legitimate because it is based on the authority that is vested in the position held. With a particular position comes the ability to reward and to punish, control or manipulate (coerce). Information is also often associated with positional power. People in higher positions usually have access to more vital and important information. Most people have heard the phrase that "information is power."

PERSONAL POWER

Expertise
Referent
Information
Communication

Personal power is another category of power that many people may not realize is open to them. There are several different types of personal power. First, there is referent power which is when someone is admired and commands respect because others want to be like him or her. Expertise or knowledge is another type of power. A person's ability or having a special skill to do a particular task well gives a person a great deal of power.

Communication ability is also a form of power. The better a person can use communication to get across ideas and persuade others, the more power that person has. How we each use our power or our influence to change ourselves and then influence those around us becomes the operative question. Some people, some managers, some friends, some parents wield power as if it were a sledge hammer, driving it deep into others, creating environments of control. When they turn their backs or leave the room their perceived control is gone. This use of power does not have a lasting effect.

Others recognize that the more power one gives away the more power one really has. Working with other people is about accomplishing goals and power becomes an enabler in this process. In this sense, people are set free and power funnels toward the tasks at hand. Motivation is strong because it comes from inside the people doing the job and their energies are focused in the right direction—toward completing the task.

Learning how to recognize what type of power works best for you in different situations and then using your power wisely is the sign of a great leader, manager, follower, member, teacher, parent, partner. If you feel you must control others, then the reality is that you have no real power. Control is just control. It is not power.

PERSONAL REFLECTION

Think of a situation at work where you have attempted to have power, or use power to get a particular outcome. What methods, motions were most successful? When did you feel most frustrated? Why did you feel the need to control the situation? Upon reflection, can you now think of another way you could have handled the situation?

LESSONS FROM GEESE from a speech by Angeles Arrien, 1991

Fact

As each goose flaps its wings, it creates an "uplift" for the birds that follow. By flying in a "v" formation, the whole flock adds 71% greater flying range than if each bird flew alone.

Lesson

People who share a common direction and sense of community can get where they are going quicker and easier because they are traveling on the thrust of one another.

Fact

When a goose falls out of formation, it suddenly feels the drag resistance of flying alone. It quickly moves back into formation to take advantage of the lifting power of the bird immediately in front of it.

Lesson

If we have as much sense as a goose we stay in formation with those headed where we want to go. We are willing to accept their help and give our help to others.

Fact

When the lead goose tires, it rotates back into the formation and another goose flies to the point position.

Lesson

It pays to take turns doing the hard tasks and sharing leadership. As with geese, people are interdependent on each other's skills, capabilities and unique arrangements of gifts, talents or resources.

Fact

The geese flying in formation honk to encourage those up front to keep up their speed.

Lesson

We need to make sure our honking is encouraging. In groups where there is encouragement, the production is much greater. The power of encouragement (to stand by one's heart or core values and encourage the heart and core of others) is the quality of honking we seek.

Fact

When a goose gets sick, wounded or shot down, two geese drop out of formation and follow it down to help and protect it. They stay with it until it dies or is able to fly aain. Then, they launch out with another formation or catch up with the flock.

Lesson

If we have as much sense as geese, we will stand by each other in difficult times as well as when we are strong.

LEADERSHIP/FOLLOWERSHIP/SELF-LEADERSHIP

It is often thought that through the definition of a term we arrive at a more solid understanding of that term. Leadership, however, is one of those concepts that defies definitive definition. Many people say that they "know it when they see it," adding that they don't see very much of it lately. There is a cry for more effective leaders in all spheres of society today: business, politics, religion, community, and of course in families. There are certainly enough people out there. Where are all the leaders?

Attempts to define *leadership* in concrete terms have proven somewhat elusive. Researchers, and people who seek to be called leader, have often cast their definition of leadership to reflect their personal biases, agendas, and interests with the topic. Most researchers and practitioners would agree that leadership denotes some type of intentional influence over others.

For the moment we will set aside a comparison of definitions of leadership, using the idea of intentional influence as a basis for presenting a brief history of leadership thought. In this module, the early frameworks for the scientific study of leadership will be presented for consideration. These fall into three categories: Trait Theories, Behavioral Theories, and Situation/Contingency Theories. Around these three categories, however, has developed a rich knowledge base about related topics like motivation, power, and the development of effective interpersonal relationships; all of which have led to furthering our understanding of leadership.

TRAIT THEORY

This theory led to the cliché that "Leaders are born, not made." For years the thought was that there were specific traits that people were born with that enabled them to lead others. Once identified, these traits could be used to screen people for leadership positions. Those people that were found to have the traits and characteristics that had been identified as "leadership traits" could then be nurtured and provided with training and opportunities to further develop these traits.

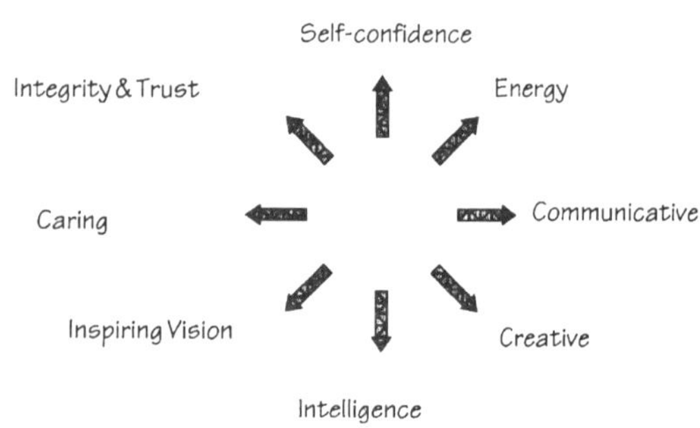

Some of the most common traits/characteristics that leaders seem to possess are shown in the diagram to the left. Of course, you may have other ideas about what traits leaders must have. This is the fun of the debate.

Think about this for a moment. What do you think are the critical traits that a leader must have? A leader's essence, if you will.

Which do you see as secondary?

What were the traits of leadership? According to Gary Yukl, a noted researcher in the field of leadership, although there are characteristics that enable the development of a person into a leader, no conclusive evidence has ever been found to link specific traits to leadership. While some people with the perceived leadership traits do develop into leaders, many others do not.

BEHAVIOR THEORIES

One thing that became clear from the search for traits that led to leadership was that leadership was too dynamic a process. Research then shifted to a focus on how leaders acted. The behaviors of effective leaders could be compared and contrasted with the behaviors of people thought to be ineffective leaders.

Behaviors were thought to have certain advantages over traits, including their visibility and the simple fact that behaviors can be taught. People could observe leaders in action and observe specific behaviors that enabled them to be successful. These behaviors could then be taught.

While there were many research projects taking place in the late 1950s and early 1960s, a few stand out and are the best-known in the area of behavioral leadership. One took place at the University of Michigan and the other at Ohio State University. Both investigated leadership behaviors on a two dimensional axis-like model. In each one, the development of personal relationships was contrasted with the tasks required to do the job. Another study in this same time period was done by Rensis Likert. The Blake-Mouton Managerial Grid (now Anne Adams McCanse) also follows similar dimensional thinking.

The Ohio State and Michigan Studies

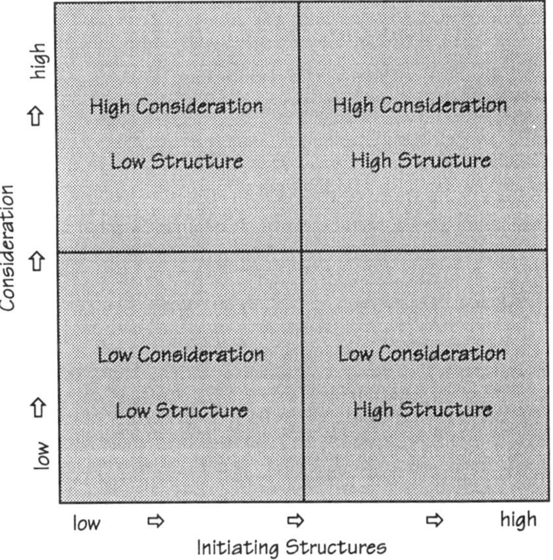

At Ohio State, close to 2000 different behaviors were identified and then narrowed to form what we now know of as the Leadership Behavior Description Questionnaire. The two different dimensions of leadership under investigation focused on consideration factors (those behaviors that are people-oriented) and initiating structures (those behaviors that are task-related). These two dimensions were plotted as an axis orientation rather than as a behavior continuum.

The University of Michigan also focused on two dimensions of leadership: employee orientation and production orientation. The original study was done at the Prudential Insurance Company following an interview data collection format. One of the most significant findings of the Michigan study was that relationship oriented behaviors and production oriented behaviors could exist together. Effective managers scored well on both dimensions.

Managerial Grid

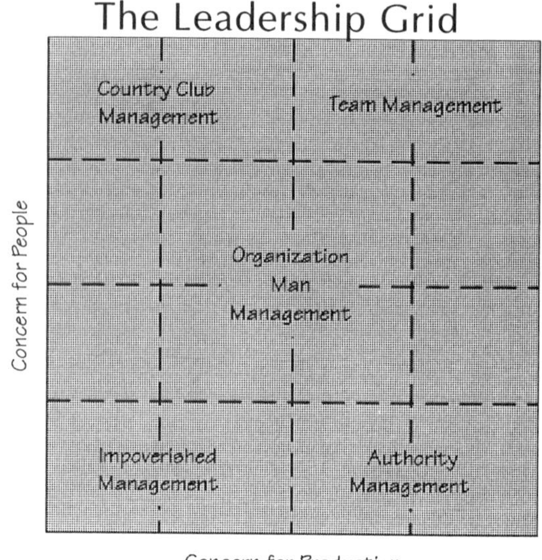

Robert Blake and Jane Mouton developed the managerial grid which also examined management effectiveness along two dimensions: concern for people and concern for production. This work was later enhanced by Blake working with Anne Adams McCanse and is known as the leadership grid. It is used extensively in organizations today to identify the style of leadership in evidence.

Results from these studies continue to be examined for consistency of findings. What has always been most challenging in leadership research is the ability to move from the theoretical realm to daily practice. Clearly, employees are more satisfied in environments where they are treated well and thus respond with better work.

While this may be a direct result of the leader's behavioral style, it could also be a result of many factors outside of the leader.

When "A" = "B"
DO "C"

CONTINGENCY THEORIES

The theories grouped under the umbrella heading of contingency take into account certain aspects of the leader, the people being led, and the variables of the situation itself. These theories attempted to add the "when" to the leadership discussions that had preceded them. Many of the theorists of the contingency school of thought felt that if a manager could isolate the relevant factors of a particular situation, there would be a "one best way" to manage/lead that would always work in situations when those same factors were present. Four of the most popular studies will be presented here for your review.

Tannenbaum—Schmidt Continuum

Robert Tannenbaum and Warren Schmidt published a seminal article in the *Harvard Business Review* in 1957 describing a continuum of leader behaviors that the leader selected from depending upon the interplay of the leader, the situation, and the followers. The dimensions used in their work were similar to those of the Ohio and Michigan studies previously discussed.

The leader's behavior choices existed on a continuum between a democratic, relationship orientation on one end and an autocratic, more task oriented style at the other end. The basis for the choice of leader style is the assumption that leaders make about the source of their power. Leaders that perceive their power as emanating from those that follow them would choose a more relationship orientation or democratic approach. Those leaders that felt their power came from their positions would be more inclined to use autocratic behaviors.

Fiedler Contingency Model

Fred Fiedler developed his contingency model of leadership based on the premise that there is a correlation between a leader's style, the task itself, and the amount of control the leader had over the task. He is best known for his development of the Least Preferred Co-Worker Scale (LPC) questionnaire. This instrument, which is basically a psychological test, assesses whether a person is task oriented or relationship oriented. Once the leader's style was understood, the situation itself was analyzed based on three elements: leader-member relations, task structure, and position power. From there the leader was matched to the situation.

Fiedler's belief that leadership styles are fixed suggests to management that leadership effectiveness can only be enhanced through a good match of the leader to the situation. If the leader's style does not "fit" the situation, one must change the leader or change the situation. The more complex variables of today's workplace also need to be considered and were not considered in the original LPC study. The study and model are important because they do emphasize the importance of "fit" between leader style and the situation in order to assure the best possible outcomes.

Path-Goal Theory

The Path-Goal Theory of Leadership uses the Expectancy Theory of Motivation as a foundational element in predicting leadership effectiveness. The premise here is that one of the primary tasks of a leader is to outline for followers the kind of behavior that will result in the accomplishment of the goal. The leader defines the "path" to the "goal."

Four types of leader behaviors were identified as those types of behaviors that would enable the leader to elicit performance from followers. They were directive, supportive, participative, and achievement oriented. Leaders would be able to choose among these approaches or styles depending on the situation and the desired outcomes. This is in direct contrast to Fiedler who assumed that leader styles were fixed.

Two sets of variables are considered in Path-Goal Theory. Environmental variables are those which are outside the control of the follower such as the task structure, the formal authority structure, and the work group, but are important as variables to ensure the ability of the follower to perform effectively. The other set of variables is in the control of the followers and includes experience, locus of control, and perceived ability.

While research is still needed to add validity to this theory, the logic of its underlying premise is important. A person's job performance and satisfaction with that job performance are more likely to be positive when the leader can compensate for environmental problems or skill deficiencies. On the other hand, if the leader is too directive in situations where it is clear the employee has the requisite skill and experience to handle it, the employee is more likely to see this as interference and respond negatively.

Hersey-Blanchard Situational Model

The foci of the situational/contingency leadership theories are the followers. The followers have the choice to accept or reject the leader. Their maturity, according to Paul Hersey and Kenneth Blanchard (of *One Minute Manager* fame), becomes the key element that needs to be assessed when selecting a leadership style. The abilities of followers to take responsibility for directing their own behavior and their willingness to do so are paramount.

The two leadership dimensions identified by Fiedler are also used here: task orientation and relationship orientation. They are placed on a four-quadrant grid and described as four different leadership styles based on whether they are high or low. The maturity level of the followers is also considered in the Hersey-Blanchard model and is divided into four stages as well.

TELLING (high task/low relationship)	**M1**
Roles are defined by the leader, people are told exactly what to do, how to do it, and when to do it.	People are unable and unwilling to take responsibility and lack confidence and competence.
SELLING (high task/high relationship)	**M2**
The leader provides directive and supportive behaviors.	People are motivated but lack appropriate job skills. They are willing but unable.
PARTICIPATING (low task/high relationship)	**M3**
Decision making is shared and the leader's role is more as a facilitator.	People are able in that they have the requisite skills, but are unwilling to do what the leader wants done.
DELEGATING (low task/low relationship)	**M4**
Little direction or support is provided by the leader.	People are able and are willing.

Vroom/Yetton/Jago

Several other leadership theories centered on the decision making process. Victor Vroom and Philip Yetton developed a decision making tree incorporating seven contingencies and five alternative leadership styles based on "yes" and/or "no" responses along the decision path. The original work was revised by Vroom and Arthur Jago several years later. The basic assumption of the model was that leadership style could be flexible and change with the situation. The three critical components of the model were

a. the specification of the criteria by which the effectiveness of the decision would be judged,
b. a framework for describing and categorizing leaders' behaviors and styles, and
c. the diagnostic variables that would describe the aspects of the situation.

PERSONAL REFLECTION

Where does all of this leave us? This is the question of all questions. So many people today seem to be waiting for new leaders to step up to the plate and be counted, unhappy with the results of previous leadership. Do we keep hoping for a savior who will lead us out of the fray into a brave new world not of our own making?

Here are some other questions to assist you as you clarify your thoughts about leadership. Jot down your thoughts so that you will be prepared to discuss these.

How does a leader's behavior cause or affect follower performance and subsequent job satisfaction?

Are there substitutes for leadership?

Is shared leadership possible?

What is transformational leadership?

What is servant leadership?

Where do good and evil play out in the leadership equation, if at all?

Are the people we call "leader" really leaders or is there some other word that can better describe these people so that the term leader can be more narrowly defined?

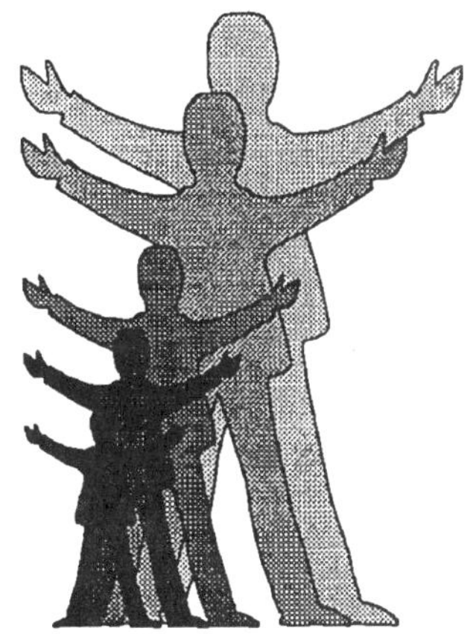

THE LEADER WITHIN

These are the questions that challenge all students of management and leadership thought. It is not enough to memorize and parrot theory. If each person is going to be more responsible and more accountable in a world of smaller, more dynamic and responsive organizations, then understanding the essence of leadership is required. We can no longer tolerate "any man" to step up to the plate because he or she talks the loudest or the longest.

Each person must initiate an internal dialogue and come to a solid understanding of what leadership is and the characteristics that make an effective leader, the kind one would willingly follow. The public can no longer be led by a blindness that tolerates the whims and fancy of those that would be kings. It is our responsibility to stand up and be counted, to develop the leader within, so that together we can create the world we want to live in. Tomorrow's workplace requires a new set of skills on the part of every person who plans to be a member of it. Companies want employees who can manage and lead themselves, who take action, who accept responsibility, who are committed to more than just a pay check, who are passionate about whatever it is they are doing.

LEADERSHIP

FOLLOWERSHIP

SELF-LEADERSHIP

SERVANT LEADERSHIP

TRANSFORMATIONAL LEADERSHIP

There is an important relationship between these words. Leadership may not really be about giving orders and being in charge. New research suggests that effective leadership requires a person to serve those he or she is leading, to balance the tremendous responsibility of being out in front with the equally important responsibility of making sure that others are able to complete their goals.

As many of the management trends of the last few years are more closely examined one can see how well "leadership as service" would fit with empowerment, ideas about participative management, and total quality initiatives. Leadership, in this sense, offers more to more people. The leader becomes one with others, not one out in front telling others what to do and then watching others work. Many of the latest trends in management thought and practice—mission, goals, collaborative work, shared rewards—fit into this style of leadership.

If a definition of management as "getting work done through others" is accepted, then those "others" become critical elements of the work process. Leaders create the vision, give meaning to work, and provide opportunities for others to become successful. This is true leadership.

FOLLOWERS—ALL FOR ONE/ONE FOR ALL

Leaders are nothing without followers. The idea of following needs to change and is, in fact, undergoing a tremendous transformation in business today. Once thought of as a passive, obedient role, the idea of being a follower seemed to be a safe haven for many. Do what you are told, follow orders, work—don't think.

Today's climate requires that followers assume new levels of authority and responsibility within the organization. Companies are asking employees to act as if they were owners. Tom Peters calls for all employees to develop ownership mentalities, to become business persons, "entrepreneurs" (Peters, 1994).

As more decisions are made outside of the executive suite and move into the general ranks of the organization, followers are really in charge. Engaged followers are critically important because they are the people on the front lines, doing the work, interacting with the customers. The employees must begin to "see" themselves as individual leaders with important responsibilities. This is the only way the new workplace will successfully engage its customers.

Followership is what we all do every day and we must hone these skills and become highly effective in this critical role.

Robert Kelley studied followers and concluded that followers are "people who know what to do without being told—the people who act with intelligence, independence, courage, and a strong sense of ethics" (Kelley, 1991, p. 12) He continues stating that, "followers . . . participate with enthusiasm . . . and self-reliance but without star billing in pursuit of organizational goals" (p. 27). Followers are the employees of an organization. Followers are you and me. Followership and leadership go hand in hand. Organizations must celebrate both. Without followers, there are no leaders. In a business environment now focused on collaboration and team projects, the role of follower is the "*sine qua non*" of organizational success.

Through Kelley's research he developed two dimensions within which followers act: independent thinking and active engagement. From these two dimensions, Kelley identified five styles of followership that people may fall into when they fulfill the follower role. He lists these as: Exemplary, Alienated, Conformist, Pragmatist, and Passive.

What does all of this mean for you today? Clearly, as organizations look to employees to add value to the operation, becoming more accountable, a partner in the action, your ability to fully exploit your follower skills will be important. Remember, followers give leaders power. Followers choose who to follow.

Exemplary followers, to use Kelley's designation, will be those employees who engage their full range of technical and mental capabilities on behalf of those they serve. They see themselves as partners with leaders, with their companies, with themselves and their actions exhibit strength, personal responsibility, accountability, and a high moral character. They are self-leaders.

PERSONAL REFLECTION

Complete both the Leadership Development Inventory and the Followership Inventory created by Robert Kelley in the Personal Development Exercises for this module. See where you fall on both scoring cards.

SELF-LEADERSHIP

Tomorrow's workplace requires a new set of skills on the part of every person who plans to be a member of it. Companies want employees who can manage and lead themselves, who take action, who accept responsibility, who are committed to more than just a pay check, who are passionate about whatever it is they are doing.

Charles Manz, a researcher in the field of self-leadership, defines the concept of self-leadership as "a philosophy and a systematic set of behavioral and cognitive strategies for leading ourselves to higher performance and effectiveness" (Manz and Sims, 1989, p. xviii). This definition brings together attributes of the leader and attributes of the follower. It places responsibility for all aspects of a person's success squarely where it has always been—on that person!

As more people recognize the critical role they, themselves, play in achieving desired outcomes, self-leadership skills will take on increased relevance. Learning these will serve each person well. Many have already been discussed, but will be restated here for emphasis.

Self-leadership is about self-control and self-influence. It requires that each person set goals for the short and long term to establish direction, focus, and priorities. Without goals, a person does not know what to spend time doing. Actions that promote goal attainment should be enhanced and those that prevent goals from being achieved should be diminished or eliminated. This must be done by the person, not an external force.

Practice is a key component to self-leadership because it leads to excellence. No one does anything perfectly the first time out. It takes practice and honest self-observation coupled with evaluation to improve the performance. Finally, the reward and/or withholding of reward must be self-administered.

As you continue to work and study, you will be confronted with decisions about how to interact with the world. Taking charge of your own personal actions is a good beginning point. Organizations place a high value on employees who not only say they are responsible but whose actions show this trait. Being able to lead yourself will be the most important skill you can develop.

> The wise leader is not collecting a string of successes. The leader is helping others to find their own success. There is plenty to go around. Sharing success with others is very successful.
>
> Tao of Leadership

What if leadership was more about serving? What if effective leadership required a person to serve those he/she is leading, to balance the tremendous responsibility of being out in front with the equally important responsibility of making sure that others were able to complete their goals?

Leadership in this sense takes on a different meaning. There is a call now for organizations with heart, organizations with soul. In the early 1970s Robert Greenleaf coined a phrase for this type of leadership—*servant leadership*. He felt that leaders should act as servants first.

From this a sense of community would develop where everyone would perform for the benefit of all. His ideas about leaders as servers of those they lead would create strong positive professional and personal communities.

CONFLICT!

CONFLICT AS CONFRONTATION

—or—

CONFLICT AS CREATIVE CHALLENGE

the choice is yours!

The final topic, *conflict*, can be both a spark to ignite creativity or a major problem that causes a great deal of stress. Conflict is nothing more than people looking at a problem from different perspectives. When many of the tools already discussed are utilized effectively, any conflict can be handled. When these tools are forgotten, conflicts can stop a project dead in its tracks.

How do you handle conflicts?

What are your "comfort zone" actions?
(*withdrawing, smoothing over, forcing, compromising*)

Do you ever find yourself in the middle of a conflict and not know how you got there?

Do you try to make peace with everyone?

Do you need to win? Do you need to be right, no matter what?

People have a conflict style that needs to be taken into account. This is how a person acts when a conflict arises. Some people attack the problem head on. Others avoid it completely, hoping it will go away. How we approach conflicts can add to achievement of successful outcomes or can lead to breakdowns in the relationships.

Communication is at the heart of any conflict strategy. Being able to talk about the issue in an open and frank manner is key. According to Stephen Covey, author of the highly successful *Seven Habits of Highly Effective People*, it is important to focus on how each party in the conflict can "win." The relationship is critical because in most situations, we will have to deal with the same people again.

Very often arriving at a winning situation for all concerned involves finding a new solution that is better than the one either of the parties involved have thought of to that point. Covey lists several elements that give win/win solutions the power to be successful over time. First, they focus on results and how those results are to be accomplished. Support and other resources needed to accomplish the desired results are identified and clear lines of accountability are established so that evaluation can take place. Finally, consequences of action or inaction are established so all parties understand both the good and the bad consequences of their actions.

Being able to generate creative outcomes from conflicting issues, opinions, goals, or situations shows a great deal of skill and strength. Anyone can walk away from conflict, clam up, play devil's advocate, force their decisions on others. It is the highly skilled person who can look at conflict as the true opportunity it is, and work through it. It takes all of the skills of the managerial artist to move from being embroiled in the issues and emotions of the conflict to generating the outcomes that will best serve all concerned.

PEOPLE AND MANAGEMENT

PERSONAL DEVELOPMENT EXERCISES

BEING A MIDWIFE

The wise leader does not intervene unnecessarily. The leader's presence is felt, but often the group runs itself.

Lesser leaders do a lot, say a lot, have followers, and form cults.

Even worse ones use fear to energize the group and force to overcome resistance.

Only the most dreadful leaders have bad reputations.

Remember that you are facilitating another person's process. It is not your process. Do not intrude. Do not control. Do not force your own needs and insights into the foreground.

If you do not trust a person's process, that person will not trust you.

Imagine that you are a midwife; you are assisting at someone else's birth. Do good without show or fuss. Facilitate what is happening rather than what you think ought to be happening. If you must take the lead, lead so that the mother is helped, yet still free and in charge.

When the baby is born, the mother will rightly say: "We did it ourselves!"

The Tao of Leadership

FOLLOWERSHIP-STYLE INVENTORY

Based on the research of Robert Kelley for his book, *The Power of Followership*, the following inventory will give you some idea of the type of followership style that you currently utilize. As most employees follow someone most of the time, developing an active, engaged follower style will enable each of us to participate more fully in the development of our chosen career path.

Directions: Using the following scale, place a 0–6 next to each of the items below to indicate the level to which the statement accurately describes your "follower" actions within the workplace. Try to stay focused on a typical "follower" situation in which you have been involved at work.

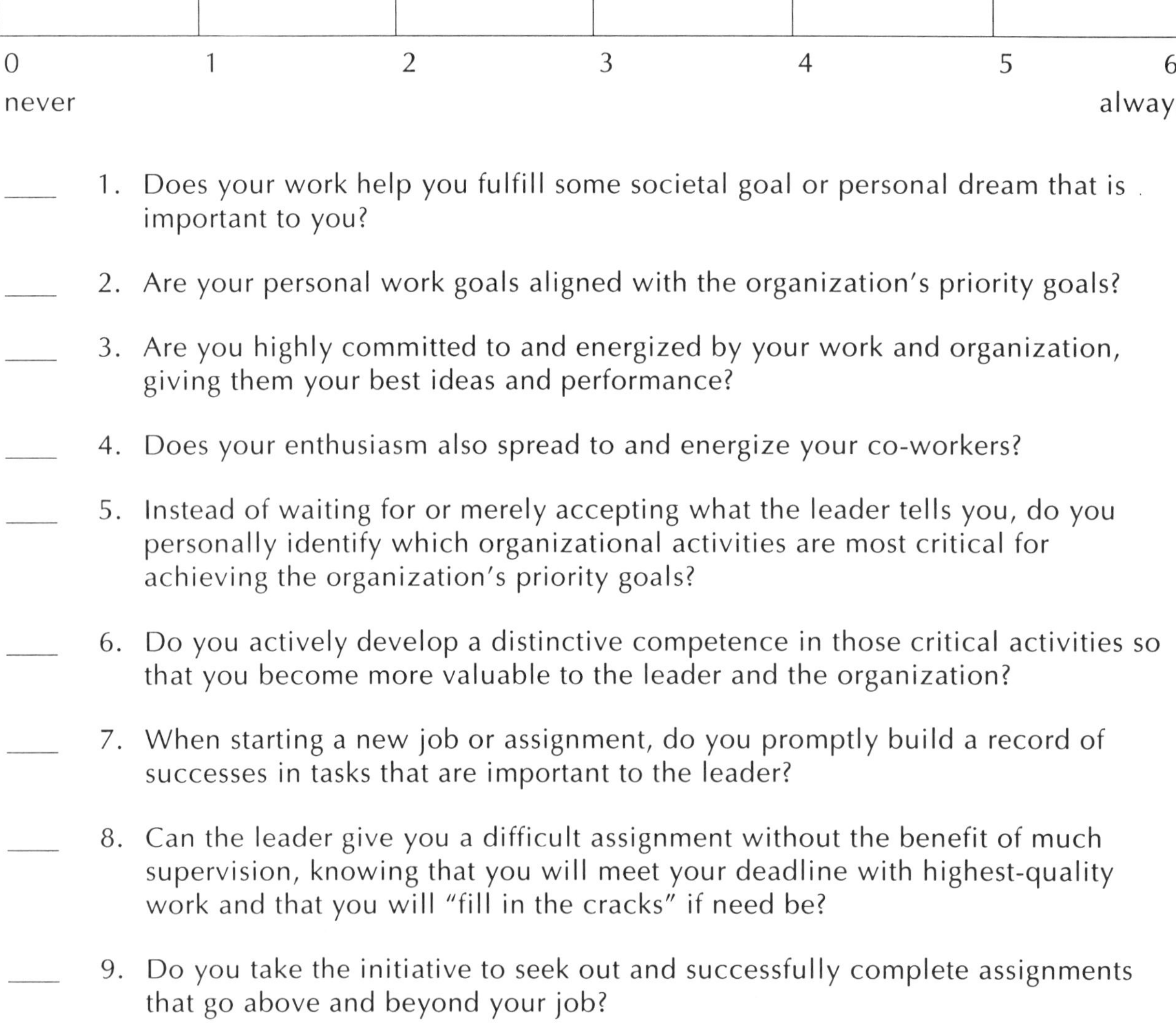

0	1	2	3	4	5	6
never						always

____ 1. Does your work help you fulfill some societal goal or personal dream that is important to you?

____ 2. Are your personal work goals aligned with the organization's priority goals?

____ 3. Are you highly committed to and energized by your work and organization, giving them your best ideas and performance?

____ 4. Does your enthusiasm also spread to and energize your co-workers?

____ 5. Instead of waiting for or merely accepting what the leader tells you, do you personally identify which organizational activities are most critical for achieving the organization's priority goals?

____ 6. Do you actively develop a distinctive competence in those critical activities so that you become more valuable to the leader and the organization?

____ 7. When starting a new job or assignment, do you promptly build a record of successes in tasks that are important to the leader?

____ 8. Can the leader give you a difficult assignment without the benefit of much supervision, knowing that you will meet your deadline with highest-quality work and that you will "fill in the cracks" if need be?

____ 9. Do you take the initiative to seek out and successfully complete assignments that go above and beyond your job?

____ 10. When you are not the leader of a group project, do you still contribute at a high level, often doing more than your share?

____ 11. Do you independently think up and champion new ideas that will contribute significantly to the leader's or the organization's goals?

____ 12. Do you try to solve the tough problems (technical or organizational), rather than look to the leader to do it for you?

____ 13. Do you help out other co-workers, making them look good, even when you don't get any credit?

____ 14. Do you help the leader or group see both the upside potential and downside risks of ideas or plans, playing the devil's advocate if need be?

____ 15. Do you understand the leader's needs, goals, and constraints, and work hard to help meet them?

____ 16. Do you actively and honestly own up to your strengths and weaknesses rather than put off evaluation?

____ 17. Do you make a habit of internally questioning the wisdom of the leader's decision rather than just doing what you are told?

____ 18. When the leader asks you to do something that runs contrary to your professional or personal preferences, do you say "no" rather than "yes"?

____ 19. Do you act on your own ethical standards rather than the leader's or the group's standards?

____ 20. Do you assert your views on important issues, even though it might mean conflict with your group or reprisals from the leader?

SCORING: Use the scoring key below to tally your results. Be careful to place the number you recorded next to the correct question number.

ITEM #	SCORE	ITEM #	SCORE
1.	______	2.	______
5.	______	3.	______
11.	______	4.	______
12.	______	6.	______
14.	______	7.	______
16.	______	8.	______
17.	______	9.	______
18.	______	10.	______
19.	______	13.	______
20.	______	15.	______
total	______	total	______

The first column total represents items which assess your *thinking*, while the second column represents items that assess your *engagement* style. Chart your scores on the graph below. The first score gets charted on the vertical axis. The second goes on the horizontal axis.

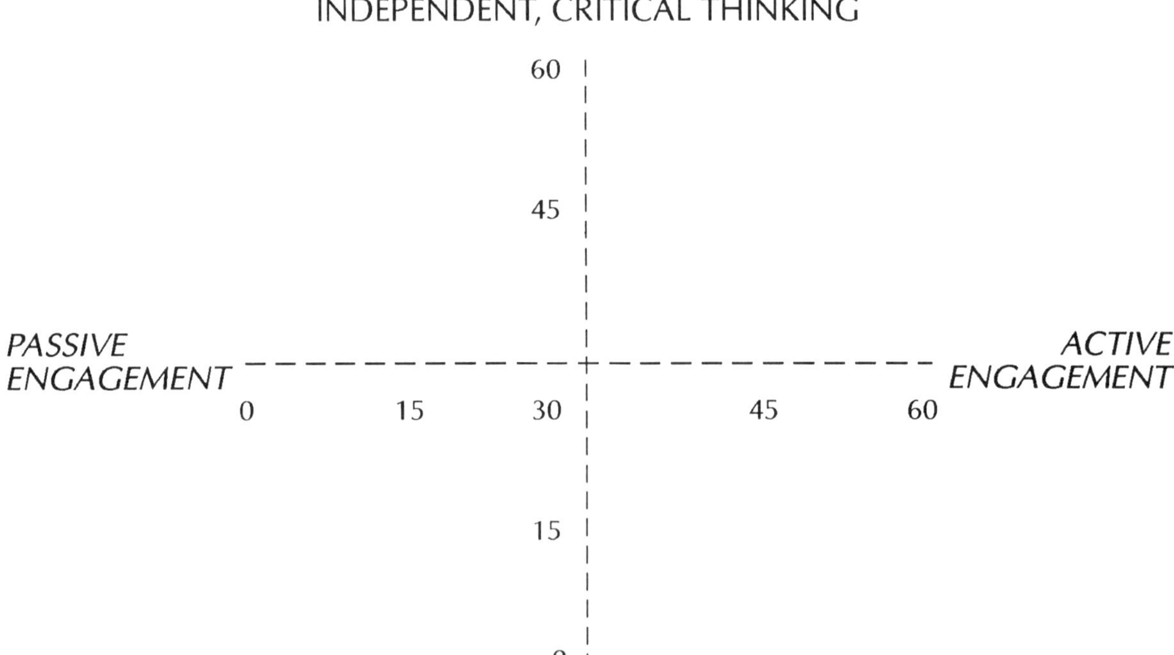

UNDERSTANDING ABOUT FOLLOWERSHIP STYLES

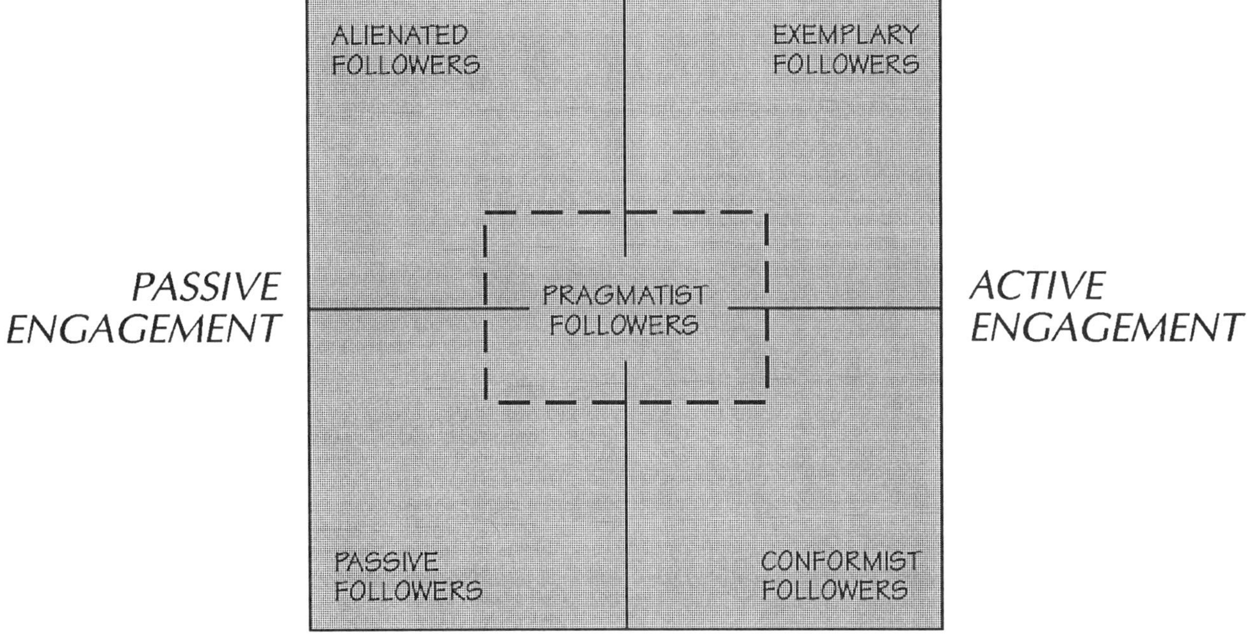

An analysis of your position on the diagram above will provide you with a wealth of information about your followership style. These categories examine how you carry out the role of follower, not who you are as a person. For more in-depth descriptions, Robert Kelley's book is highly recommended reading.

Organizations are looking for active, engaged entrepreneurial thinkers who add significant value to the achievement of organizational goals. They also recognize that personal goals need to fit into this picture. The days of an employee just "doing" and not also "thinking" are long gone. The days of companies controlling and navigating employees along a particular career path are also long gone.

The good news is that the skills needed to move into the *exemplary follower* style are learnable. As you examine the table on the next page, think about what you could do to change your current style of operation to become the *exemplary follower* so prized by business today.

STYLE DESCRIPTIONS

FOLLOWERSHIP STYLE	INDEPENDENT THINKING	ACTIVE ENGAGEMENT	BASIC CHARACTERISTICS
Alienated	High	Low	Unhappy about the work situation—sees self as victim, used, not recognized for talents Hostility created by lack of trust with leadership/management Often have unmet expectations Perceived by others as troublesome, cynical, or negative; not a team player
Conformist	Low	High	Eagerly takes orders and pleases; engaged and committed contributor Defer to leader's authority, views, and judgment; little self-thinking Finds comfort in knowing place and structure Adds little value in today's complex workplace
Pragmatist	Middle	Middle	Coping response to unstable and changing work situation Keeps things in perspective Can play political games and manipulate others to personal benefit Seen as rational and safe follower style because of change dynamics
Passive	Low	Low	Looks to leader/management to do thinking Can be a response to overly controlling manager or one who does not reward contributions of others Lacks initiative and a sense of responsibility; requires constant direction Never ventures beyond given assignment parameters Poorly developed follower skills lead to this type of follower behavior
Exemplary	High	High	Is able to balance independent thinking and active engagement skills Puts full range of talents to work for organization; sees how job relates to "big picture" Makes positive value-added contributions above and beyond job scope Focused, committed, enthusiastic Is strong at self-evaluation and implementing corrective personal actions

Source: Kelley, R. (1991). The Power of Followership. New York: Currency Books/Doubleday.

LEADERSHIP DEVELOPMENT

Developing leadership skills is something that each person can work on as he or she moves through work and personal activities. This instrument will give you an assessment of how you balance concern for the task itself with your orientation for people. It is just another piece of information from which you can focus your skill development program.

Instructions: The following items describe aspects of leadership behavior. Respond to each item according to the way you would most likely act if you were the leader of a work group. Circle whether you would most likely behave in the described way:

A	>	always
F	>	frequently
O	>	occasionally
S	>	seldom
N	>	never

If I were the leader of a work group . . .

A F O S N 1. I would most likely act as the spokesperson of the group.

A F O S N 2. I would encourage overtime work.

A F O S N 3. I would allow members complete freedom in their work.

A F O S N 4. I would encourage the use of uniform procedures.

A F O S N 5. I would permit the members to use their own judgment in solving problems.

A F O S N 6. I would stress being ahead of competing groups.

A F O S N 7. I would speak as a representative of the group.

A F O S N 8. I would needle members for greater effort.

A F O S N 9. I would try out my ideas in the group.

A F O S N 10. I would let the members do their best work the way they think best.

A F O S N 11. I would be working hard for a promotion.

A F O S N 12. I would be able to tolerate postponement and uncertainty.

A F O S N 13. I would speak for the group when visitors were present.

A F O S N 14. I would keep the work moving at a rapid pace.

A F O S N 15. I would turn the members loose on a job and let them go to it.

A F O S N 16. I would settle conflicts when they occur in the group.

A F O S N 17. I would get swamped by details.

A F O S N 18. I would represent the group at outside meetings.

A F O S N 19. I would be reluctant to allow the members any freedom of action.

A F O S N 20. I would decide what shall be done and how it shall be done.

A F O S N 21. I would push for increased production.

A F O S N 22. I would let some members have authority which I could keep.

A F O S N 23. Things would usually turn out as I predict.

A F O S N 24. I would allow the group a high degree of initiative.

A F O S N 25. I would assign group members to particular tasks.

A F O S N 26. I would be willing to make changes.

A F O S N 27. I would ask the members to work harder.

A F O S N 28. I would trust the group members to exercise good judgment.

A F O S N 29. I would schedule the work to be done.

A F O S N 30. I would refuse to explain my actions.

A F O S N 31. I would persuade others that my ideas are to their advantage.

A F O S N 32. I would permit the group to set its own pace.

A F O S N 33. I would urge the group to beat its previous record.

A F O S N 34. I would act without consulting the group.

A F O S N 35. I would ask that group members follow standard rules and regulations.

Source: Pfeiffer, J. W. What kind of a leader are you? *Handbook of Structured Experiences*, Volume I. San Diego, CA: Pfeiffer & Company, 7–12.

SCORING: Follow the directions below to score your leadership style inventory. These may seem confusing so take your time as you work through each item.

1. Using a highlighter or colored marker, circle the item numbers for items 8, 12, 17, 18, 19, 30, 34, and 35.
2. Write a number "1" in front of the items above where you responded with an "S" for Seldom or an "N" for never.
3. Write a number "1" in front of all other inventory questions (not circled or highlighted) where you responded "A" for Always or "F" for frequently.
4. Circle the "1's" which you have written in front of the following items: 3, 5, 8, 10, 15, 18, 19, 22, 24, 26, 28, 30, 32, 34, and 35.
5. Count the circled "1's" from #4. This is your score for concern for people. Record that score below.
6. Count the uncircled "1's." This is your concern for task score. Record that score below.

CONCERN FOR PEOPLE: __________ CONCERN FOR TASK: ________

Now refer to the diagram. Find your score on the *concern for task* dimension line and mark that location. Then find your *concern for people* score on the right hand dimension line and mark that spot. Draw a straight line that intersects the two scores. The point at which that line crosses the *shared leadership* dimension indicates your score on that dimension. All three dimensions together will give you a sense of your leadership style.

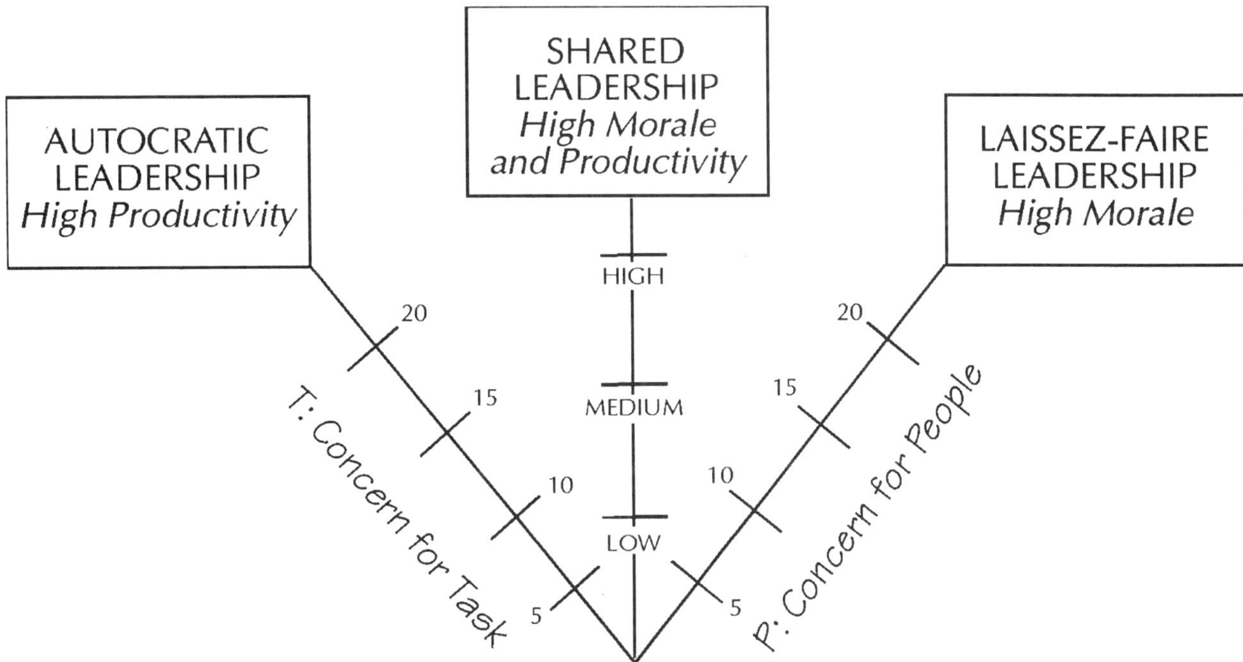

REFERENCES AND SUGGESTED READINGS

Bennis, W., and Mische, M. *The 21st Century Organization.* San Diego, CA: Pfeiffer & Company, 1995.

Block, Peter. *Stewardship: Choosing Service over Self-interest.* San Francisco, CA: Berrett-Koehler, 1993.

Bridges, William. *Managing Transitions.* Reading, MA: Addison-Wesley Publishing Company, 1991.

Brodie, Richard. *Virus of the Mind.* Seattle, WA: Integral Press, 1996.

Covey, Stephen R. *Seven Habits of Highly Effective People.* New York: Simon & Schuster, 1989.

Crosby, Philip, and Associates. *The Quality Improvement Management College Workbook,* Palm Beach Gardens, FL: The Creative Factory, 1991.

Csikszentmihalyi, Mihalyi. *Creativity.* New York: HarperCollins, 1996.

Dumaine, B. Distilled Wisdom: Buddy, Can You Paradigm? *Fortune* (May 1995): 205–206.

Ettorre, B. Benchmarking: The Next Generation. *Management Review* (June 1993): 10–16.

Frankl, V. *Man's Search for Meaning: An Introduction to Logotherapy,* 3rd ed. New York: Simon & Schuster, 1984.

Gale, Bradley T. Quality Profiling: The First Step in Reengineering and Benchmarking. *Planning Review* (May/June 1995): 37–38.

Grant, R. M., R. Shani, and R. Krishnan. TQM's Challenge to Management Theory and Practice. *Sloan Management Review* (Winter 1994).

Greenleaf, R. K. *Servant Leadership: A Journey into the Nature of Legitimate Power and Greatness.* New York: Paulist Press, 1977.

Hammer, Michael, and James Champy. *Reengineering the Corporation.* New York: HarperCollins, 1993.

Heider, J. *The Tao of Leadership: Leadership Strategies for a New Age.* New York: Bantam Books, 1985.

Katzenbach, J. R., and D. K. Smith. *The Wisdom of Teams.* Upper Saddle River, NJ: Prentice Hall, 1993.

Kelley, Robert E. *The Power of Followership.* New York: Doubleday, 1992.

Kriegel, Robert, and David Brant. *Sacred Cows Make the Best Burgers: Developing Change-Ready People and Organizations.* New York: Warner Books, 1996.

Lawler, E. E. III. *The Ultimate Advantage: Creating the High Involvement Organization.* San Francisco, CA: Jossey-Bass, 1992.

Levitt, Theodore. *Thinking about Management.* New York: Free Press, 1991.

Manz, C. C., and H. P. Sims. *Superleaderhsip.* Upper Saddle River, NJ: Prentice Hall, 1989.

Peters, Tom. *The Tom Peters Seminar: Crazy Times Call for Crazy Organizations.* New York: Vintage Books, 1994.

Senge, Peter M. *The Fifth Discipline: The Art and Practice of the Learning Organization.* New York: Doubleday, 1990.

Shechtmann, M. R. *Working without a Net: How to Survive and Thrive in Today's High Risk Business World.* Upper Saddle River, NJ: Prentice Hall, 1994.

Sheridan, J. H. Where Benchmarkers Go Wrong. *Industry Week* (March 15, 1993): 28–34.

Steil, L. K., L. L. Barker, and K. W. Watson. *Effective Listening: Key to Your Success.* New York: Random House, 1983.

Wheatley, Margaret. *A Simpler Way.* San Francisco, CA: Berett-Koehler, 1997.

Wheatley, Margaret. *Leadership and the New Science.* San Francisco, CA: Berrett-Koehler, 1992.

Whetton, D. A. and K. S. Cameron. *Developing Managerial Skills,* 2nd ed. New York: HarperCollins, 1991.

Zaleznik, Abraham. *The Managerial Mystique.* New York: Harper & Row, 1989.

SELECTED READINGS

THE EVOLUTIONARY VISION OF DEE HOCK: FROM CHAOS TO CHAORDS

By Bonnie Durrance

Ready or not, the millennium is coming. Will your organization look like chaos? Dee Hock—thinker, rancher, organizational visionary, founder and CEO Emeritus of VISA—hopes so.

Wait. Don't turn the page. The chaos Hock would like to see is not the collapse that he believes threatens organizations today, but the complex, unpredictable, and eminently orderly disorder that mystics for centuries (and scientists fairly recently) recognize as nature's way.

But first, a brief tutorial on chaos theory: Chaos, as science refers to it, is a revolution in our understanding of the way the world works. Its revelations have overturned Newton's law-abiding universe and replaced it with a world of infinite complexity, in which everything is connected in a vast and ever-evolving web.

One of the first connections chaos made was among the disciplines of science. Traditionally, mathematicians and physicists, not to mention mystics, had little to say to each other. They worked within the sacrosanct walls of their own intellectual castles, guns on the turrets aimed at the contrary opinions of others.

In the 1960s, however, certain meteorologists, mathematicians, physicists, and biologists began to find, and gradually exchange, undeniable evidence that caused them a range of chagrin, excitement, awe, and even anger. Nature can't behave in the way they were seeing, could it?

According to their experiments, nature's behavior seemed unpredictable, forming random and complex patterns described by equations that would not resolve into straight lines but that bifurcated at odd points and had their way with preconceived notions. Clouds. Lightning. Bubbles at the foot of a waterfall. Weather. Population. Those last bastions of nature's secrets finally, under scientists' insistent probing, yielded a shocking truth: Mother Nature is erratic. Not at all what science since the Middle Ages has wished her to be: a rational and eminently orderly extrapolation of the human mind. Not at all what Descartes declared she was: spiritless matter whose whole could be grasped by analysis of her parts. Not even what Newton assured us she was: a well-behaved machine set in motion by God and driven by laws that, if we just found them all, would deliver her to our control.

No. Our sun may rise daily, but nature does not run like clockwork. Nor is nature a summary of physical parts. Nature is complexity itself: chaos.

THE PARADOX OF CHAOS

Chaos. The word is deceptive. The band of baffled, chagrined, disbelieving, and sometimes almost evangelical scientists that first recognized it had a hard time settling on a name, for there was a paradox involved. At the edge of chaos, on a very narrow band, lives a kind of sublime order.

Picture a snowflake: a bit of moisture drifting to the ground and crystallizing into a unique, unrepeatable form distinct from every other snowflake. Yet, a snowflake is always recognizable. We see one and know right away what it is. Order in chaos, chaos in order.

Dee Hock, who works to bring organizations into harmony with nature and life, resolves the paradox linguistically and philosophically by joining the opposites and by calling the situation and organizational model he draws from it, "chaordic."

What does a chaordic system look like? I ask Hock, knowing that he won't describe a traditional organizational pattern. Still, I'm surprised when he says, "Look out the window!" with a sweeping gesture past the serene stacks in his library toward the tangled hillside beyond.

"Show me the chairman of the board of the forest," he says. "Show me the chief financial fish of the pond. Show me (tapping his head) the chief executive neuron of the brain!"

"In chaordic systems," Hock says with enthusiasm and wonder, "order emerges. Structure evolves. Life is recognizable pattern within infinite diversity."

Keep thinking about snowflakes. Patterned idiosyncratically by the turbulence through which they drift, snowflakes and other chaordic organizations exhibit what scientists call "sensitive dependence on initial conditions." That means that unlike the linear idea of cause and effect—which you can visualize as a set of falling dominoes—in a chaordic system, a tiny change early on can create vast and unpredictable changes down the road—a road never straight but endlessly branching, like the pattern of a ganglion or lightning across a western sky.

"If it is truly chaordic," Hock says, "it won't look like anything else. But there will be a pattern you can recognize, coherence and cohesion within infinite diversity. Nature has never repeated a single human being, yet we know one when we see one."

STIRRUPS, COMPUTERS, AND NEWTON'S APPLE

Organizations, snowflakes, human beings. Can we really compare societal structures to principles observed in science? We not only can, says Hock, but we must. The very idea of organizations must change and be brought into harmony with what we now know of the world, if the future we hope for is to emerge. The study of chaos offers a map.

Unlike quantum physics, which deals with submolecular happenings, chaos (or complexity theory, as it is also called) offers metaphors that are readily applicable to the human scale. Nobel Laureate Ilya Prigogene observes in his book, *Order Out of Chaos,* that human societies, like chaos models, are immensely complex systems highly susceptible to fluctuations. Witness the variety of cultures that have evolved in the short span of human history.

Technical advances (fluctuations) have changed the course of history in countless unpredictable ways. Think of the invention of the stirrup in the 11th century. That simple device enabled William the Conqueror's mounted knights to stand in their saddles, hurl their lances, and devastate Saxon foot soldiers—winning the Battle of Hastings, delivering England to the Normans, and revolutionizing the way battles and horse raising (bigger horses were needed to carry the knights) were done.

Or, if you prefer, look closer to home. Think of the little computer screen glowing on your desk. Try to remember what life was like before it or what it would be like without it. The phrase "complex and highly sensitive to fluctuations" means that a small invention can alter a nation or revolutionize the way a society works.

That reassures us: Individual activities make a difference. "On the other hand," says Prigogene, "our universe (the security of stable, permanent rules) seems gone forever." That security and the mechanical model on which it rests have been with us since Newton's apple fell. They were created by two things: Descartes's rational method of inquiry that severed mind from matter with the decisiveness of a guillotine and Newton's laws of motion, which reduced the universe to a divinely managed, law-abiding machine.

Newton's certainty in a mechanically predictable universe—pull this lever here, get that result there—revolutionized the world and married the Scientific Revolution to the Industrial Revolution. Newton's certainty is like the certainty of the blind men in a well-known fable: Each tries to describe an elephant by grasping a different part. The blind man that feels the trunk describes the elephant as a flexible tube. Not wrong, just incomplete. Newton's certainty was hailed in the 1600s by scientists hungry to control their world.

"Where does the compulsion to control come from?" Hock wonders. "Let's pretend that I can take my desire for control and develop it to the ultimate. What would that mean? I'd have to know every event that ever happened in the past and everything that could possibly happen in the future. I would have to know every possible past and future thought. Emotion would have to go, along with desire, hope, love, and hate, if I [were to] reach that state of total and complete control. What would it be like?"

(Imagine generals pointing bug-eyed at their maps, faces contorted over chess boards, sweating.) Says Hock in disgust, "I'd be dead! Life *is* mystery. And uncertainty. To wish absolute control is to wish you were not alive." That thought hangs in the quiet air as he repeats, "At bottom," desire for control is a death wish.

Newtonian structures, the musty smell of which any of us can recall if we've ever tangled with a bureaucracy, require a vast hierarchy exerting ever-more control and using evermore resources to keep the antiquated behemoth alive. "The important thing to remember," says Hock (reflecting on what he calls the Age of Management that Newton's assumptions ushered in) "is not that we became a society of expert managers but that the nature of our expertise became the management of constants, uniformity, and efficiency while our need has become the coordination of variability, complexity, and effectiveness—the very process of change itself."

ORGANIZATIONS 'R US

Think about change for a moment. There is a natural interval between invention and its assimilation into society, which Hock calls *float*, a term from his banking days that refers to the time that can be used to advantage in which a check makes its way through the system. Now whether in banking or in information, float has shrunk to nanoseconds. Life speeds in fast-forward; innovation and change chase each other into one continual digital blur. Change is not going to happen, nor is it likely to happen. Change is the very nature of what is happening.

"What has not changed," laments Hock, "is the mechanistic, hierarchical, command-and-control idea of organization that originated with Newton, Descartes, and the Industrial Age. That concept of organization," says Hock (not to mention the world view that spawned it), "is not only increasingly archaic and irrelevant but it's also antithetical to the human spirit and destructive to the biosphere. It has become a public menace."

Examples are all around us: the extinction of species, loss of forest, global pollution, global warming, genocide . . . genocide? According to a recent *New Yorker* article, it was the hierarchical structure of government—the "intricate pyramidal pecking order of coercion and obedience refined by the old feudal, colonial order and retooled under the post-independence Hutu dictatorships"—that created, in the author's chilling phrase, "an engine of genocide" in Rwanda.

Our organizations are us. Our organizations and behaviors reflect the way we see the world. If you believed that the Earth is flat, would you set off on an ocean voyage? If, as the Newtonian system describes, cause and effect can be traced neatly in a linear chain and everything is controllable from the top down, then hierarchical organizations are the way to go. But if instead of a straight line, the organizing pattern of the universe is revealed to be an ever-complexifying web of bifurcations and connections, then how do you behave? Who's in control?

Picture a line of boxcars. If you take out the engine, what happens to the train? Now picture a flock of birds. Which bird would you shoot to destroy the "mind" of the flock?

A flock, in Hock's terms, is a chaordic system. In chaordic systems, hierarchical control is traded for dynamic possibility. The whole is greater than the sum of the parts. Every intelligence is an asset; every individual counts.

In Newtonian systems, hierarchy is preserved at the cost of flexibility and individuality. Compare Newtonian systems with chaordic systems: Machines break down; chaordic systems evolve. Machines dehumanize people: chaordic systems empower people. Machines are vulnerable and expensive to change: chaordic systems thrive on change. Machines cannot be retrofitted to resemble chaordic systems; chaordic systems begin at the heart of the matter. There, at the heart of the matter, is where you will find Dee Hock.

THE ORIGIN OF A CHAORD

Around the time that mathematicians and physicists were tearing their hair out over unresolvable equations, a momentous change was brewing in the realm of business. In the late 1960s, an innovative, unconventional, and independent-minded vice president of a small bank in Seattle was about to revolutionize the bank-card industry.

Hock, whose career up till then had been characterized by mold-breaking innovation leading to results and profits (followed, ironically, by attempts from higher-ups to force him back into the mold), was representing his bank at a meeting of Bank of America officials and its credit-card licensees. It was 1966, and the fledgling bank-card industry was in trouble. Ferocious competition, fraud, and massive losses were driving the industry under. After watching a range of unworkable solutions being argued back and forth, Hock suggested that the members consider creating "an orderly method of addressing all problems." Bank of America agreed, a committee was formed, and Hock, as he puts it, "was elbowed into the chair." VISA was not created overnight.

In the first six months, Hock's committee expanded into a complex of regional and national committees that invited the emergence of "organized information about the problems." The picture that emerged was grave: losses in hundreds of millions of dollars. Not only were the problems worse than anyone had thought, but also Hock saw that what was needed—a means of enabling lifelong, global, and electronic monetary exchange—was beyond the capability of any existing organization.

Says Hock, "All of the 'rees' now so popular—reorganizing, recapitalizing, reengineering, and reinventing—were the wrong 'rees.' They implied yet another version of that which [already] is. [Instead,] it was necessary to reconceive the very idea of bank, money, and credit cards. Once we did that, it became obvious we would have to reconceive the idea of [an] organization itself."

How does one "reconceive" the ideas of an organization?

Before Hock tells the audiences of his management seminars how to go about that, he wants to be sure that they know what an organization really is.

"Think about your organization. What is its taste? Sweet? Sour? Don't know? How about its texture? Rough? Smooth?" At this juncture, audience members tend to stare with faces as pleasant and blank as stickers on a refrigerator door.

"Still don't know?" asks Hock. "That is because your institution has no reality, save in your mind and spirit. None whatever. It's a mental construct. It's a concept to which people and resources are drawn in pursuit of a common purpose."

He lets that sink in. "Every institution is nothing more than a manifestation of that ancient idea, community." (Nods of recognition.) "And if that is true, then the success of any organization has infinitely more to do with clarity of shared purpose and principles, and strength of belief in them, than it does with management practices or resources, important as they may be. Without the hearts and minds of people, all assets are just so much inert chemical and mineral material." (Smiles throughout the room.)

Shared purpose, by definition, is not something that can be imposed on people. It emerges: it evolves. And so, in 1966 Dee Hock, faced with a crippled bank-card industry, invited three other people to focus with him on a single question: If anything imaginable was possible, if there were no constraints whatever, what would be an ideal organization to create the world's premier system for the exchange of monetary value?

That was beyond what they could imagine and certainly beyond what they could engineer. But Hock, an original thinker whose interests range without boundaries from the classics to modern science, took his cue from the natural world. "After all," he says, "evolution routinely tossed off much more complex chaords with seeming ease." And so, he and his group began.

After much discussion, agreement emerged that the ideal organization should be based on biological concepts. It would have to evolve, in effect, to invent itself. It would have to balance competition and cooperation. What better model than nature?

Now, Hock would remind you, when you start to think of an organization in terms of biological metaphors, you must acknowledge the whole human being—body, mind, and spirit. Not the segregated entities of Newton's time, but the whole person, with emotions, intuitions, beliefs, and thoughts. When you bring all that to the table, an interesting thing happens: Discussions of change become value-based.

Over the next two years as values were dragged out and wrestled over slowly and painfully, some guiding principles emerged:

- "The organization must be equitably owned by all participants."
- "Power and function must be distributive to the maximum degree."
- "It must embrace diversity and change.

Eventually, those and other principles became a concept, and the concept became a structure. In 1970, the structure became an entity, and VISA, a nonstock, private, for-profit membership corporation, came into being.

THE VISA STORY

VISA is part of the commerce of many people's lives. Since 1970, the company has grown 10,000 percent. Today, with a staff of about 3,000 in 21 offices on four continents, VISA is a trillion-dollar business serving more than half a billion clients. Yet, as Hock loves to remind audiences, you don't know where it's located, how it's operated who owns it, or where to buy its shares. That's because VISA is a new kind of organization—decentralized, nonhierarchical, evolving, self-organizing, and self-regulating. It's composed of 20,000 financial institutions operating in more than 200 countries and territories. Bound by no political, economic, social, or legal theory, its services reach across national and cultural boundaries. It is a chaordic system that thrives on a balanced diet of competition and cooperation—much more like a flock than a train.

Now, we see chaordic organizations everywhere, from patterns in nature to business. But in 1970, the idea was unique. Says Hock, "Virtually everyone thought it was technology that made VISA succeed. Or because it was in financial services. They didn't even see the significance of the organization—that its success was about a new way of creating relationships."

Hock smiles. "Think of it as social sculpturing."

He describes the structure: "Money and power should flow not *up,* as in hierarchical structures, but *out* to the most peripheral or smallest part, which then has commensurate responsibility to surrender back the minimum amount necessary to achieve common purpose."

Picture a root system and a fruiting tree.

Says Hock, "The whole heart and soul of VISA were in conceiving an organization on the basis of purpose and principle, and allowing the structure to evolve from them."

In less than 30 years, VISA evolved out of disaster into a large, successful business. But Hock doesn't seem satisfied.

"In 1969, I believed, and I believe today, that we were creating an archetype of institutions for the 21st century. But I don't think we got it more than 20 percent right." Hock is serious.

"The power inherent in that way of thinking about institutions is immensely greater than even the success of VISA would indicate. I've been working with these ideas most of my life, and I am barely beginning to understand them. I'd like to think we did the best we could, but I can now see so many flaws and failures along the way that I have a compelling sense we should have done better."

Hock's idols are the giants: Marcus Aurelius, Lao Tse, Francis Bacon, Thomas Jefferson, Gandhi, Goethe, Einstein, Shakespeare, Milton, and Montaigne. Hock works in the middle of his 5,000-volume library, shelves crowded with the writings and biographies of those great thinkers.

"Those people seemed able to put themselves into the future, to conceive of the world as it ought to be. They were able to bring that future into the present and live as though it were true. In a sense, their consciousness was a causative factor in creating the future."

You wonder if that's how Hock conceived of the chaordic organization of VISA. "I had a sense of direction," he says, "and an idea." Hock recalls the story of Einstein's response when asked how he conceived the theory of relativity. "Well," Einstein replied, "I thought deeply about how the universe ought to be organized, and so it was."

Order emerges not from decree, but from the depths of our beliefs and principles.

"We have to sop searching for some expert out there to solve our problems," says Hock. "Shakespeare said, 'First of all, to thine own self be true, and it follows as the night the day thou canst be false to no man.' Emerson used other words: 'Trust yourself, every heart vibrates to that iron string.'"

RECONCEIVING ORGANIZATIONS

Hock's inside-out vision for the reconceiving of organizations, founded on the absolute integrity of inner conviction, is consistent with the way he conducts his life and manages his organizations.

Listen as he talks to managers about management:

"I used to have sessions with my employees once a week. Anyone could come, and we'd talk about anything on their minds. They always wanted to talk about management. 'How do you do it?' 'What's the best way?' So, I would ask them, 'What is the single most fundamental responsibility of a manager?'

"And I'd get a thousand different answers, all having one thing in common: They would be downward looking. They always had something to do with controlling those folks over whom they had power."

At this point, Hock's audiences usually smile expectantly: Isn't that what management is about?

"Dead wrong," says Hock, who waits for the confusion to settle in. "The first responsibility of anyone that purports to manage is to manage themselves." *What?*

Hock continues, "Their own integrity, their own knowledge, and their own ability, conduct, knowledge, ethics, and wisdom. Unless you do that, you're not fit for authority, no matter how much you acquire. You're not fit; you're dangerous. You're going to be destructive.

"And then I'd ask what the second responsibility is. And, boy, they'd think they were going to get those folks now. Dead wrong. The second responsibility is to manage your bosses. If they don't trust, respect, and support you, how are you possibly going to do anything with your people? Managing your staff is useless if you can't manage your boss.

"So, then I'd ask for the third responsibility of anyone who's a manager—downward looking again. So, I'd say, 'Dead wrong! Manage your peers, those over whom you have no authority and who have none over you. If you can't manage them, how are you going to do anything with your people?'

"Then I'd ask, 'What's the fourth responsibility?' And by then, everyone would be looking around. No one wanted to be wrong again. The fourth responsibility is to manage your staff."

Hock likes to test his audiences. "If you hire good people and teach them the theory and if they manage themselves, you, and their peers well and they hire good people and are willing to be well-managed by them, what do you have to do but recognize them, reward them, and get out of the way?" (Laughter, relief, and a few questioning looks.)

Hock responds to the unasked questions: How do you manage your boss? How do you manage your peers? He faces a sea of wide eyes with a calm smile.

"Well, the answer is incredibly simple. You can't. There's no way. You have no power over superiors and peers. But can you understand them? Can you motivate them? Excite them?

Persuade them? Influence them? Set an example? Inform, forgive, and interest them? Disturb them? Of course you can. And eventually the word will emerge. Can you lead them? Absolutely."

Hock contends that there is nothing that can stop anyone from setting an example. He tells audiences, "The truth is that you were born a leader." (Raised eyebrows.)

"You think not? Then, one of you stand up and deny that you managed your parents." (Laughter.) "You were leading yourself, your superiors, and your peers from the day you were born until you were sent to school and taught to manage."

That's the paradoxical dance of a conversation with Dee Hock. You swoop along in the rightness of his vision, feeling euphoric because it's so obvious. Then, you suddenly let fall some comment, maybe pointing a finger here or pronouncing the blame there, and you trip over your big, Newtonian feet. "Ah ha!" he says, "Now, that's Newtonian!" And you know that your inner paradigm hasn't yet changed.

You're probably thinking, "That wouldn't happen to me. Why, I'm not Newtonian or mechanical." Oh no? Listen to Hock's samples of telltale Newtonian terms:

- *jump-start*
- *out of sync*
- *high-powered*
- *shift gears*
- *exhausted*
- *turned on*
- *went ballistic.*

Enough? Sound familiar? The mechanical metaphor lives in our language and drives our thoughts, and we're not going to change overnight.

Dee Hock knows that. Failure, he'll tell you, is an integral part of growth. No need to point fingers; no need to deify or demonize anyone. Just begin where you are. Just start. Imagine the world as it ought to be, and behave accordingly.

FOUR CONDITIONS, THREE CHAORDIC GROUPS

Hock left a flourishing VISA 13 years ago for a life of nature, family, and reflection on the VISA experience and the future of organizations. In 1994, he was sought by the Joyce Foundation, a philanthropic organization concerned about the prospects of institutional failure and inspired by the story of VISA. It asked Hock, "If anything imaginable were possible, if there were no constraints whatever, what would be required to catalyze chaordic institutional change throughout society to avoid massive institutional failure?"

Hock suggested four conditions that would have to be well underway within five years:

1. At least six extremely successful, new examples of chaordic organizations, similar to VISA and the Internet, would have to evolve, spanning such diverse areas as education,

government, social services, and commerce to demonstrate universal applicability. Organizations ready and willing for such change must be sought and methods developed to help them through the process.

2. Sophisticated, four-dimensional physical models of such structures would have to be created so that people had the means to compare the new concepts with their existing organizations. The fourth dimension is the spiritual, ethical dimension. Additions to the physical models, computer models, would have to be created, collapsing time and graphically demonstrating how such institutions organize themselves and evolve and how, based on similar fundamental principles, they could link with new patterns for a peaceful, equitable, and constructive 21st-century society.
3. The models would have to be supported by an impeccable intellectual foundation. The economic, scientific, political, historical, technical, and philosophical rationales for such organizations would have to be documented. Though a great deal of work has already been done, it's far from complete, and it lacks coherence and clarity. Nor have the necessary common language and metaphors evolved for massive dissemination and understanding.
4. A global organization would have to emerge whose sole purpose would be the development, dissemination, and implementation of new chaordic concepts of organization, linking in a vast web of shared learning, information, and ownership, as well as all people and institutions committed to institutional and societal reconception. The global organization must be organized on the chaordic principles it espouses and itself be one of the successful examples.

The Joyce Foundation asked whether, if it were to cover costs, Hock would contribute his time to investigate as freely and broadly as he liked whether the four conditions were possible and what might be required to set them in motion. At first, he refused. But thoughts of his seven grandchildren and the future that lay before them, should the present course continue, changed his mind.

After a year and a half traveling the world searching out people concerned and committed to change, Hock became convinced that there was at least a chance that the four conditions could be set in motion. He accepted the mission.

Fostering chaordic institutions is now Dee Hock's life work. Since 1995, he has been talking, meeting, listening, and learning about the chaordic organizations that are beginning to emerge everywhere. He has founded the Chaordic Alliance to further his efforts. In a world hungry for life and purpose, Hock's ideas are increasingly in demand.

The groups that Hock has chosen to work with have gone through the same soul-searching process of discovering their purposes and principies that he and his associates went through at VISA. It's not easy. Three groups in particular have taken a year each to complete their statements of purpose and principles.

One group, the Northwest Atlantic Marine Alliance, is an unlikely union of fishermen, environmental lawyers, and academics drawn together by the impending collapse of local fisheries. Each had vested, though different, interests in marine resources. Each was in cut-throat competition with the rest. To bring them together, much less elicit their deepest beliefs, was a feat in itself.

After months of arguments, tears, and table-pounding, NAMA has arrived at a statement of common purpose that is inspiring to everyone in its clarity and balance. A structural concept for a self-managing, community-based management system founded on those beliefs is nearly complete.

At the Massachusetts Institute of Technology, Peter Senge's group of highly evolved management specialists, the MIT Center for Organizational Learning, has been wrestling with the chaordic process for a year and a half. The group now has a solid statement of purpose and principles, and a new organizational concept based on its beliefs. It expects to bring its new organization into being this month.

A third group, the Appleseed Foundation, was founded by Ralph Nader and a group of Harvard law graduates to bring about needed change. The foundation has formed its purpose, principles, concept, and structure and brought into being its new organization.

After a group agrees on its purpose and principles, the actions of the organization grow continually and organically from the shared purpose. The result will be flexible, changeable, and viable with a core of integrity shared by each member—a community in balance with itself and its environment.

By now, you know that Hock is not talking about simple, surface, overnight change. This is a path, a way, a kind of evolution.

"I've been thinking about and implementing these ideas all of my life, and I'm just starting to learn about them." Hock notes that it will take a huge commitment of education and learning by people and institutions from top to bottom to bring this change into being.

"I think this is an emergent phenomenon," says Hock about chaordic groups. "I see it springing up everywhere."

This is no optimist with rose-colored glasses talking, but someone that sees the way of the future balanced on the "edge of a knife" and that could go either way.

"If the current epidemic of institutional failure continues," Hock warns, "we are quite likely to see a regression to even more dictatorial organizations in a blind effort to impose control—a modern Dark Age. But one thing is certain: It's far too late and things are far too bad for pessimism."

It is late, and the sun is raking over the dull winter green of Hock's Pacific hillside. There's not much time, Hock has miles to go and promises to keep, if he is to leave the kind of world he wants to leave for his seven grandchildren.

THE UNPLANNED ORGANIZATION: LEARNING FROM NATURE'S EMERGENT CREATIVITY

by Margaret Wheatley

We live in a world that is self-organizing. Life is capable of creating patterns and structures and organization all the time, without conscious rational direction, planning, or control, all of the things that many of us have grown up loving. This realization is having a profound impact on our beliefs about the nature of process—in interpersonal relations, in business organizations, as well as in nature itself. In this article, I will focus on some of the recent shifts in our understanding of the way things change.

> In my work with large organizations, one of the questions we often ask is, "How would we work differently if we really understood that we are truly self-organizing?" The first thing we recognize is that, just like individuals, the organizations we create have a natural tendency to change, to develop. This is completely counter to the current mantra of organizational life: "People resist change. People fear change. People hate change." Instead, in a self-organizing world, we see change as a power, a presence, a capacity, that is available. It's part of the way the world works—a spontaneous movement toward new forms of order, new patterns of creativity.

Three images have changed my life—one, a picture of a chemical reaction, another, a termite tower in Australia, and a third, an aspen grove in my new home state of Utah. Each image in its own way represents a profound shift in my understanding about the nature of change in organizations. I will explain their significance later, but first I want to discuss eight tenets of what I call "unplanned organization", inspired by these images.

We live in a world in which life wants to happen.

This is a simple, though profound, realization. You might not think it is such a remarkable notion, but we grew up in a culture influenced by Darwinian evolutionary theory which said life was an accident. Now, if life is an accident, that means there is nothing here to support us; so we do it all alone, and if we don't get it right, we get killed because the world is an inhospitable place. I believe this kind of thinking led to the heroic image of he great corporate leader who would craft organizations and *make* things happen—nothing would happen without this great impetus of human ingenuity and human control.

We used to believe that for the first seven-eighths of the planet's existence there was no life, that it showed up about 600 million years ago. Now scientists agree that life seems to have emerged almost instantaneously with the creation of the planet. This is a very important realization. For me, this means that I belong to a whole planetary community of life, and that I am supported in my own small efforts by a deep natural history spanning between four and five billion years—*life wants to happen as a community and we are all part of it.*

Organizations are living systems, or at least the people in them are living systems.

I sometimes feel embarrassed to point this out because it seems so obvious. We're moving away from a terribly deadening image of who we are and how we should organize. The image of the world as a machine that came into our consciousness in the seventeenth century was a wonderful metaphor that then went out of control. Ultimately, we came to believe not only that the world is a machine but that people can best be understood as machines.

One of the interesting things I learned recently is that since about 1850 we have described our brains in terms of our current technology. So, in the middle of the nineteenth century brains were thought of as hydraulic pumps. Then they were thought of as telegraph systems, then as telephone switchboards, and now we're up to neural nets. But these are all technological machine metaphors for understanding ourselves.

When we say that organizations or people are living systems, we're saying that, unlike machines, people have intelligence. Again, this is not a profound thought, except we've strayed so far from it. People are capable of change, whereas machines have no capacity to change apart from their programs or designs devised by some smart engineers. Machines have no intelligence. They're created for specific tolerances. It is stultifying to think about life this way, and yet this way of thinking is so deeply embedded in our culture that it's going to take a while to think otherwise.

We live in a universe that is alive, creative, and experimenting all the time to discover what's possible.

This is my favorite realization. We see this at all levels of scale, whether we're looking at the smallest microbes or looking out into the galaxies. We live in a world which is constantly exploring what's possible, finding new combinations—not struggling to survive, but playing, tinkering, to find what's possible.

People are intelligent. We're creative, we're adaptive, we seek order, we seek meaning in our lives. When we really start to understand this, when we *really* start to change our perception of who people are, then it changes how we think about organizing.

It is the natural tendency of life to organize—to seek greater levels of complexity and diversity.

One of my own beliefs, inspired by different readings, is that everywhere you look you see that life is system-seeking. We are rediscovering our interconnectedness; there are no isolated individuals in the natural world. Life seeks to affiliate with other life, and as it does that it makes more possibilities available, it makes more diversity possible. I believe (and this is just my own perspective right now) that the reason life seeks to organize is so that it can explore its diversity, so that it can explore its creative potential. It doesn't seek to organize to protect itself, to defend itself—that seems to me a 300-year-old Western conceptual overlay.

I think life seeks systems because systems allow more diversity, they allow individuals to thrive, and they give each of us (when we're in a healthy functioning systems) more freedom to experiment with what we want to be—as long as we remain conscious of our connections to the *whole of the system*. To repeat: Life is self-organizing. It seeks to create patterns, structures, organization, without pre-planned directive leadership.

Life uses messes to get to well-ordered solutions.

Life is incredibly messy. We could even sat it is unbelievably wasteful. But shift perspective and judgments, and what at glance what may appear to be messy and inefficient may actually be *life experimenting*—discovering what is possible. If you have ever tried to create an aquarium, you'll know how messy that can be. You keep trying to put in new life forms and hoping that the whole will suddenly take hold as a system. Then your fish die. But if you keep messing around, sooner or later the aquarium takes as a system, and sustains itself.

This is a recurring phenomenon in the re-creation of ecosystems. Scientists say it takes a lot of messes to finally discover what works. But underneath is the realization that all of those messes are tending toward the discovery of a form of organization that will work for multiple species. Life uses messes, but the direction is always toward organization; it's always toward order.

Life is intent on finding what works, not what's right.

I find this very liberating. This is where playfulness can enter into our own human relationships in a different way, because the task of the moment, of any moment, is to find something that works, but not be so ego-attached to it that we believe it is the only solution, the only right answer. How many relationships split up because of arguments about who is right? Yet when you look around, you see life tinkering, experimenting, playing, as if to say, "If it works, fine; and if it doesn't work, let's see if we can find a way that does work." For me it's a different sensibility, and it creates a much greater sense of playfulness in my own work.

Life creates more possibilities as it engages with opportunities.

A phrase I often hear used in business is that life—or some project, or the market—presents a "narrow window of opportunity." This is not true. Systems don't work that way. Every time we try to make something work, we are creating more possibilities within the system—we open many different "windows of opportunity". If a particular opportunity is not fulfilled, there are always many others to engage with. Each path of opportunity leads to its own pattern of order. It may be unpredictable, but life is attracted to order. It is the nature of natural systems.

Life organizes around identity.

Out of all of this blooming, buzzing confusion of life, how do we decide to pay attention to certain things, or to make sense of certain things? We look for information that is meaningful to us in some way, given who we think we are.

Someone once asked me, "What's the 'self' that gets organized in 'self-organizing'?" These two words are equally important. Life organizes spontaneously and creatively, but it organizes around a self. It is making self. For me, this feels like further evidence that consciousness is at work in everything because you can't organize around a self without being conscious that you are a self. So when we see self-organization, I believe what we're watching is consciousness forming itself into different identifiable beings.

Thus, we live in a world which is truly co-creative, in which you and I cannot exist in isolation. Richard Lewontin, a geneticist whose work I admire greatly, once said that "environment" is a strange concept because we talk about it as if it exists independently of us. We even talk of "saving the environment". He said that the environment is an organized set of relationships between individuals. We're constantly affecting one another, constantly being changed by the process of being in relationship with one another by our choices. For those of us who have tried to save the world, I think this is a humbling thought. There's nothing out there to save. There is a lot to be engaged with.

BEYOND THE MACHINE IMAGE

This brings me to the three images that have changed my life. The first is a chemical process called the Belousov-Zhabotinsky (B-Z) reaction. We've known about its existence in Western culture, particularly in Russia, since the 1940s. It was so revolutionary to scientific thinking that its existence was denied for a long time.

This wonderful little chemical reaction is saying that the universe is not all "downhill". This is contrary to the Second Law of Thermodynamics, which says that the natural tendency of any system is to run down from a state of order to disorder, from energy to entrophy. The Second Law says that with every change you give up useful energy, and you have no way of recouping it, so you fall into a state of entropy—where all you can do is wait for death and disorder to overtake you. Someone recently defined the Second Law as "You can't win, and you can't get out of the game." That's a terrible burden on our Western way of thinking.

Yet what these surprising little chemicals showed is that there is a self-organizing capacity in matter. When confronted with turbulence and change, it's not all downhill. For example, in the B-Z reaction, red and white chemicals had blended in perfect equilibrium. The next discernible state for this system, given the traditions of Western science, was that it would disintegrate, or at best remain in disordered equilibrium. In fact, when scientists added chemicals, stirred it up, lit a flame under it, and poked a hot wire into it—a lot of change if you're a chemical—what happened was that the system separated out into its constituent chemical groups, red and white, and instead of falling apart and dissipating, the chemicals restructured themselves. Beyond dissipation, there was spontaneous reorganization—self-organization.

This is quite startling because what these inert, (allegedly) unconscious chemicals created were intricate spirals. How do you explain this if these chemicals, which are supposedly dead, are not communicating, if they're not conscious in some way? Many scientists disagree with this attribution of consciousness, but they all agree that the B-Z reaction is a stunning image of the self-organizing capacity of our world.

What this says to me is that when confronted with change, you and I have a choice between two options, and we are not doomed to an inevitable course of action as the old belief system would have had us believe. The old myth was that we would disappear, that we would die, that we would dissipate—and that would be the end of it. But the new recognition of a self-organizing world tells us that we can use any period of chaos and dissipation to reorganize ourselves to a structure better suited to the environment.

The whole quest to understand the world of self-organizing is really a quest to realize that there is a deeper, more elemental force at work behind the structures we see. What cause is behind the patterns of organization we see in the world—where organization occurs without directive leaders or planning? What deeper elemental force gives rise to it all? The answer, it appears, is that behind the organizing patterns we recognize as life is self-organization—a spontaneous capacity to generate pattern and organization from within. And this, of course, is one way of defining consciousness.

According to Fritjof Capra, who is publishing a new book on self-organization, we've had four or five billion years of experience with this; this is how life discovered the possibility of creating more and more life. So there is this deep, elemental capacity for organizing in all of us. Knowing this, when we see resistance to change—and we certainly see a lot of that these days—we can understand what's happening in a different way. It seems to me that resistance always reflects the need of each of us to understand who we are in the moment—our identity. When we see a change being forced on us, we recognize it as threatening our sense of self. Resistance reflects our need to protect our sense of dignity and identity as presently defined. Resistance does not represent a fundamental tendency toward inertia, which is the old belief about human nature.

If you start to think about this for a while, and you're engaged in a change process or a change strategy, this alters the way you relate to change. If identity is a key issue, then it seems to me inescapable that we involve people from the start in whatever the change is going to be. Then they have the chance to reorganize their own sense of identity to fit the changed reality. You can't change people, but people change all the time. That's who we are.

Realizing that we live in a self-organizing world is to recognize that so much more is available for us as groups, as organizations, as communities. So much more is available to us in the form of a naturally occurring energy—the self-organizing capacity we all have. We have to learn how to engage it, how to evoke it.

TERMITE TOWERS AND LEADERLESS GROUPS

And so to life-changing image number two: a termite tower on the Australian savanna. The one I have a picture of is about 20 feet high, so if you think of the size of the termite, these are the tallest structures on Earth, relative to the size of their builders. A particularly interesting one is called a "magnetic tower" because the termites always build it on a north-south axis. The interior is a very complex structure. It has tunnels and arches. Their function is to move air into a darkened interior where it is cooler, because even though termites live in hot places they don't do well with heat. The nests are also designed to move moisture in so the termites can farm a form of fungi they require for digestion. These are very sophisticated structures.

Entomologists who study termites looked at these for years, and, recognizing a very complex structure, wondered, "Where's the leader? Where's the engineer? Where's the brains behind this operation?" The search for a leader was a long and futile quest. What is interesting is that the leaderless phenomenon wasn't even pointed out until some women started critiquing the history of science, and came up with the stunning realization that there didn't have to be a leader.

Termite colonies are examples of a wonderful self-organizing process, and can be highly instructive about human endeavor as well. For instance, individual termites are capable only of digging dirt piles. They don't do anything sophisticated. This is true of most social insects. If you think of the hive as a brain, and the social relations as a mind, individual termites are like single neurons. Isolated, they barely have any significance. But as a coordinated group they perform like a hive-mind. Like neurons, they emit chemicals for communication. Termites emit scents that attract other termites. They are constantly aware of what's going on in their environment; they're very tuned in. They wander at will, bump up against one another, and then they respond.

I think this is an excellent maxim for organizational life. You wander at will, you bump up against one another, and you respond. But you're developing so much more consciousness of what's going on in your environment, and you're tuned to so much more information than we have allowed people in those "org. chart" disasters.

So after a certain number of termites collect, their behavior shifts, emerging into something with an entirely new capacity, and they start building their towers. A group of termites over here will start an arch, another group over there will notice it, and they'll start the other side of the arch. Spontaneously, it meets in the middle, and there was no engineer present.

Termites build towers only because the "self" they're organizing around is very clear to them. But the way in which they create elaborate complex structure is in the moment. Entomologist Edward O. Wilson compared it to dynamic programming in computers: You do something, you notice its effect, you do the next thing. This is a view of life beyond conventional strategic plans, planners, goals, objectives, and Myers-Briggs tests. Let me explain that last remark: Myers-Briggs is a system for assessment of psychological types. It's a way of understanding who you are, how you take in information, how you thrive. Like all such tests, it is focused on individuals—when we're just out there digging dirt piles, so to speak.

But as far as I can tell, right now, none of our personality assessors or indicators let us know who or what we are capable of being when we are in community with one another. I believe it is a travesty to think we can understand ourselves or another human being independent of being in a relationship with them. And one of the wonderful things the termites show is that we live in a world that has emergent properties, which means that when a group is together it is capable of behaviors that simply are not knowable when you study the individuals. It doesn't matter how well, how deeply, or how long you study the individuals, you would never see the potential for the tower in the individual termite. I think this is true of human behavior as well. So why do we spend so much time trying to understand our self (little s), since that self changes—whole new capacities come forward in us—when we are together in our communities?

The reason I think this is so problematic for us is that you cannot plan; you can only watch once you're in the process of being together. You can only notice what's happening, and then tinker with it. Instead of creating dream teams, you just get into the process of organizing and see what emerges. That feels unplanned, it looks messy, it smacks us in the face; it goes against all the ways we have been taught to be effective leaders, or effective individuals. In contemporary society, we've gone crazy with goal-setting and planning and thinking about our lives in a linear progression.

We would do well to learn from the termites. There is a lot of wisdom available in the study of emergent behavior. And it is available only because we live in a world which is self-organizing. We live in a world in which, when we come together, we can discover new possibilities. And we live in a world in which the discovery of new possibilities is, I believe, the reason for existing.

This says something about organizing activities that I want to stress. If you think of life as a network, then you don't have bottoms or tops. Emergent solutions can come from anywhere, but they are always very situational, always highly contextual, and therefore they're going to be quite variable, and always unplanned.

I also want to emphasize that emergent organizations are leader-full, not leaderless. Leaders emerge and recede as needed. Leadership is a series of behaviors rather than a role for heroes.

ASPEN TREES AND HIDDEN CONNECTEDNESS

I recently learned from my son's fifth grade teacher that the largest known living organism on the planet lives in Utah, where we now live. My son got excited and thought it was Bigfoot, but it's not. It's a grove of aspen trees that cover thousands of acres. When we look at them, we think, "Oh, look at all the trees." When botanists looked underground they said, "Oh, look at this system, it's all one. This is one organism." You see, when aspen trees propagate, they don't send out seeds or cones, they send out runners, and a runner runs for the light (there's wonderful imagery in all of this), and we say, "Aha! There's another tree . . ." until we look underground, and we see that it is all one vast connection.

Before I was aware of the Utah aspens, I used to think that the Michigan mushroom, which covered 37 acres, was the largest organism. What was interesting about that was when mycologists looked at these mushrooms they couldn't figure out how they survived, because they didn't have all the "functionality" they needed to be healthy mushrooms. When they looked underground they found the answer—it was just one large organism.

In a self-organizing world, one of the things that works on our behalf is not only that we have a natural tendency toward change, that we can constantly reorganize, or that we can structure ourselves without leaders (as long as we're well connected and informed and focused) but that, underneath it all, what we're doing is discovering our connections.

One of the great teachings in chaos theory is that a very slight twitch in a connective system will create convulsions elsewhere. I'm sure you've had a negative version of this experience in which you made an offhand comment to somebody, and later it blew up in your face. Whereas you may have presented your life's work, thinking it was the greatest gift to humankind, others just looked at it and said, "Well, that's very nice, dear."

Biologist Francisco Varela has said that you cannot direct a living system, you can only disturb it. In a system, the most we can do, when we are trying to serve, is to contribute a little twitch, be a little disturbance. One of the great things about living systems is that not only can they not be leveraged, they cannot be directed. You cannot tell another human being or a human organization what to do and expect it to do it. Yet this is not a lesson we have learned. It has been in our faces all our lives—especially if you're a parent of a teenager (actually it starts much younger, with two-year-olds)—that we can't direct living things.

If we really start to sense the self-organizing capacity that is around us, we could realize that our efforts to foster change or to midwife change—not to manage change—have much support.

In my own work, I'm trying to feel more playful about it, and to take away some of the drama—"If we don't get it right now, we're all going to perish." I believe that's a true statement, but it doesn't help me play with life the way I want to, the way in which I see life playing with us. I would like us just to be more experimental. We are not looking for the solutions, we're just seeing what works for this system, with a deep respect for its interconnections. When it doesn't work, we move on and try something else, and when it works, we feel very blessed.

Margaret Wheatley is president of The Berkana Institute (a research foundation supporting the discovery of new organizational forms), and a principal of Kellner-Rogers and Wheatly, Inc. A former professor of management at Brigham Young University, she has consulted with a wide variety of Fortune 500 clients, educational institutions, nonprofit organizations, and health care organizations—from CEOs to assembly line workers.

Her book Leadership and the New Science: Learning About Organization from an Orderly Universe *(Berrett-Koebler, 1992) was named "Best Management Book of 1992" in Industry Week. Her next book,* A Simpler Way, *written with Myron Kellner-Rogers, will be published in summer 1996.*

THE SOUL OF THE HOG

by Bob Filipczak

It was his first day on the job, two years ago, and Ken Sutton was at a vending machine getting a cup of coffee. Behind him, a machinist he had never met asked, "You're new here, aren't you?"

Sutton allowed that he was.

"Well, let me buy you a cup of coffee," the machinist offered.

It was a simple gesture, but two years later, as vice president and general manager at Harley-Davidson's power train plant in suburban Milwaukee, Sutton remembers what it was like to be welcomed to the family. He learned quickly that "relationships" were an important—maybe the most important—component of Harley-Davidson's corporate culture.

Relationships? Isn't that a bit warm and fuzzy for a work force full of hard-core bikers building power trains for motorcycles? Here's a factory full of tough-looking, tattooed and (except for the women) bearded workers. They're producing the most infamous icon of go-to-hell individualism in America, and it turns out they're all worked up about relationships?

Well, yes, says Margaret Crawford, corporate director of training and employee development. "We are very much a relationship-based company." Building strong working relationships—between coworkers, between unions and management, between supervisors and the supervised, between executives and machinists—is a core concern at Harley-Davidson.

That doesn't mean you'll hear phrases like "I hear what you're saying" or "Thanks for sharing" from Harley workers. They are a little more *direct* than that. Harley-Davidson's idea of a healthy working relationship is embedded in five formal values that fit easily on a 3- by 5-inch laminated card and constitute a code of behavior for everyone. Most workers at the power train plant seem to know them verbatim:

- Tell the truth.
- Be fair.
- Keep your promises
- Respect the individual.
- Encourage intellectual curiosity.

OIL PUDDLES

You can't get so much as a shoeshine anymore without receiving a card engraved with somebody's mission or vision or values, of course, and all of this would be neither here nor there except that Harley-Davidson is something of a special case.

Not to put too fine a point on it, Harley was at death's door in the early 1980s. The company had a reputation for poor quality, it had lost most of its market share to the Japanese, it was beset with debt, and it was generally going the way of many American manufacturing businesses that are no longer with us. The period from 1969 to 1981 is still referred to as the "AMF years," when Harley was owned by American Machine & Foundry. The history of the AMF years, and the subsequent resurrection of the company, is documented in the book *Well Made in America* by Peter C. Reid

Reid doesn't attribute Harley's troubles solely to AMF as many observers have, and in fact argues that much of Harley's current success is due to investments made by AMF. But while the bike's reputation for reliability was far from unsullied even before AMF bought the company—bikers took perverse joy in pointing to any oil puddle in the street and speculating that a Harley must have been parked there—the quality of Harley-Davidson's products indisputably suffered during the AMF years.

Reid describes how AMF began to turn this around during the last years of its stewardship with a triad of quality techniques learned from the Japanese: just-in-time inventory (JIT), statistical process control (SPC), and employee involvement. Even so, when AMF put the company up for sale in 1981, it looked to be a death sentence for Harley. Only a last-minute leveraged buyout by 13 of Harley's top managers saved the business. Company veterans still talk about how current CEO Rich Teerlink scrambled from investor to investor on Dec. 31, just hours before Harley would be forced to declare Chapter 11 bankruptcy.

The rest of the tale is now famous as a classic American turnaround, a Cinderella story. Harley survived constant setbacks to reclaim its market share, eliminate its long-term debt, and regain the respect of its customers. It did so by producing bikes of the highest quality and reliability. In 1994, the company had $1.5 billion in sales and a return on equity of 27.5 percent. It owns about 56 percent of the U.S. super-heavyweight motorcycle market—and the only reason its share isn't higher is because the company can't produce enough motorcycles to meet demand. Depending on which bike you order, you'll wait six to 18 months to get a new Harley.

Part of the reason for Harley's success is, of course, a uniquely fanatical brand of customer loyalty. Even during the AMF years, Harley riders kept the faith—though it was sorely tested—and kept buying the company's motorcycles. Employees like to remind people that their company logo may be the only corporate symbol that customers actually tattoo on their bodies. It's also a testimony to the Harley mystique that more than half of all employees own a bike. Most of the executives, including Teerlink, are Harley riders. Workers know that the machine they are currently building might turn out to be their own . . . or the CEO's.

LIVING QUALITY

Because Harley-Davidson was one of the first victories of the American quality movement, and perhaps the most dramatic, the company has become a poster child for total quality management (TQM). But you don't hear many people at Harley talking about quality anymore; it's so ingrained in the culture that it has become a way of life.

Many employees have been around long enough to remember the AMF years, however, and there is a palpable sense that nobody wants to take his eyes off the ball ever again. Lest anyone forget that poor quality almost destroyed the company, the other side of the laminated values card presents a fist of "issues" or continuing concerns:

- Quality.
- Participation.
- Productivity.
- Flexibility.
- Cash flow.

The one TQM phrase that seems to have survived in the vocabulary of employees is "continuous improvement." It has come to mean not just process improvement on the factory floor, but a more personal improvement of the relationships between people. That's where the "values" kick in. And when people agree to tell the truth, be fair to each other, keep promises, respect each other and encourage curiosity, there is nothing necessarily "soft" about their ensuing interpersonal dealings. As Curt Kapugia, senior quality engineer, puts it, "I could hate your guts, but I still have to respect you as an individual at work so that we can work together."

Here is how some of those values work in practice.

TRUTH

The five values were initially hashed out in the late '80s as part of a bigger plan called the Business Process, an umbrella concept that Teerlink has been pushing for the last four years as a way to educate employees about all aspects of the business, including its strategic direction. Executives held discussions with employees at every level about what it meant to "tell the truth" at Harley. Did it mean everybody must tell the whole truth and nothing but the truth all the time? It was generally conceded that sometimes managers couldn't tell everyone all they knew. But if a manager or anyone else had information he couldn't release, it was unacceptable to dissemble. He had to look the person straight in the eye and tell her that he couldn't give her the straight scoop—and, when possible, *why* he couldn't tell her what he knew.

Manufacturing engineer Dave DiJulio tells the story of an improvement that he and some other engineers wanted to make to the arrangement of a workstation. It was a change that the operators might not like, and the engineers were wondering how they were going to finesse it. Finally someone pointed out that "telling the truth" was supposed to be standard operating procedure. So they decided to lay it on the line: Tell the workers exactly what they were planning and elicit ideas on how to do it better.

"Instead of jamming it down their throats," says DiJulio, "we went through it, got ideas, and actually didn't implement quite what we were talking about." This seemed remarkable to DiJulio, who joined Harley just two years ago. Now, he says, he's used to it. "That's kind of the way it is around here. Somebody will have a concept, we'll go through it, and by the time it gets implemented it doesn't look anything like [the original idea."

FAIRNESS

There are two unions at the power train plant, and the cooperation they practice with management may be unparalleled anywhere else in America. General manager Sutton remembers that one of the primary concerns when he started at the company was productivity. There was talk of opening a new plant. Then, as now, most manufacturing companies tended to build new plants in the South, where unions don't have as strong a presence.

Instead, the leadership of the company went directly to Harley's unions and presented them with the problem of expanding production. The theme Sutton kept hearing from veteran managers was that the unions had stuck by Harley when times were tough, to the point that machinists brought in their own drills because the company couldn't afford to buy new equipment. Management's attitude, he says, was: "We're not going to try to go get the fast dollar or the low labor wage someplace else. We're going to stick with the people who stuck with us." In the end, the company decided to expand production in the existing facility instead of building a new plant.

Bob Klebar is president of Lodge 78 of the International Association of Machinists and Aerospace Workers (IAM), one of Harley's unions. His inclination to view management as a partner instead of an adversary was born when the 13 Harley executives bought the company from AMF in 1981. At that point, says Klebar, the managers legitimately could have asked for a new contract from the unions. They stuck with the negotiated contract instead.

Management's good-faith dealings with the unions have continued. Harley-Davidson has a history of in-sourcing, which means that it tries to bring as much work as possible into the plant to forestall any layoffs. And Klebar's union has considerable control over what kind of work is outsourced to other companies. By choosing the work that his group does in-house, he bolsters the job security of his people. Contrary to the practices of most companies, "When times are good, we'd outsource it. But if things get tougher, we'd look at those [projects] and maybe bring them in-house to keep the employment," says Klebar.

Largely as a consequence of management policies and actions like these, the machinists and tool and die makers Klebar represents are willing to take terms like "customer focus" seriously. "Instead of focusing on what we think we have a right to," Klebar says, his people work closely with the production department, and everyone concentrates on the final customer. "It really binds us together and makes us go in the right direction."

The union sometimes will even censure its own workers for shoddy performance, Klebar says: "Instead of protecting someone who's not doing the work, we take him aside and say, Hey, we really need your help to make this successful, and from what we see, you're not pulling your weight.'"

That willingness among workers to police themselves may become more crucial as Harley's power train plant begins a move toward self-managed teams this year. As training manager Darlene Rindo describes it, the plan is to create "semiautonomous work groups." These teams won't be completely self-managing, but team members will set their own schedules and be crosstrained. The change will be gradual, Rindo says; for one thing, it would violate the company values to dump a lot of new responsibilities on employees all at once. Management and the unions are cooperating in the creation of these work groups.

RESPECT

Harley's employee-involvement commitment, started in the late '70s, contains an element of respect for the individual. But this value becomes most apparent when employees talk about the company's process for consensus decision making.

You'd think that a bunch of Harley workers would have as much use for facilitated, consensus-driven meetings as they would for Hondas. After a few conversations with employees, however, you come to understand that these meetings are anything but calm affairs. People tick off multiple examples of meetings that became forums for workers to express dissenting opinions to executives. In meetings with CEO Teerlink, says Sutton, "I've seen machine operators do what in other companies would be considered 'talking back to the president.' I've also seen that he didn't flinch. He listened."

This brand of respect goes both ways. Executives confront employees in straightforward terms, too.

A training course called "Meetings Harley Style" teaches employees how to run meetings and how consensus decision making is supposed to work. According to training manager Rindo, the basic idea is that while not everyone in the group will agree with a decision, they have to be able to go out and support it on the factory floor. That means never moving on to another agenda item without reaching closure. But there is a stylistic element to all this that the course covers as well, Rindo says. "It's very much teaching the Harley culture at the same time, meaning that when people lay it straight—and people at Harley lay it straight a lot—it's OK."

"We get a lot of resistance in meetings," says Sutton, "and something we call 'push back,' where if you don't like something, it's your obligation—not just your right—to state what you don't like, what you think is wrong, and get that out in the open."

There is one caveat to this open meeting style, Sutton says: No foul language.

No cussing? At Harley-Davidson? That's right. Foul language has nothing to do with respecting other people, says Sutton, so it isn't allowed at the meetings.

CURIOSITY

The final statement in the declaration of values is "encourage intellectual curiosity." Harley-Davidson's Learning Center is a facility dedicated to lifelong learning. Its primary role is to serve employees who want to keep their skills current. In some cases, this means remedial training in basic skills, but mostly the center is a place to come with requests for specific job-training courses.

John Boyd works as a powder-coat operator at the power train plant, powder-coating being essentially a painting process. As Boyd explains it, all you have to do is come up with a course you want taught, enlist other employees who have similar interests, and appeal to the Learning Center. It will organize the course.

Harley also sponsors a Leadership Institute, a separate program set up by Marquette University in Milwaukee in which employees can take college courses for credit on the company's premises and get a baccalaureate degree in leadership at the end of four years.

The Leadership Institute also offers a course on values, in which employees are encouraged to take a hard look at their own values in an effort to see where they match Harley's declared values. Corporate training director Crawford, who teaches the course, says it isn't just a feel-good exercise but a very serious examination.

Originally the values course started at the top of the organization. Later Crawford decided that this kind of soul-searching would benefit everyone. CEO Teerlink is himself certified to teach the values course, and co-presented with Crawford when they took the vice presidents through the program.

A striking example of someone whose intellectual curiosity was encouraged is training coordinator Gail Rosenthal, a member of United Paperworkers International Union Local 7209. A quick look at her career path is a lesson in lifelong learning. During her 26 years at Harley, she has been in the electronics department, worked in golf cart assembly, progressed to snowmobile assembly (both during the AMF years, when Harley manufactured a variety of products), was the first woman engine tester and the first woman engine repair mechanic. Now she's a trainer who teaches a course in interpersonal skills and loves it. Rosenthal was selected for the job because interpersonal skills can be a dicey subject for bikers. "[Management] felt people on the floor would trust someone 'who's been there'," she says.

There's so much training in progress at Harley, in many different areas, that it has become Rindo's mandate to keep track of what's going on in all the departments and collate everything into an integrated plan. For example, says Rindo, there's safety training, environmental training, apprenticeships, training programs developed at the power train plant, programs developed at the corporate level, the Leadership Institute, values training, product-knowledge training, and all the programs going on at the Learning Center. She's got her work cut out for her.

STAKEHOLDERS

This is a word that comes up often in conversations with Harley workers. The corporate values aren't intended solely for interactions between co-workers but are meant to include all the stakeholders of the company. That means workers, managers, unions, the community, the environment, the government and, most importantly, the extended family of Harley-Davidson: its zealous customers. Employees are encouraged to attend some of the rallies the company sponsors (major annual events include gatherings in Sturgis, SD, and Daytona, FL) to talk to customers and find out what they want. And like its employees, Harley-Davidson's customers aren't shy about expressing their opinions.

That may help account for the surprising lack of complacency at Harley. Nobody is smug about that 18-month waiting list for a new bike; everyone we talked to agonized about keeping customers waiting that long. And no one seems to take the company's present success for granted. Talk around the factory is that if they don't constantly change, constantly improve, constantly keep an eye on the competition, they could all quickly find themselves in the unemployment line. "What's our competition doing?" asks DiJulio rhetorically. "Our competition is doing a lot of things to try and get our market share. Where we have a problem is we can't make enough bikes."

One quick recession, Boyd remarks, and that 18-month list of orders could vanish overnight When times are tight, worries powder-coat technician Jimmy Kilbourn, the toys are the first thing to go.

Another surprise at Harley is that so little of the talk you hear about the corporate values is self-congratulatory. Rather, everybody wants to be the first to admit that they aren't fully living up to the ideals. Does every decision achieve a perfect balance of all stakeholder interests? No. Does everyone tell the truth every time? No. Are they always respectful of individuals? No. Do they always keep promises? Boyd comments that one manager promised a monthly party as an incentive for more productivity; Boyd hasn't seen any parties yet.

Engineer Kapugia produces a notebook and displays a list of concerns that employees have raised with him. It's a pretty long list, but he doesn't want to forget even one of these issues. "All you've got to do is forget somebody," says Kapugia, "and before you know it, that somebody is going to say to somebody else, 'Hey, don't bother talking to him. He never gets back to you.'"

THE MISSING PIECE IN REENGINEERING

By Nicholas F. Horney and Richard Koonce

Is your organization suffering from reorganization fatigue? Have you restructured, downsized, outplaced, and outsourced until all that remains is a skeleton staff of stressed-out employees and senior executives, still waiting for the promised gains in productivity to materialize?

In recent years, hundreds of business books and management articles have been written about downsizing and restructuring: how to do it right, how to do it well, how to use it for sustainable change, and how to squeeze corporate vitality and productivity gains out of reengineered work processes and a slimmed-down workforce. Many of those articles spotlight the stage-setting importance of energetic CEO leadership and "envelope-pushing" missions and visions.

Leadership and organizational goals are important. But something is missing from the literature. Despite the media attention, the verdict on many reengineering efforts today is mixed at best. In fact, a recent business survey by a leading human resources consulting firm suggests that nearly two-thirds of all restructuring efforts are clear failures.

The reasons vary. Many restructuring efforts suffer from poor planning and have paid only scant attention to the importance of clear, consistent, and ongoing communication as part of restructuring initiatives.

Another problem is that workplaces have dealt inadequately with the "people variables" that are always at play in organizations in times of rapid change. Executives and managers need to pay more attention to the stress and anxiety that people feel during transition.

Still another reason for the failure of many restructuring and reengineering efforts is a lack of penetration to the deepest organizational levels. In essence, these initiatives ignore the issue of how people actually do their jobs each day. In other words, they fail to address one of the key ways for people to become engaged and energized as individual agents of change.

What we call competency alignment is a critical underpinning of successful business-process reengineering initiatives.

At its best, BPR involves a fundamental rethinking and radical redesign of "core business processes" within an organization. It necessarily implies taking a hard and systematic look not only at the organizational structures, management systems, beliefs, and values that are part of an organization's culture, but also at the jobs that people do on a daily basis and the systems that support and reinforce them.

Reengineering efforts should be targeted toward the specific goal of changing employee behaviors, processes, and systems at the "transactional" level in an organization (the level at which day-to-day business is actually done, according to change-management consultant and theorist W. Warner Burke).

Unless BPR examines the business at that level, all the CEO exhortations in the world aren't likely to bring about significant, long-term changes—either in organizational effectiveness or in a company's financial performance. Unless BPR pays attention to employees' day-to-day work, people are unlikely to fall enthusiastically into line to support new marketing goals, to work toward achieving the CEO's heartfelt desire to "go global," or to pursue more ambitious customer-service objectives.

Most organizations display an implicit (and sometimes explicit) systemic inertia. Systems and people resist change unless an organization address barriers methodically and systematically.

That's why competency alignment is critical. It gets you right down into the heart of an organization. It helps you focus time, energy, and attention on the details of how people work and interact on a day-to-day basis—with each other, with customers, with other stakeholders, with competitors, and with various human-resource processes and information systems in the organization.

By paying attention to how people interact "transactionally" in your company, organization, department, or work group, you put yourself in a powerful position to make changes that can reinforce reengineering goals or dramatic process improvement.

THE COMPETENCY-ALIGNMENT PROCESS

Coopers & Lybrand's competency-alignment process, or CAP, involves the systematic study, analysis, and assessment of job functions, tasks, and skills required by an organization that is reengineering one or more of its work processes. It focuses on analyzing, understanding, and optimally deploying people in the reengineered organization, ensuring the best job fit for everyone.

To do that, it methodically examines employee skill sets in order to determine where and when skill gaps exist and what can be done to remedy deficiencies—either through employee training, skill enhancement, redeployment, outplacement, outsourcing, or other efforts.

CAP provides a baseline methodology for retooling work processes at their most fundamental level—the level of the individual and the small work team.

CAP is an ideal mechanism for bringing employees into closer alignment with strategic organizational goals and objectives—a key success factor in creating a high-performing, improvement-driven organization, according to a recent C&L survey.

And it provides a means of refining and recalibrating that alignment over time—as job requirements change, as the structure of work within an organization changes, as production or manufacturing processes incorporate new technology, as employee skill sets age, and as external factors come into play.

A systematic and methodical approach can help you implement competency alignment in your own organization as a component of other reengineering efforts you are planning or implementing.

Where does competency alignment fit into the reengineering process? Think of it as a critical subset of larger-scale business-process redesign or reengineering efforts that are in the works or recently completed. It should be a part of any BPR initiative—whether the goal of the reengineering is to redraft your organization's entire mission or to overhaul one key business process such as research and development, marketing, manufacturing, or product distribution.

For many organizations, competency alignment has been the missing element or link in reengineering efforts. Even if it fell through the cracks in years past, it still may have influenced the outcome of productivity-improvement and change-management initiatives.

Nowadays, organizations can't afford to ignore it. The cost of employee recruitment, training, turnover, retraining, and poor job fit have become clearly driving the need for organizations to get the most out of their BPR efforts, at a minimal cost.

FOUR STAGES OF CAP

An important outcome of completing competency alignment is the identification of current employees the organization can successfully place in new jobs or on new teams, as part of reengineering a key business process. Doing so takes great care, careful planning, and systematic implementation.

Most organizations should implement CAP in four stages: assess, deploy, learn, and align.

In stage 1, the assessment, it's important to conduct a task analysis of the reengineered process to determine the knowledge, skills, abilities, and competencies people will need in order to be effective contributors. You also will examine the suitability of current job holders to do that work.

A critical outcome of stage 2, deployment, is the identification of peoples' skill gaps. With this information, you can begin to make decisions about which employees to retain in their current functions and which to slate for outplacement or redeployment elsewhere in the organization.

Stage 3 of any CAP initiative deals with learning. This stage involves the development of skill-acquisition plans (such as training, outsourcing, or recruiting) to fill the skill gaps identified in stage 2.

You might, for example, decide to institute new training programs to help retained employees work more effectively in teams. You might also decide to import at least some new talent from outside the organization through targeted recruitment efforts. Or you might choose to outsource certain tasks that the organization through targeted recruitment efforts. Or you might choose to outsource certain tasks that the organization no longer considers essential core functions.

Stage 4 of CAP is alignment. It focuses on developing and aligning an organization's human resource systems (such as the performance-appraisal system and the compensation system) to sustain the performance of people in the newly reengineered process.

Following this road map can help you ensure successful implementation of competency alignment in your organization. Now, let's take a detailed look at each of the four stages, which are summarized in the figure.

The Four Stages of the Competency-Alignment Process

Stage 1: Assess

- Assess your process.
- Assess your people.
- Determine necessary tasks.
- Determine necessary skills, abilities, and competencies.
- Create a gap-analysis matrix.

Stage 2: Deploy

- Develop skill, ability, and competency profiles.
- Use the profiles to deploy people into reengineered jobs, to redeploy them elsewhere in the organization, or to outplace them.

Stage 3: Learn

- Create training and career-development plans for employees.
- Explore the use of different training approaches, formats, and methods.
- Outsource non-core functions.

Stage 4: Align

- Align HR systems, including reward and recognition, compensation, and performance appraisal.
- Conduct pilot tests.
- Review, assess, and revise as appropriate.

STAGE 1: ASSESSING THE PROCESS AND THE PEOPLE

This stage is divided into two parts: assessing the competencies that the newly reengineered processes will require, and assessing the competency of existing employees to carry out the processes.

PROCESS COMPETENCY ASSESSMENT.

Let's say that your company or organization has decided to reengineer. You might be planning to reengineer your entire organization as part of a comprehensive change-management initiative (one that involves the systematic reengineering of all business processes, your business strategy, and your information-technology capabilities). Or you might plan to redesign only selected departments or work processes.

In any case, you'll need to get a clear bead on the kinds of tasks that will need to get a clear bead on the kinds of tasks that will need to be done. And you'll need to know which skills and competencies people will need if they are to do the work in the future, after reengineering efforts are fully implemented.

In years past, you might have used job and task analysis to get at the heart of productivity problems or to understand better the different elements in a work process. You might have asked job holders to provide the following information:

- the core knowledge, skills, and abilities necessary for doing their jobs
- the amount of time spent each day or week on specific tasks
- ratings of tasks, in terms of relative importance.

That approach to job analysis was valuable in the past. But it becomes difficult to do when you are in the middle of reengineering a core business process—primarily because you don't yet have job holders or "incumbents" in the reengineered process. Instead, you'll need to use subject matter experts within the organization to help identify tasks and to describe the knowledge, skills, and abilities that are likely to be required of job holders once a map of the new process is fully developed.

SMEs can include current job holders, "process owners," key line managers, and others you deem to have broad knowledge of organizational goals as well as of specific processes and work content.

Now let's imagine that you are reengineering your company's order-management process. A key objective in stage 1 of CAP is to develop a process description, showing how work is performed now and how it will be done in the future. So you'll need to break the process down into individual tasks (for example, planning, order generating, scheduling, and shipping) and ask SMEs to identify the competencies people need for each task.

Initially, what you come up with may resemble a step-by-step view of the order-management process, with lists of specific skills tagged to each of the principle steps or tasks.

Next, work with members of your reengineering team and with the SMEs to map out the way in which work will be done in the future. Ask such questions as these:

- What additional skills and competencies will people need to have?
- Will people work together differently than they do now? (For instance, will they spend more time in teams and on collaborative decision making?)
- What new technology will be integrated into the way work is done?
- What new skills will the technology require of workers?

To get answers to those questions and others, try conducting focus-group sessions, using groupware technology to catalog and organize peoples' responses. See the accompanying box, "A New Kind of Tool for Groups," for a discussion of groupware as a means for facilitating group sessions and collecting and analyzing data.

What typically emerges from an in-depth focus-group process is a detailed list of tasks, skills, and competencies that will be part of employees' work in the future.

A groupware session with subject matter experts will probably yield a sheet of formatted information that looks something like the table shown on this page. This example was developed as the result of some work with a large financial institution to determine its employees' work tasks, knowledge and skill requirements, and competencies.

JOB TASKS FOR BANK EMPLOYEES, WITH RELATED SKILLS AND COMPETENCIES

TASKS

- Gather closing information.
- Identify, read, review, and interpret loan documentation.
- Identify legal issues.
- Review and interpret loan histories and amortization schedules.

KNOWLEDGE AND SKILL REQUIREMENTS

- reading comprehension
- knowledge of loan-servicing systems and loan documentation
- knowledge of asset types and loan-classification schedules
- knowledge of loan documentation, ranking and legal issues, terminology, and definitions.

REQUIRED COMPETENCIES

- detail orientation.

What also frequently emerges from such data-gathering sessions are broad themes that suggest how much the nature and structure of work is changing.

For example, nowadays everyone from the boardroom to the loading dock needs hands-on familiarity—and preferably, a high comfort level—with computers. And today's workplace requires many people to have specific experience with such relatively new technology as local-area networks, "shareware," the Internet, and Windows applications. Such competencies will be even more essential in the future.

Another competency that people increasingly need in the workplace today is the ability to work effectively in groups. Since more and more work is team-based, you'll want to make sure that subject matter experts in your focus groups fully map the constellation of team skills and competencies that work will require in a newly restructured area of your organization.

By the time you've done all that, you'll have a clear handle on the competencies people will need for doing their jobs in the context of a reengineered work process. And by eliciting comments from process owners, supervisors, and others who are familiar with current processes, you create strong buy-in for the important employee-deployment decisions to come.

At the same time, you may acquire a sense of the work that lies ahead of you in actually implementing competency alignment in your organization, and of the tactics and strategies you'll need to use.

For example, say you oversee training and development programs in a craft environment (such as a tool-and-die manufacturer) where the tradition and emphasis has long been on individual skill. Now, such factors as speed-to-market and concurrent engineering (the simultaneous development of a product and of the process for development of a product and of the process for developing it) have emerged as critical to success.

You may face tough challenges if you intend to introduce team principles or large-scale, technology-assisted design into a manufacturing process in a traditional environment. Employees may be unfamiliar with (and even hostile to) new technology. They may lack an understanding of teamwork principles; they may have no interest at all in working on teams.

The people-assessment process that makes up the next part of stage 1 addresses such concerns by giving you tools for appropriate selection and retention of employees. It will also help you determine an individual employee's motivation to do new work, so that you can assess his or her suitability for working in an environment of changing norms and expectations.

EMPLOYEE COMPETENCY ASSESSMENT.

At this point, you've inventoried the skills and competencies people will need once a work process has been reengineered. So you have a road map with which to assess the suitability of current job holders to perform future jobs in your organization.

Your goal now is to assess the individual skills and backrounds of current job holders.

Start by developing an assessment tool that looks at their interests and skills in the key areas you identified in the process of competency assessment.

A helpful tool at this stage is a 360-degree survey that lets supervisors, co-workers, and subordinates provide input on job holders. The responses will form accurate profiles of individual employees and their suitability to fill new jobs in the reengineered workplace.

Many of the questions to ask at this stage are specific to the process being reengineered. Others relate more generally to the work values and work styles of employees and to how well specific people are likely to perform in a reengineered environment. Still others seek to assess peoples' compatability with, interest in, and motivation to do tasks in the reengineered job context.

For example, you might ask supervisors, co-workers, and subordinates to rate a person's ability to work with new technology, to think creatively, to deal with new situtations, to handle stress, to solve problems, to work as part of a team, and lead a team.

Some traits tend to predict success in almost any job—especially in organizations that are in states of constant reorganization. See the box, "How Do You Spell Success in a Reengineered Workplace?" for a rundown.

The outcome of assessing employees' backgrounds and skill levels is a gap-analysis matrix that includes each person who is involved in the work process as it stands before reengineering begins. The martix covers a spectrum of skill areas that earlier steps have identified as important to the work process in question. For each competency, indicate whether each employee's skill level is weak, moderate, or strong.

HOW DO YOU SPELL SUCCESS IN A REENGINEERED WORKPLACE?

So, you've been charged with leading the effort to assess current employees' suitability for working in a reengineered job context. Surveying those who work with the employees in question can give you a 360-degree view of worker competencies.

Of course, many of the questions you'll ask are specific to the job you have in mind. But several factors tend to predict exellent performance in any job. To be successful in a job today—particularly in organizations that are undergoing incessant internal change and process improvement—a person typically must display the following traits:

- the skills and abilities to do the actual work
- the inclination or inherant ability to learn and adapt to a changing environment over time
- motivation to do the work
- compatibility with the organization's overall operating and management style
- a sense of self-confidence about her or his ability to perform in the job over time.

STAGE 2: DEPLOYING PEOPLE IN A REENGINEERED WORKPLACE

In essence, the matrix you created at the end of stage 1 enables you to assess the range of peoples' individual and aggregate abilities across a typical profile of what you need from an employee—both as an individual contributer and as part of a team.

You've now provided people with an overall "rating and ranking"—comparing their strengths and weaknesses with those of their co-workers, and taking into account the skills that are critical to the reengineered jobs. Armed with that information, it's possible to determine each person's suitability for training, for redeployment elsewhere in the organization, or for outplacement.

Determine people's scores on the matrix by taking the responses gathered from their supervisors, co-workers, and subordinates. Subject those responses to computer analysis that gives weighted averages to different skills and to the relative skills of one person compared with those of his or her co-workers.

That information will help you make the tough decisions about where and how each employee can best contribute in the reengineered work environment.

STAGE 3: CREATING THE MEANS FOR LEARNING

You've determined the competencies people need for success in performing newly reengineered tasks. And you've profiled current job holders to assess their individual skill levels and their skill gaps.

Now you're in an ideal position to create training and career-development plans for employees, using the information you've collected. You also have the information you need for developing a plan to outsource specific tasks and functions that can now best be done outside the organization—for instance, benefits administration and payroll.

People from human resources, training and development, and various line operations should work in tandem to create training plans for employees. Those plans can be regularly updated and revised as needed. For instance, the introduction of new technology might necessitate additional training. So might the implementation of new work practices, whether they are specific to a single process or common across the organization.

This may also be the time to develop jointly a new learning philosophy for your organization—a philosophy that specifically supports job-redesign and process-reengineering priorities. For instance, you may want to inaugurate just-in-time training, computer-based training, distance learning (if you serve multiple geographic sites), or other training strategies to help support continuous-improvement efforts, whether they are process-specific or people-specific.

A NEW KIND OF TOOL FOR GROUPS

Groupware, or electronic meeting-support, is a kind of software that organizations are using more and more often in brainstorming, data-gathering, and focus-group situations.

Groupware technology can help you electronically capture and catalog large amounts of participant input, typically gathered in classroom sessions or through teleconferences. Usually, participants use lap top computers or keypads to input their answers to questions. The technology provides an accurate and quick way to capture data, compile statistics, set priorities for goals and objectives, and build action plans.

When using groupware with focus groups, you may find it helpful to ask participants to review an existing list of tasks, developed ahead of time by the reengineering team. Have focus-group members verify that the list is complete and that it accurately reflects all the transactions likely to be required as part of implementing a new work process.

Once participants have signed off on the list, group the tasks and "subtasks" together in clusters. From those clusters, the focus-group participants can determine what knowledge, skills, and abilities people will need to have in order to perform future tasks in the organization.

One common groupware feature, rank-order voting, may be especially useful in helping focus groups to determine the relative importance of various tasks, skills, and competencies.

BPR presents an excellent time to develop, pilot, and roll out new training initiatives. They are another way to reinforce new work requirements and performance expectations in the reengineered environment.

What kinds of training do employees need to receive?

In addition to process and task-specific training, it's likely that your employees will need to develop better teamwork and communication skills. They may need updated management skills, or training in new technology.

In all likelihood, CAP will by this time have fully delineated the kinds of training you need to offer. Indeed, you may see a "before" and "after" picture emerging—one that gives a clear view of the skills that served employees well in the past, compared with the ones they now need to learn. That picture can point you in the direction you need to go in order to give employees the highest possible skill levels for performing reengineered jobs.

See the figure on this page, "Moving People Into the New Workplace," for an example of changing skill and knowledge requirements in a reengineered workplace.

STAGE 4: ALIGNING THE SUPPORT SYSTEMS

Clearly, no amount of job reconfiguration is going to work unless you put systems in place to reinforce new behaviors and help support the design of new functions. Key systems include the reward and recognition system, the compensation system, and the performance-appraisal program.

That's why stage 4 of the CAP process must deal with building the right kind of infrastructure to support newly designed jobs.

You'll need to develop new philosopies and policies for performance appraisal, compensation, rewards, and incentives. Your reengineered environment probably includes more collaborative work, so the new systems should use measurements that are more team-based than in the past. You may need to retool your systems to reflect critical success factors such as customer-satisfaction levels, cycle time, quality improvement, and team performance.

But you'll also want to leave room for some measurements that key into individual contributions and effort on the job. For instance, what criteria will you build into your performance-appraisal process to recognize and acknowledge individual initiative?

In the Coopers & Lybrand survey of improvement-driven organizations, respondents from high-performing organizations in both the public and the private sector said their workplaces put a lot of stock in recognizing and rewarding individual as well as team efforts in the workplace.

MOVING PEOPLE INTO THE NEW WORKPLACE

In the past, employees...	Now, they need training in...
were familiar with mainframe computers and individual PCs	use of local-area networks, Windows, Lotus Notes, and other advanced computer technologies
worked as individual contributors, performing jobs defined by formal written job descriptions	how to work cooperatively on teams to perform project-driven work assignments; conflict-resolution and project-management skills are a must
dealt with very little change in their jobs	how to deal with constant technological and organizational change
did what they were told, each person reporting to one boss who as a supervisor.	serving many different "customers," both inside and outside the organization.

In those organizations, quality-improvement accomplishments figure prominently in people's annual performance reviews. Job empowerment is a key operating philosophy. You might want to build such objectives into your own performance-appraisal process, as well.

To undergird your competency-alignment, you'll need to field test the HR systems you are putting in place. Fully test each separate system (such as performance appraisal and measurement, compensation, or recognization) in a trial-period shakedown. Testing can help you ensure that each system is performing to expectations and is helping to reinforce the new work norms.

After you conduct separate tests of the different systems, evaluate the results and make revisions as necessary.

MAKING IT ALL COME TOGETHER

How do you ensure that competency alignment becomes a highly effective component of your reengineering efforts?

Success begins with a realization that increasing corporate profitability or organizational effectiveness requires more than cutting costs or shedding staff. Instead, organizations must be purposeful in the ways in which they develop and leverage people as part of reengineering efforts.

Ultimately, the outcome of all this is to increase the bottom line or whatever other measurements your organization uses to gauge profitability or organizational vitality.

It is often easier, in the short term, to increase net income by reducing costs or head count. But true growth and vitality come from sensing new opportunities in the marketplace; building new competencies within the organization; and leveraging the skills, talents, and adaptiveness of employees to achieve organizational aims.

"Any company that is a bystander on the road to the future will watch as its structure, values, and skills become progressively less attuned to industry realities" and to the needs of the marketplace, note Gary Hamel and C.K. Prahalad in their book, *Competing for the Future*.

Pay consious and purposeful attention to the importance of competency alignment as part of your reengineering efforts. Not only will it boost your organization's sustained vitality and profitability, but it also can enhance the resilience and resourcefulness of your organization and its employees in a climate of constant change.

GROUP GENIUS

by Paul Roberts

Frustration. It's 7 p.m. on the second day of a two-day seminar on South Carolina, and the entire executive team from New York-based AM Cosmetics is incredulous. Smack-dab in the middle of a brainstorming session that was producing a concrete business plan, creativity guru Matt Taylor has pulled the plug. As the executives look on in astonishment, Taylor's colleagues silently pile candles, rubber bands, paper clips, Play-Doh, wing nuts, fishing line, and 40 other items unrelated to cosmetics at the front of the workshop space.

Then it gets worse. Taylor instructs them to equip themselves at random from the pile of objects and to use those items to make . . . a toy. And not just any toy. The toys must do things. They must propel themselves up or down or sideways. They must make sounds. Or change color. Or change smell.

The cosmetics executives look at one another, then back at Taylor, who is now standing on a chair. "Oh, come on," says a serious-looking accountant-type who's here from New York for what was advertised as a workshop on the business paradigm of the 21st century—but which now looks like a scene from "Romper Room." "You have got to be kidding."

Taylor isn't kidding. After spending four decades studying, modeling, and testing the character of creativity, the 59-year-old architect-cum-futurist knows how to work the innovative spark: how to find it, coax it out, then build it into a collective blaze that can transform companies and reenergize organizations. He and his wife, Gail Taylor, a former school teacher whose radical notions about learning and creativity nearly got her drummed out of public schools, have broken the creative process into a series of steps, or "states," through which they can guide any person, team, or enterprise to accomplish any creative project—from bringing out a new product to remaking an entire company.

Admittedly, it is seldom a smooth trip. Participants at the Taylors' DesignShops get frustrated, angry, and rebellious. They also find that the process works, that it unleashes what the Taylors call "group genius," a collective creativity so powerful, energizing, and transformative that organizations ranging from restaurant chains to the U.S. military's aerospace test program have turned frustrating dead ends into hugely successful ventures—in a fraction of the time required by conventional management.

And yet MGTaylor Corporation is tiny and virtually unknown. For most of the 1990s, it chalked up roughly $1 million in annual revenues. But this year MGT is operating at a rate between 10 and 15 times that. The firm is developing an agreement to create an alliance with Ernst & Young to pioneer a network of creativity-focused management centers. It already has 13 design and construction projects under way, building creativity centers and field offices for various clients. Its calendar is chock-full of dates for workshops and creativity seminars. "Up to now," Matt Taylor says, "our strategy has been stealth. We've shunned public exposure and worked by word of mouth. We are a distributed, ad hoc, sapient organization, and intend to remain so."

That a self-described stealth creativity organization would find itself on a growth bender and attracting the interest of Ernst & Young is, in the context of today's business world, both instructive and predictable. After spending most of the last two decades trying to slash their way to profitability, most companies have come to realize that a corporate strategy of self-mutilation is not the path to longevity. Nor, for that matter, is a pure technology play, since there's virtually nothing you can invent, license, or buy that your rivals can't match. The only real margin is your workforce, or more precisely, how well it works. Which explains why companies now spend billions annually on various team-building programs.

What those programs are teaching them is that there's something more important than how employees work together: how they think together. It's the prospect of this cerebral collaboration, creating patterns and products that otherwise couldn't be imagined—this "massively parallel processing," as the Taylors put it—that brings companies to Hilton Head. "Smart companies now realize they must innovate their way to profitability," explains Matt Taylor. "And after that, they have to keep on innovating."

Easier said than done. Creativity is hard to measure, difficult to quantify, and nearly impossible to justify. So companies have identified their creative types and squirreled them away, confining creativity to a "safe" place. Worse, when companies have needed creativity, "they have assumed it was a singular event—that they didn't need to have creativity happening all the time," says Gail Taylor, a diminutive 58-year-old with short, grayish hair and dark direct eyes.

Even now, when the idea of creativity has been rehabilitated, corporate America still isn't sure what to do with the real thing. Workshops, books, and gurus extolling creativity are often long on metaphors and light on concrete techniques. Even the change-hungry managers who see creativity as essential still regard innovation as a mystery, a condition that afflicts only certain people.

All of which, the Taylors say, is wrong. Creativity may be exceedingly complex, but it is neither accidental nor unique. It is in fact a natural human state. The right tools and conceptual models—and the Taylors have plenty of those—can draw out, accelerate, and apply creativity to any problem or challenge, from the smallest office glitch to the most pressing global concern. Indeed, the Taylors are not particularly timid in explaining their mission. "Our goal," says Matt Taylor, "is to transform the model of working."

Monday, 7:15 a.m. Two dozen design-shop participants from AM Cosmetics, a $150 million personal care company, start arriving through the front door of "KnOwhere," MGT's headquarters and one of the more unusual work environments these participants have ever seen. The front half of the 5,000-square-foot space is a retail outlet, selling everything from relevant books—*The Third Wave, The Art of War, The Dilbert Principle*—to distinctive, hyperfunctional office furniture.

Toward the rear of the building is the actual workshop area, a warmly lit space with curved walls, a large gathering area, and alcoves for break-out groups. Wall shelves are packed with children's toys, dolls, puzzles, and hundreds of books—many on business, but others on topics that vary from tide-pool ecology to the art of Walt Disney. Most of the walls are finished in a smooth, gray surface that can be written on—massive notepads for brainstorming sessions. Ceiling microphones and video cameras record the proceedings, piping them back to the Knowledge Deck, a raised corner where a half dozen staffers energetically turn the DesignShop into a massive, multimedia document.

Matt, wearing jeans, an open collar, and his trademark vest, opens the DesignShop, outlining the session's two-day schedule. Participants, he says, have entered not only a new work space but also a new context, where hierarchy doesn't exist, ideas are welcome, and opinions can be expressed safely, without fear of reprisal—guarantees that Matt always wrings from company brass before hosting a DesignShop. "There are no chiefs here," he says.

Then the first lesson begins. Michael Kaufman, a tall, friendly-looking Californian who will be cofacilitating with Matt, holds up a wooden toy airplane. "What's this?" he asks.

TESTING THE FUTURE

For the workers at the Arnold Engineering and Development Center (AEDC) in Tullahoma, Tennessee, the Cold War's end brought little reason for celebration, The federal facility, which tests aerospace systems, saw its budget slashed in the post-Cold-War build-down; worse, its main customer—the U.S. Air Force-also had less money to spend on testing.

Outside consultants offered little hope. As the 1990s began, many AEDC managers were ready to accept their fate, convinced they should shrink their operations voluntarily and prepare to fade away gracefully. Not the commanding officer, Col. Bill Rutley. Instead, Rutley brought in MGT and, after several Design Shops, concluded that the best course was to *expand* operations—dramatically.

Was such a move possible? In the first phase, Rutley's management team "scanned" the entire AEDC operation. They assessed the center's strengths: a world-class wind tunnel, a collection of sophisticated, expensive testing equipment, and a team of highly skilled personnel. Their conclusion: AEDC had the right stuff to compete outside the military sphere and in the thriving *commercial* aerospace industry. There were, however, obstacles: low morale, bureaucratic fatalism, and most significant, a pricing clause in AEDC's authorizing legislation making it nearly impossible to vie competitively for nonmilitary customers. The DesignShop's key recommendation: change the legislation.

The next question was how to justify such a move to the U.S. Congress. Rutley and his team discovered that Europe's Airbus was becoming surprisingly well positioned to take aerospace business from American companies—the kind of development Congress might respond to. AEDC also compared the demand for testing facilities with testing capacity in he United States, and found a serious gap. If AEDC could price its services competitively, there would be enough demand for the center to expand its testing operations substantially.

Next, team members built what the Taylors call a "value web," a diverse network that included AEDC's suppliers, various military customers, as well as commercial giants like Boeing, NASA, and McDonnell Douglas. Then they convened value-web meetings, some including officials from rival firms. From the meetings, AEDC learned what testing services commercial clients would need, and potential clients gained reassurance on issues such as test-data security.

Finally, with the help of a powerful political network created by the value web, AEDC began lobbying Congress. It took less than 18 months to amend the limiting law—a remarkably short time for a process that involved both the defense bureaucracy and Congress. Among AEDC's first "outside" projects: testing engines for the Boeing 777. Because of AEDC's superior testing, the FAA certified the 777 to fly overseas two years early, a significant competitive boost for U.S. airline manufacturers.

As important as the new business is the new sense of control and confidence that the AEDC management team can now apply to other projects. Rutley, who is careful to point out that he's not speaking for the Air Force, thinks there is a larger lesson from the MGT approach. "You either design your future," he says, "or you can just let it fall on you."

The point is not to test people's toy knowledge but to introduce the notion of models—a central aspect of the MGT approach. Over the years the Taylors and their colleagues have created detailed, highly graphical models of every major aspect of business: how workers absorb information, how education and training occur, how corporations are structured—and how they must restructure to survive in the next century.

The models are multifunctional, providing ways to view and correct different aspects of a business, organization, or enterprise. The Taylors' Seven Domains model, for example, lays out the key dimensions of a company, from its physical workplace to its communications technology to its corporate philosophy; locates where managers are most likely to find barriers to creativity; and helps eliminate them. Another model, the Seven Stages of the Creative Process, offers an elegant description of the discovery process—a circular route that begins with the identification of a need; moves through the envisioning, building, and testing of a solution; and winds up back with identification. MGT's models are not for the faint of heart: an advanced version of the Creative Process model, for example, has 294 steps.

Most participants usually cut their teeth on something called Scan, Focus, Act (SFA), a simple, three-part, nature-based model that anyone can use immediately. "Scan" is the information-gathering phase, where existing conditions and needs, opportunities, and options are assessed. In "Focus," options are scrutinized, debated, and winnowed down to a chosen course of action—which is then tested in the "Act" phase. The results of that test are re-scanned, and the cycle repeats.

Though simple in appearance, the SFA model has broad applications and immediate benefits. For many program participants, it's the first time they've seen the creative process as a series of steps. And the first time they've been a part of that process.

Monday is Scan day, and AM Cosmetics executives spend much of the time gathering information and assessing options. In one exercise, each participant makes a detailed assessment of AM's status, mission, strengths, and options. Nothing is off-limits. Everything is a potential inspiration, a potential tool, a potential model. Even learning about the concept of models is a natural Scan exercise. And not only models of business.

After lunch participant teams scan the ecologies of tide pools, rain forests, beehives, and the human body, discovering parallels between these living systems and their company. Later they scan the present from an entirely new angle: the future. Each is assigned a cultural, political, or business trend—such as political freedom or information exchange—and then told to go 50 years into the future and report where that trend is and how it got there.

It's a technique the Taylors call "backcasting," and it illustrates one of the Taylors' favorite axioms: "You can't get *there* from *here*, but you *can* get *here* from *there*." "There" is an imagined future—where you want your enterprise to be 5, 10, even 50 years from now. "Here" is where you are now. "The trick," says Gail Taylor, "is to try to bring back a piece of 'there' to 'here'."

Gail has been hauling in great chunks of "there" ever since the late 1960s, when as a second-grade public-school teacher in Kansas City, Missouri she discovered that her students could learn faster than the normal curriculum could teach them. After a pupil posed a question Gail couldn't answer ("Why do soap bubbles have colors?"), she asked the class for any questions they had, about anything they wanted to know, and let them figure out how to find the answers—giving them access to all information sources, including those off-campus.

The kids went wild, inventing information-seeking methods with more enthusiasm than she had previously witnessed. "I could literally *see* their thinking, it was so intense," recalls Gail. "For the first time I realized I didn't have to 'teach' creativity—that it was innate and that every kid in the class had it."

By year's end her students were beating fifth- and sixth-graders on test scores. The results were so spectacular that school officials drew their own conclusion: Gail, already known as something of a maverick, had to be cheating.

Disgusted, she quit and in 1972 set up the Learning Exchange, a marketplace for educational innovation in an old warehouse space. While doing projects in this large open environment, Gail discovered what came to be known as the "working big" principle—having participants write or sketch ideas on huge poster boards rather than 8 x 11 notepads. "Small paper leads to small vision," Gail explains. "You can't see the complexity emerging from a project when everyone works from a tiny piece of paper. And you can't collaborate."

In 1976 Gail took a class entitled "Rebuilding the Future." The instructor was Matt Taylor, a designer who had begun training to be an architect when he was 12 and who seemed unable to look at a product or process without trying to make it better. An Air Force brat, Matt had grown up on bases around the world, always on the move yet never lacking for a community. In Matt's view, military culture is one of the few instances of an intentional community: a close-knit, planned enclave whose members are educated and dedicated, accustomed to high technology and "can do" practicality, and most important, committed to an overarching goal. "When I finally got out in the real world," Matt recalls, "I was shocked at the lack of rigor, at what was taken for granted, and mostly at the mindless, chasing-the-dollar mentality that served no larger purpose."

Part of Matt's interest in architecture and design was the power it afforded to recreate the kind of rigorous, purposeful community that had provided such comfort in his past. When Matt was 16 and his family lived in California, he began working in architecture firms. He apprenticed with Frank Lloyd Wright, whom Matt admired not only for the broad social reach of his vision but also for his almost Victorian insistence that an engineer—the quintessential figure of action, numbers, and hard-nosed decisions—be a person of passion, artistry, and creativity as well.

In the early 1960s Matt entered the construction industry, which he found incredibly exciting though badly managed, terribly organized, and hugely wasteful. Drawn by the possibilities of prefabricated construction, he devised a fast-track construction system and an early version of today's just-in-time delivery. He also created what he now calls a "value web," a network of all the players in a given project, from owner to laborers, that fosters communication and collaboration and makes it easier to solve problems.

By 1960 it occurred to Matt that the entire business paradigm—the centralized, medieval—hierarchical system that he later called the "second wave," after futurist Alvin Toffler—needed fast-tracking. Not only was business organized around a dying model, but the element that could save it, the capacity for innovation, had systematically been excluded from the process by corporate America's growing reliance on structure, chains of command, and a top-down culture. The great engineers of the late 19th century, in whom art and action found harmony, had been replaced by organization men, bureaucrats who had no interest in or understanding of the creative temperament. The feeling was mutual: creative types who once might have been drawn to the adventure and romance of business now eschewed it as crass and vulgar, says Matt, "something that you went into only if all else failed."

Matt found himself on a mission to reunite business and creativity and to create a community that could integrate the two. He went on a reading binge, sucking up everything he could find on systems theory, information, cybernetics, psychology, and economics. Then he distilled his view of the way things should work into equal parts elaborate models and corny axioms.

Matt and Gail were two of a kind. Just before they met, Matt had founded the Renascence Project, a "futures-oriented" research and community-development center in Kansas City devoted to urban renewal and entrepreneurship. In 1977 they married, moved to Boulder, Colorado, and began a systematic search for the conditions under which creativity flourishes. By 1980 they had produced the first DesignShops, drawing a small but committed following. Practicing what they preached as futurists, the Taylors saw a new complexity emerging. "For the first time in our history, creativity is required of all of us, all the time," says Matt. "And that requires not only a different way of thinking about management but also a completely new methodology and a new level of discipline."

But it was the go-go '80s. The rest of the world wasn't ready for the Taylors' version of "Montessori for adults." Corporate America wanted manly merger mania, not wimpy creativity, and Matt and Gail had no interest in pushing the issue. They rejected the usual management-guru shtick: write a book, make a video, do the lecture circuit, repeat the same speech endlessly. Instead, they elected to wait for the change to come.

Matt recalls asking an R&D team at a Big Three auto company how many hours a week they actually spent doing productive, value-adding work. "They thought about it and finally said, 'About four hours.' Four hours. The rest of their time was spent in meetings and other useless crap." Matt sighs. "Structure wins." Finally the wave broke: reengineering crashed, slash-and-burn wiped out, and a new management explosion created a new business movement—one with a hunger for creativity and for the knowledge MGT was offering.

CREATIVE DOMAINS

The Taylor mantra on managing for creativity goes something like this: All employees are inherently creative. That creativity is typically blocked by *structural* elements within a company. Eliminate the blockages, and you enable "group genius." In other words, you don't manage people; you manage, the world in which they work, a world the Taylors divide into seven key components, or *domains*.

1. **Body of Knowledge** know what you know. Recognize that your team's collective knowledge and experience are among your most valuable resources. Assess your body of knowledge; find out where—in whom—it resides. Spread it around—ensure that everyone knows "what is known" to eliminate duplicate efforts and build unity.
2. **Process Design and Facilitation** Clear the pathways. In most companies the creative process happens by accident. Find out how it happens in yours. Discover your enterprise's internal processes, or pathways, and clear them of obstacles. Don't let tradition dictate how things are done. Meetings, for example, should be times of intensive interaction. They should be called only when a project or problem requires actual collaboration and group creativity.
3. **Education** Learn how you learn. Discover the processes by which your team gathers information or explores new ideas, and assess your attitudes toward learning. If success depends on maintaining your body of knowledge, then learning must be a constant activity.
4. **Environment** Establish the physical and psychological field for work. Creating a functional environment means departing radically from workplaces left over from the industrial era. Creative space must be adaptable to multiple uses—from large meetings to small breakouts. It must be comfortable, healthy, homey, but fully functional—a place that supports multiple styles of work and creativity, from writing on wall panels to pacing back and forth. Above all, your environment must allow team members to "work big and work collaboratively."
5. **Technology** It works for you, not the other way around. Used appropriately, it lets an enterprise leverage its creative work But technology is also a false "quick fix" that will simply magnify and accelerate whatever flaws remain in your creative processes. Make your technology yours. Customize it to your needs and systems.
6. **Project Management** Manage the environment, not the people. Make sure that the environment maximizes creativity, that the body of knowledge is rich and accessible, that the team is as diverse as possible. Most important, facilitate. Lead team members through a clearly enunciated creative process—like Scan, Focus, Act—and evaluate the project and the team's progress at each step.
7. **Venture Management** The big picture. Develop a specific corporate vision to bring "there" to "here." Choose a preferred future state, then determine how to modify daily actions and processes to achieve it. It also means maintaining your organization's health, preserving functional aspects, and searching for new, more effective, and creative methods.

Tuesday, 10:33 a.m. Five members of an AM Cosmetics team stand before the rest of the group, struggling to explain how they killed their own company. It's part of a "scenario challenge," a variation on backcasting in which players are handed a realistic business outcome from 1998 and asked to explain how it happened. This team's scenario: they represent AM's real-life rival, which has devised a strategy that killed AM in late 1997. "Describe the basic elements of your strategy," reads the assignment. "What made AM vulnerable? What innovations did you use? How did your strategy roll out? How did you catch AM so completely off guard?"

The objective here is several-fold. Players are being pushed out of the box, made to see their company and all its frailties in brutally honest terms. And it's not an exercise in goofy fantasy: each alternative reality a team concocts has to be backed by realistic measures. Other teams have happier scenarios in which their company is kicking its rivals' butts. Their task is to figure out, step by step, how that happened—lessons they can immediately apply to their strategic planning.

By lunch the DesignShop's atmosphere is electric. Without waiting for the energy to subside, Matt moves into the next exercise: Vision/Mission/Strategy. Teams regroup in the main meeting area to hammer out where AM is going and how it's going to get there. There is excited talk about new product lines, new markets, new strategies. Then out of the cauldron of ideas comes a real solution to an actual marketing problem: AM will turn away a large but brutally troublesome customer, and hand over the business to its chief rival. And with the energy and resources the "loss" frees up, AM will aggressively pursue its rival's more valuable customers. It's a risky strategy, but it's in sync with the DesignShop's creative inspiration: what looks like a defeat, if executed relentlessly, will turn into a double win.

Teams break out again, each assigned a separate chunk of the company's vision: technology, marketing and image, distribution. They spend the next several hours huddled in groups, then reassemble in the main room to report out. As each team explains its contribution, ideas prompt more ideas, as well as concerns, from the others. It's a riff of massively parallel processing that could easily continue through dinner—except for that frustratingly clever interruption called Inventions, and the challenge of building a toy.

Inventions starts promptly at 7 p.m. By 7:08 the pile of objects at the front of the main meeting area has been picked over. Teams line up to receive specs for their toys, which are designed to serve as AM marketing gimmicks. The specs are so outrageous—moves up 12 inches, moves down 12 inches, changes color, or changes shape—that participants cannot imagine creating these toys in a toy shop, much less from a pile of household detritus. And yet, within one hour, grown men and women are pawing intently through screws and tape and Styrofoam, scavenging the environment for furniture and other materials, and fashioning outlandish machines that, even at this early stage, are clearly meant to do things.

"It'll never work," says one older gentleman as his group struggles with a handmade spring mechanism. Finally, he can hold back no longer. "Let me do that! Outta my way." At 10:30 that evening, to great cheering and laughter, the toys are rolled out.

As with every other DesignShop phase, Inventions operates on several levels. There is huge parallel processing, with each team member working on a different aspect of the toy. As the evening progresses, players gain a startling new perspective on their colleagues. The exercise also provides a refreshing view of collaboration. The AM executives begin to experience work as fun, and this becomes another possibility, something to draw on when they're back at "real" work. And finally, there's the feeling of creative success, something many have never felt before.

Wednesday. 7:06 a.m. Map day. Participants sip coffee and munch bagels, powering up for the final push, the Act that comes after Scan and Focus. One by one, they lay out their new takes on the company's vision, its mission, and its strategy, including 30-day, 90-day, 6-month, and 12-month goals. This raw material is then sifted through collectively—debated, taken apart, and reassembled—until there is complete agreement over what will go on the Annotated Network Diagram, the ANDMap. The ANDMap is a corporate schematic and action plan, a blueprint showing exactly where the company is going, project by project, decision point by decision point, benchmark by benchmark.

Now there is tentativeness in the room. The group has been together less than 50 hours, and here they are trying to set goals that will have implications for two, three, and four years. What they're really feeling, for the first time, is the tension between talking and doing, between Focus and Act. To act is to test, and to test is, possibly, to fail. But it is also to learn, to put more feedback into the process. As Matt, the former architect and contractor, puts it, "You start building when you can't learn any more from the drawings."

Despite such tentativeness, ANDMaps are surprisingly potent documents. Forged in such a high-energy collective process, they accurately reflect the management team's sense of the company and its direction; equally important, they forge a tacit agreement that these goals are correct, worthy, and appropriately ambitious. Most companies emerge from the MGT experience with a set of goals far larger than any they had when they began: One-year plans to persuade Congress to change a critical law. Three-year plans to quadruple earnings. Indeed, although the Taylors can see a time when they'll leave DesignShop facilitation to colleagues and move on to new paradigm-shifting projects, they can't imagine losing their appetite for the gusto of such plans.

Noon. The Designshop is over. MGT'S staff members scramble to finish documenting AM Cosmetics's DesignShop product—a detailed blueprint of where the company will be in three months, six months, one year—and how they will get there. Participants, still buzzed from the 50-hour ride, gather in a circle of chairs to share their impressions. "I like what I see here," says one veteran manager. "I wish this could have happened to me 20 years sooner."

THEORY IN ACTION: THE CITIBANK PRIVATE BANK'S PORTFOLIO BALANCING ACT

by William A. Brindley & Michael J. Bear

While downsizing was the rage in the first part of this decade, it is becoming increasingly clear that in the 21st century companies won't be able to cut their way to profitability. Cost cutting alone only saves money; it doesn't build a business. Unless cost savings are reinvested in the business, there can be no real, sustainable growth. Operations and capabilities pared to the bone rarely can respond to market opportunities, and so are vulnerable to competitors who can. In addition, costs must be reduced in a systematic and strategic way, with the focus on designing or redesigning processes for cost management.

Companies that undertake one-time "cost-cutting" often find that when it ends, if no permanent process changes have been made, people fall into the same old ways of doing business and costs reappear. But at the Citibank Private Bank, we have found that by working on process changes and by tracking the resulting business improvements for three years after implementation, our efforts become "baked into" the business.

The Citibank Private Bank, with offices in more than 30 countries catering to the top tier of individual net worth, is enjoying revenue growth of better than 20% per year. We've worked hard to integrate Citibank's strategic cost management (SCM) focus into our strategy of global franchise growth. SCM is one of the five elements of the Citibank's balanced scorecard of performance measurements, which gives every manager strategic direction. At the Citibank Private Bank, we have linked SCM with our business performance improvement (BPI) effort, thus connecting cost management and franchise growth, a powerful combination.

We have adopted and adapted a number of elements from others' reengineering methods, taking full advantage of best practices. But we have added a new twist, creating a "portfolio of projects." We actively manage this portfolio as we would any other portfolio of investments, because our BPI/SCM efforts really are investments in our business franchise, enabling us to reach our financial and nonfinancial goals.

BPI/SCM is far more than cost cutting. While simple cost cutting aims at reductions across the board, with no regard to how they might affect the franchise, our goal with strategic cost management is to improve efficiency in a way that never sacrifices client quality. Our SCM efforts focus on improving service and quality on a global basis for our clients, redesigning processes to speed account information turnaround, reducing mistakes in information input, and streamlining the development of new products and services. While the way we undertake efforts may vary slightly by region, depending on culture and the regulatory environment, we strive for global improvement in all of our efforts. At the end of the day, our SCM efforts are aimed at increasing private bankers' productivity—as well as productivity and quality in all areas that support them—in order to grow the business.

To be sure, we are in an enviable position, since private banking is a relatively young and rapidly expanding global industry. Other companies in stable or declining industries apply cost management in a different way than we do. But we believe that some of the strategies and approaches we have taken can be transferred to businesses in other industries and can be adapted to be successful in their environment.

THE PROJECT PORTFOLIO AS A RISK MANAGEMENT TOOL

The concept of a portfolio is one that comes naturally to us as bankers. But we believe it is a notion that those in any industry can use in their performance improvement and cost management efforts.

Performance improvement—often addressed through such approaches as business process reengineering or business process redesign (both called BPR)—is a concept that comes from total quality management (TQM) and systems thinking, both of which were developed in the 1940s and 1950s. At present, most practitioners of these approaches come from either a manufacturing or an information technology (I/T) discipline.

The financial services industry was late to get into performance improvement. While some believe this put us behind the curve, we think it gave us a better opportunity to adopt and adapt best practices from other industries. For instance, our approach to quality uses methods also is used successfully by Motorola Corp., and we have adapted a "work out" technique similar to General Electric Company's.

Generally speaking, the I/T faction sees BPR primarily as an opportunity to "obliterate" strings of manual activities within a process and replace them with a technological solution. To these folks, until there is a full technological installation, there is no success. Those who approach BPR from the manufacturing point of view see it as an opportunity to redesign a macro process, such as "new product development," from start to finish. These people see success only when there is a complete reengineering of the entire core business process.

Both of these approaches—which are all-or-nothing in nature—run significant risks. Some of these risks are technological, but many more have to do with organizational culture and change management. Practitioners from both schools argue this point in their writings and in their public speaking, yet none have found the key that really opens up the door to successful change management.

We couldn't agree more that the biggest risks in performance improvement initiatives are organizational, and that managing organizational change is difficult. But as bankers, we are specialists in portfolio management and risk management, and we believe these two concepts can be used effectively to manage organizational change. At the Citibank Private Bank we have applied both of these banking principles to create a powerful business performance improvement and strategic cost management tool: the portfolio of initiatives.

Portfolios are inherently about choice and balance. By considering the tradeoffs—effectiveness vs. efficiency, organizational change vs. comfort, cost management vs. franchise growth, developed vs. emerging markets, and resources vs. needs—we can create a balanced portfolio of SCM initiatives. The portfolio approach allows us to best allocate our resources, including those of our senior line managers, who have ultimate authority and responsibility for each initiative, and those of our cadre of 15 BPI specialists, who bring project management expertise to the undertaking. While line managers "own" the individual projects in their portfolios, the BPI specialists take the project management burden off the line managers and their immediate staff.

Our portfolio of SCM initiatives is designed to yield, on balance, a high return on investments and full payback within one year. Not every initiative yields a high return—some are in our portfolio specifically because they offer more modest returns, but with little or no organizational or financial risk. Others are in the portfolio because they offer quick returns, which can be used to fund longer-term efforts.

We believe that applying the portfolio concept to our strategic cost management/business performance improvement effort is one of the keys to its success. Our record, with a tenfold payback on investment since 1995, has clearly demonstrated the practicality of the portfolio approach.

THE FOUR STAGES

Our portfolio of SCM undertakings does not magically appear, but rather is the outcome of a structured, disciplined four-stage approach. The four stages are

- identify,
- dimension,
- rank, and
- choose.

IDENTIFY: GATHERING OPPORTUNITIES

At the private bank, we get ideas for improving our cost structure from the whole spectrum of our business. We have both formal and informal ways to collect these thoughts. Some ideas come from project teams and from diagnostic assessments, some grow out of other improvement efforts. Input also comes from the PBG Forum, a select group of some 150 business managers and front-line employees who bring their businesses' ideas to light. By generating these ideas from the operating units instead of from a centralized corps of "expert reengineers" or outside consultants, process changes that are eventually undertaken already have sponsors within the relevant business units. Senior BPI officers cull the list for obvious duplicates and combine aspects of a number of similiar ideas to create the full set of unique opportunities. This is a continuous process; we reconsider them monthly.

CITIBANK AND THE CITIBANK PRIVATE BANK

Citibank is divided into two major global operations: the consumer franchise, which had revenues of $13.5 billion in 1996, and corporate banking, which accounted for $7.2 billion in revenues in 1996. The consumer franchise consists of three businesses, Citibanking (branch banking), Cards (credit and charge cards), and the Citibank Private Bank, which targets the top tier of the consumer financial services market, providing wealth management for individuals with high net worth.

The Citibank Private Bank is one of the largest private banks in the world, with offices in more than 30 countries and $96 billion in assets under management. Products and services are delivered to clients worldwide through five market regiom: United States, Western Hemisphere, Europe/Middle East/Africa, Asia-Pacific, and Japan.

The private bank's revenues (almost $1.1 billion in 1996) and net income ($279 million) are growing rapidly, at a rate of more than 20% last year. Assets under management increased 11% in 1996.

Ideas run from the simple—reducing the cost of photocopying by using both sides of the paper—to the more comprehensive—outsourcing all back-office operations. Many of our projects are "follow ons" to other projects.

For example, we were looking for a way to reduce the cycle time in underwriting decisions for mortgages for a particular niche of U.S.-based clients. We had been putting all mortgage applications through a rigorous, cumbersome, and time-consuming underwriting process, because we would be holding the risk-associated mortgages. Using input from the underwriters, we reduced cycle time by streamlining the process, forming co-located underwriting teams, and adding some technology. This combination reduced handoffs and eliminated steps that didn't add value. The project was very successful.

But during the project, the team realized that we could tap additional opportunities for improvement. We created a predictive model that can filter loan-application data and make the "first pass," approving or rejecting the most obvious decisions, and sending only the more difficult applications to underwriters. An analysis was done, the software designed, and when the project is finally implemented, about 40% of these applications will now go through the streamlined approval process, with no additional risk to the bank.

DIMENSION: DETERMINING THE POTENTIAL REWARD

Once unique opportunities have been identified, both line executives and BPI officers perform a brief business case analysis to determine their potential. While cost management is the point of SCM, we also analyze ideas for how much effectiveness they could add to the process, thereby creating the possibility for additional margin benefits, even if the cost reduction gains are small. Since it is important that everyone working on these efforts speak the same language, we have created a standard format that allows us to quantify potential gains consistently across regions.

We conduct this business case analysis by measuring known activity costs against known activities. We mapped all of the private bank's processes, down to the activity level, and collected these maps in what we call the "anchor process set." Combining these process maps with our SCM database, we can perform an activity based costing analysis of all of activities within the scope of the proposed project. Armed with this information, we can gauge roughly how much savings can be accrued by particular suggestions.

RANK: QUEUING UP ON THE "RUNWAY"

The private bank's senior line management and BPI executives rank initiatives in order of importance with the help of a proprietary computer-based model called the "PGB diagnostic filter." This filter scores each prospective undertaking on six dimensions. The first three dimensions—strategic alignment, contribution, and risk—speak to the question: Should we do this project? The other three dimensions—capacity, capability, and timing—speak to the question: If so, when? The diagnostic filter, in effect, builds the business case for each prospective undertaking.

Briefly, the six dimensions ask:

- *Strategic alignment:* How well does the proposed initiative fit with Citibank's and the private bank's overall objectives?
- *Contribution:* Will the proposed initiative add value for clients or for shareholders; and will the effort help build the private bank's franchise?
- *Risk:* Is there a high, medium, or low organizational and change management risk to the proposed initiative? We assess risk on two dimensions: risk to the franchise and business and risk to the initiative.
- *Capacity:* This is the share of the organizational plate available. Can we take on another project of the proposed size and magnitude? Do we have the necessary resources available to accomplish the effect? How much capacity of both the senior line management responsible and BPI staff would the proposed initiative use? What is the capacity of the organization to absorb the changes that would occur with this proposed initiative?
- *Capability:* Does the senior line management, with help from BPI officers, have the skills, such as project management, necessary to make this proposed initiative successful? If not now, are the necessary capabilities being developed?
- *Timing:* What is the time frame in which the proposed initiative would generate results? Is it short term (e.g., three months), medium term (three months to one year), or longer term (more than one year)? All of our BPI/SCM initiatives must show significant return within eight quarters, or two years.

Using the ranking generated by the answers to such questions, the PGB diagnostic filter then adds the new prospective initiative, based on priority, to the existing queue already on the "runway" of projects to be undertaken.

THE BPI UNIT

Business performance improvement (BPI) is not something you have done to you. It is something you do to yourself. So it is important that the business unit in which a BPI or strategic cost management (SCM) effort is being undertaken have "ownership" of the project.

Our BPI officers work closely with global and regional senior management to both design and implement BPI/SCM efforts. Sometimes these efforts are the outgrowth of requests made by the senior manager, asking the BPI unit to come and do an analysis and business case of an issue he or she has identified. Other times an issue has been identified in some other way, and the BPI unit is looking for a place to institute a pilot that can then be rolled out globally. Ideas also come in via other routes. But however the project is initiated, in all cases the line management—not the BPI unit—sponsors and owns each initiative. We provide analytical assistance, business advice, project management, and a dispassionate eye.

We like to think of the BPI unit as a "rapid deployment force." Our force officers are armed with practical tools and techniques, and deployed in four locations around the world to cover Asia, Europe, and North and South America. Our people are embedded within each major business in the private bank. We all use the same approach and report benefits the same way. We can support critical projects from any of our locations.

While we have worked assiduously in the past three years to first reduce, then eliminate, the use of outside consultants, we have at the same time built these capabilities in-house so that our BPI officers are, in effect, internal consultants to senior line managers.

CHOOSE: MAINTAINING BALANCE IN THE PORTFOLIO

While the diagnostic filter gives each new prospective idea an objective ranking, what project to put into the portfolio and when to do it is still a business decision—one that must be made by a human being. It takes human decision making and business judgment to keep the portfolio in balance.

The total portfolio includes both global and regional initiatives. Each regional portfolio is different, depending on local needs. One region may need an infusion of quick successes in order to build credibility or fund longer-term projects. Another region may have some "must-do" undertakings, driven by regulation. But whether the particular project is global or local, our BPI practitioners use the same approach to analysis, business case building, project design, and implementation.

Business analysis skills are essential. Creating a properly structured portfolio of projects requires the ability to look at potential undertakings in a dispassionate way, both as an outsider to the regional organization and as an insider to the goals and aims of the Citibank Private Bank.

ACTIVELY MANAGING THE PORTFOLIO

SCM doesn't stop at selecting the initiatives and waiting for business managers to show results. We in the BPI unit work with line management to keep the portfolio moving. To us, active management means knowing what is happening in every undertaking at any given time. Efforts can speed up or slow down; they can narrow or widen in scope; the expected benefits can change. Portfolio management—teams constantly adjust and refocus resources—rebalancing the portfolio—to produce dependable, defendable benefits and minimize risk. While the business unit has ultimate responsibility for the benefits generated by the portfolio, the BPI officers work closely, as co-managers, to deliver those results.

We track revenues, expenses, and accrued benefits for each project in the portfolio, using our proprietary benefits identification and tracking software (BITS). We monitor where each undertaking in the portfolio stands every month. The private bank executive who "owns" the project, a financial controller, and the senior BPI officer each review and sign off results. We also analyze, in real time, the risk and opportunity of each project in the portfolio. If a project is not working, we may need to launch additional initiatives to make up the shortfall. In this way, we constantly refine the expectation of senior management with regard to delivery of SCM benefits, and we present tradeoffs in terms of what benefits can be delivered at what resource investment.

A few illustrations show how we can leverage strategic cost management into value for our customers and growth for our business franchise.

We were asked by the senior line manager in our Asia-Pacific region to have the BPI unit perform a strategic market assessment of his on-shore investment business (that is, for clients who invest in the country in which they hold citizenship) in Thailand. We found a capacity mismatch. While the market for private banking in Thailand was growing, we did not have enough private bankers there. At the same time, we had an overcapacity in Singapore for processing investment transactions.

We transferred the processing of some kinds of product transactions from Thailand to Singapore—making sure to stay within local regulatory requirements—and reallocated our resources in Thailand to allow for more private bankers. In effect, we traded the resources it would cost to have five processing employees, and all of their premises and equipment, for more private bankers. In this way we saved 10% of the processing costs, while adding private bankers to capitalize on the growing Thai market and thus increase the revenue line. The combination of reduced cost and increased revenue equates to significant margin benefit for this SCM initiative.

It's not always a question of cutting a lot of support personnel and replacing them with private bankers. In Hong Kong, for instance, we found that we had far too many high-level people in treasury and financial control. By consolidating treasury functions under one person, and then "insourcing" some work—contracting with the corporate banking arm of

Citibank to perform the services for us—we were able to free up resources to add a product specialist in our Singapore office in order to meet customer needs.

Again, the premise is not cost cutting, but right-sizing and creating the proper balance of resources where and when they are needed.

Sometimes it's important to make a "quick hit" in order to gain credibility with a senior manager in a region, especially if he or she is new. Such was the case in a project involving loan rollovers. The BPI office analyzed the loan portfolio in one of our regional markets and found that 77% of the loans being processed were rollovers of previous loans. Yet we were sending rollovers through the same detailed credit approval process as new loans. This was causing our clients time and anxiety, and eating up capacity we could be using making new loans to current and future clients.

We were able to help the regional manager create a new process for rollover loans that took out many of the underwriting steps and, in effect, merely checked to see that the client's financial conditions were not radically different than when the original loan was made and that the interest rate on the rolled-over loan would be appropriate. The regional manager was able to use freed-up underwriting capacity to expand services to current clients and to market for new clients. The BPI team showed people in the field that—even if the gains are not tremendous in dollar terms—we will support and carry out projects that make their jobs easier and help solidify their client relationships, making it easier to do business with the bank.

Finally, an example from Europe. Citibank manages a number of mutual funds, holds securities, and does currency transactions in a European country that offers its investors a number of tax advantages, under strict secrecy laws. Costs are very high, and the country has limited human resources. Our processing capacity was being taxed. Because of our global technology platform, we were able to offload processing to our regional operations center in another European country while still adhering to all secrecy and banking regulations in the first county. We were able to redirect the talents of 17 people there who had formerly done processing work. By retraining them, and in many cases upgrading their skills, we were able to fill needed openings in compliance, marketing, and other areas, while also increasing the business's profitability.

OUR RESULTS SO FAR

We are very proud of the results achieved from our efforts. Over the past three years, 1995 through 1997, we project that our SCM/BPI efforts will yield approximately $120 million of cumulative margin benefits. Remember that to us margin benefits are reductions in cost and increases in attributable revenue above all required investments in the project. Payback on invested costs almost always occurs in less than one year, and often occurs in six to eight months.

We use conservative calculations of benefits and liberal calculations of project cost to make sure we are not creating an overly optimistic scenario. Since we began in 1995, our BPI/SCM efforts have paid back more than 10 times the investment we have made in them. In 1997 alone, SCM projects in the portfolio will yield incremental year-on-year cost savings in excess of 7% of our expense baseline, exceeding the corporae goal. And because we are in a high-growth business, we are able to redeploy those savings into growing the franchise. In fact, on our project "runway" at the present time, we have a ranked list of potential SCM projects that represent more than 20% of our cost base.

We believe those seeking performance improvement in any industry can adopt and adapt our methodology, using our four-stage approach to build their own portfolio of process and performance enhancement efforts. Once selected, active management of the portfolio should lead to delivery of results.

PERFORMANCE APPRAISAL: CAN WE "MANAGE" AWAY THE CURSE?

By Chris Lee

"Performance appraisals are that occasion when, once a year, you are reminded of who owns you."

—Peter Block, consultant and author.

"Remove barriers that rob people in management and in engineering of their right to pride of workmanship. This means, inter alia, abolishment of the annual or merit rating and of management by objective, management by the numbers."

—Point 12B of W. Edwards Deming's Famous 14 Points.

"A city electrician—angered over a poor performance evaluation and fearing that he might be fired—hunted down and shot to death four of his superiors at Los Angeles' downtown technical center Wednesday before he was disarmed and arrested, police said."

—Los Angeles Times, July 20,1995.

Ah, performance appraisals. The one organizational ritual that is universally despised. Call them appraisals, evaluations, or reviews, the ugly truth is that most employees dread receiving them almost as much as managers hate giving them.

Appraisal horror stories abound, though, thankfully, few culminate in shoot-outs. There's the one about the auto-industry manager who received his annual review while he and his boss sat in adjoining stalls in the men's room. The boss was pleased with the manager's performance; he just hated giving face-to-face reviews. Or there's the one about the ex-IBM employee who received the lowest-possible performance rating after years of receiving the highest rating. When pressed for an explanation, her manager pointed to her admission in a meeting that getting laid off wouldn't be a big blow to her. Since the lowest-rated employees were to be marked for layoff, the manager manipulated the appraisal system to meet his downsizing quota. And there are innumerable stories of people who found completed review forms surreptitiously slipped onto their desk chairs after work hours or who consider their annual appraisal meeting an ambush in which they are held to previously unknown performance criteria.

IT'S A CROCK

While much of the human resources profession concentrates on trying to improve the performance appraisal process, a few lonely voices out there insist that the whole thing is a toxic practice that should be eliminated altogether. One of them belongs to Peter Scholtes, president of Scholtes Seminars & Consulting in Madison, WI. "It's a crock," he says flatly.

Not only does performance appraisal fail to fulfill its primary objective, to improve performance, Scholtes contends, but organizations that use it are revealing their true beliefs about people: They don't trust them to do a good job. So they introduce a remote control way for the organization's leaders to control employees' goals and hold them accountable. "It's not leadership," says Scholtes, "it's stupidity. It's the abdication of leadership. Performance appraisals are a quick and dirty way to do something [managers] don't have time to do well."

In most discussions about performance appraisal, he says, "there's an unspoken assumption that if only we knew how to do it right, we could fix what's wrong. What's not understood is there is no right way. Performance appraisal is inherently the wrong thing to do. The alternative is not some other form of performance appraisal, but an entirely different way of thinking about work."

The teachings of the late quality guru W. Edwards Deming point the way, Scholtes says. "You have to learn to think differently. The key word is system." If you understand the business as a system, then you can see that performance appraisal is not a way to improve the system."

Ninety-five percent of quality problems are built into an organization's system, Scholtes says, citing Deming. And you can't improve the performance of a system by improving the performance of individuals. Above average, outstanding or even heroic efforts on the part of individuals can't compensate for an inadequate or dysfunctional system. So why are you rating individuals?

To eliminate performance appraisal, Scholtes recommends something he calls "unbundling." Examine your performance-appraisal process and ask, why do we do this?

You'll likely come up with a list that includes: to give feedback, to decide who to promote, to create a basis for merit pay, to identify training needs to create a paper trail in case of legal action and so on. Decide which of those purposes are important to you and how you can best accomplish them without using appraisals. "Remove the various purposes from the fragile cart called performance appraisal, and devise ways to do them that will succeed," says Scholtes.

Impossible, you say? Talk to Dorothy Gill, vice president of human resources at Parkview Episcopal Medical Center in Pueblo, CO. She was aware of Deming's warnings about the destructive impact of performance evaluation and attended a Scholtes workshop on eliminating the practice. She says she came back raring to go, but without a clear idea of how to begin unbundling.

She served on a task force of HR people from other health care organizations that created a model to follow for eliminating evaluations. She modified it to fit Parkview's culture, and went at it.

One of the avowed purposes of Parkview's performance evaluations was to give employees feedback. Gill substituted a process that came to be known as APOP. "We didn't like the word feedback—it's so unidirectional—so we said that until we figure out something else well call it 'the annual piece of paper,'" she says. "And it stuck."

This is no simple matter of a cute name change for the same piece of paper. The new system is 180 degrees different from the old evaluations, she says. Employees get a one-page agenda before the annual meeting with their managers. It includes questions such as: What things get in the way of you doing your job the way you'd like to be doing it? What kind of learning would you like to do? What quality-improvement process are you working on that you need help with?

Employees are not rated. "The intent is not for employees to come out hearing what their leader thinks of the quality of their work," says Gill. Some of that may come up in the conversation because of employees' need to know how they're doing, but the focus is on communication between manager and employee. "I always conceived of APOP as a temporary process, but when I mention doing away with it, I get resistance," she says. "Leaders feel they get good information, and employees like the individual attention. When I ask leaders why they need the process, they say, 'I'm so blooming busy, if you don't make me, I won't do it.'"

Gill admits that Parkview's attorneys were horrified at the idea of doing away with performance evaluations—until she asked them for examples of when evaluations actually helped them resolve a legal problem. "That's how I got them to back down," says Gill. "If there is a legal issue in separations, and 10 years of evaluations that say [the employee] met the standard all those years, they're not going to help you." Besides, she adds, the hospital has a discipline process in place that provides for coaching and counseling, and then verbal and written warnings. "A discipline process documents [performance problems] in real time, not on an annual basis" she adds.

Gill anticipated that dealing with compensation issues would be tougher. The merit pay built into the hospital's old evaluation system had always produced ill feelings; the difference in merit pay between people rated outstanding and those rated "meeting standard" was "maybe half a percent," she says. Still, "When we did away with [merit pay], we thought we would have unhappy people. But we talked to employees about Deming's philosophy and Scholtes' ideas—and we got nodding heads and agreement."

Of 1,300 employees, she says, maybe 30 felt they worked harder than anyone else in their positions and should get paid more. Gill continued to talk to those folks and gave them reading materials that explained the rationale for eliminating merit pay. Debate over the issue has largely disappeared, she says. "Maybe they just got tired of talking about it"

After it eliminated merit pay Parkveiw put into place a shared comp plan that gives each employee an equal share in a percentage of the budgeted bottom line. It's not a huge amount, says Gill, but employees pay attention to the figures that affect their shared compensation.

Clearly, organizations can find less-onerous alternatives to performance appraisal if they look for them. According to Scholtes, more companies are seeking alternatives or attempting too eliminate performance appraisal altogether. "Ten years ago, when I would talk about this, people looked at me like I was talking about burning the flag," he says. "Today, they're rarely so shocked or antagonistic about it They're genuinely puzzled about how to get rid of appraisals."—C.L.

What is this process that causes employees sleepless nights and leads *Fortune* 500 executives to cower in bathroom stalls? It often consists of a form, which the human resources department demands every manager complete on every employee every year. Bosses rate subordinates on how well they fulfilled a list of objectives, and the rating bestowed determines employees' annual salary increases. The annual appraisal meeting between boss and subordinate is also supposed to be an opportunity for the boss to give positive and negative feedback, to discuss training and development needs, and to set new objectives that will be evaluated at next year's meeting.

That's a generic summary of the components of a "traditional" performance appraisal. The shortcomings of this annual cataloguing of bouquets and brickbats are obvious to anyone who has ever been on the giving or receiving end of one: a once-a-year "event" doesn't improve performance, it's too time-consuming for the benefits it provides, employees have no say in the process, and ratings are ill-defined and inconsistently applied. What's more, fear (on the employee's part) and loathing (on the manager's part) seem inevitable when salary and promotional decisions rest on one individual's judgment of another.

It's no wonder that a performance appraisal can be the single most demoralizing event in an employee's work year. Part of the problem is simple human nature. Most of us prefer to think of ourselves as denizens of Garrison Keillor's mythical Lake Wobegon, where the women are strong, the men are good-looking, and all the children are above average. "If you think you're above average, and you're rated 'competent' on a five-point scale, you're likely to be devastated or at least demotivated," points out Darcy Hitchcock, principal of Axis Performance Advisors in Battle Ground, WA, and a faculty member of the Association for Quality and Participation.

Hitchcock knows whereof she speaks. As a leader of AQP workshops on peer review around the country, she hears a litany of appraisal horror stories. She also recalls her own painful introduction to performance ratings when she was working in an organization. "I was a goody-two-shoes, Pollyanna employee," she says. "I looked at my rating, and my boss had given me a four on a five-point scale. He'd been giving me positive feedback on everything I did, but he hadn't given me a five. I didn't know what I needed to do to get a five, and he couldn't tell me what was wrong." Hitchcock was so upset by the rating, she says, she went AWOL—"a very big deal for me at that time"—and sat in a nearby park until she had collected herself. Looking back, she says, "My boss took an employee who was highly motivated and made me highly unmotivated in the space of a one-hour meeting." This was the reaction, mind you, to a *good* performance rating.

This kind of perverse effect, so easily set into motion by the dynamics of performance appraisal, has not gone unnoticed by those who manage and create such systems. Probably since performance reviews were introduced, which The *Wall Street Journal* credits to Lord & Taylor Company in 1914, they have been revised and refined. If anything, that tinkering process is accelerating. These days, most tinkerers recommend performance management, a more or less elaborate structure that provides for ongoing feedback between boss and employee and more frequent reviews of performance. Meanwhile, some contend it's time to stop refining a practice as damaging and demoralizing as performance appraisal. It's time, they say, to eliminate the whole thing (see sidebar).

COMMON PRACTICES, COMMON PROBLEM

Since that first performance review at Lord & Taylor 82 years ago, the procedure has become endemic in corporate America. The *WSJ* estimates that some 70 million U.S. workers receive annual performance evaluations

A 1995 survey among executives at 218 companies, conducted by New York-based William Mercer Inc., found that managers and technical/knowledge workers are virtually always subject to formal performance evaluations. The survey paints a picture of the most common performance-evaluation practices:

- Immediate supervisors conduct the reviews at 99 percent of the companies, although employees also evaluate themselves at two-thirds of the companies. Sixty percent make no use of less-traditional evaluators—peers, subordinates, or internal and external customers.
- Employees are most often rated on goals (at 78 percent of the companies) and results (72 percent); other common measures include responsibilities (65 percent), competencies (61 percent), and behaviors (58 percent).
- The most popular rating system is a narrative evaluation with an overall numeric score, used by 60 percent of respondents. Other systems include: using an overall numeric score (33 percent), writing a narrative description with no numeric score (26 percent), and ranking each employee in a work group from best to worst (20 percent).

The majority of Mercer's respondents had either made changes to their performance-evaluation system in the last two years or planned to do so. The most common reason cited: simple dissatisfaction with the existing one.

A 1993 survey conducted by the Pittsburgh-based training company Development Dimensions International (DDI) and the Society for Human Resources Management among 1,149 respondents—human resources managers, and managers and nonmanagement employees in their organizations—found rampant dissatisfaction with the peformance-review system. And the distress cut across job types; managers and nonmanagers alike were equally critical of their systems. The top frustrations:

- Lack of ongoing review. An annual review is "about as pleasant as a trip to the dentist" one respondent observed. Without periodic updates, people don't have the information they need to understand their ratings or to improve their performance.
- Lack of employee involvement. Respondents didn't feel they had control over their goals and objectives, nor did they understand how their objectives related to the organization's overall business goals.
- Lack of appropriate rewards. Respondents complained that they were neither compensated nor recognized for good performance.

So the surveys confirm what we might suspect: Traditional performance evaluations are frustrating to all, if not downright destructive. Which brings us back to the often-asked question, why have the damn things anyhow?

Everyone seems to have a list of answers to that question, but we'll distill them down to these general categories: to align individuals' goals and objectives with the organization's; to give individuals feedback on their performance, the ultimate goal being, of course, to improve that performance; to pinpoint training and development needs; to provide a basis for merit increases and promotional decisions; and to document poor performance in case it becomes necessary to defend personnel decisions in court.

STRETCHING THE ENVELOPE

How well *any* performance evaluation can satisfy those objectives is a matter of some debate, but most agree that a once-a-year appraisal simply can't be stretched to cover all of them. The standard solution to that problem is performance management, which includes performance reviews, coaching sessions, performance-tracking and goal-setting. Alice Pescuric, vice president of training and development technologies at DDI, offers a succinct definition of performance management: "A system that helps people manage their actions to help their organization achieve its goals."

That would also be a pretty good definition of management in general. Essentially, a performance-management system is a blueprint for the classic approach to effective management. Its requirements and steps—set objectives with employees, measure their progress, offer regular feedback on how they're doing, find out where problems lie, coach them when they need help, and offer rewards and reinforcement—guide managers who might be less than willing or able to take those steps on their own.

While there's nothing new about performance management, it seems to be gathering momentum. It provides a way to build accountability into the goal-setting and feedback process, and it can encourage manager and employee to share responsibility for understanding the business, gathering data, and evaluating performance. "There's a huge emphasis these days on performance management," says Susan Gebelein, senior vice president at Personnel Decisions International in Minneapolis. While formal performance appraisals are still a part of that process, she says, performance management focuses on ongoing performance and employee development, and assessments are more likely to come from multiple sources—team members, peers or customers—as well as an individual's boss.

"Ongoing" is a key to making performance management work. For one thing, frequent performance checks make reviews less onerous for both employee and manager: An employee who is getting off track has a chance to improve, and the manager can offer assistance before the employee derails. For another, the day of cast-in-stone objectives is past, says Charlene Reiss, a New York consultant with Boston-based Forum Corp. "Ever-changing business and customer requirements demand a more flexible and fluid system."

The performance goals you define in April may not be valid in January, she points out. "Look at AT&T Credit [one of the operations AT&T is in the process of spinning off]. What was a priority to them when they set goals last year is totally irrelevant today. Now they want to make the organization look attractive to buyers." The nature of business today demands a performance-management system that will accommodate sudden changes in strategic direction, she adds.

A CULTURAL SHIFT

Just as many organizations expect employees to take responsibility for their own career development, they also want employees at least to share responsibility for managing their performance. Instead of waiting for the annual review time to roll around, says Reiss, people need to learn to ask, "How am I doing?"

"Every time I ask for feedback, I get a review on my performance," she says. "Given the nature of my work, I have to be able to elicit feedback from the people I work with. When I go out on a call with an account executive, I make it a regular part of my working with that individual to ask what went well, what could have gone better. It's my responsibility to ask. I can't sit back and wait for my performance review at the end of the year."

The nature of organizations has changed, she points out, and that cultural shift has changed relationships. Managers who once had six direct reports now have 30—and half of them may be working on projects with which the manager is only tangentially involved. The upshot is that employees must learn to initiate requests for feedback or coaching on their own. For their part, managers need to create an atmosphere that encourages such individual initiative and to communicate this shift in the relationship, says Reiss: "In order for me as your manager to help you improve, I need your assistance. You need to take ownership."

EMPLOYEE-DRIVEN

When Ceridian, an HR services and defense electronics company in Minneapolis, substituted performance management for its old appraisal system, it added a twist: Its forms reside on a LAN system, so employees and managers can update objectives and their progress on them continuously. The electronic tool makes the process as efficient as possible and drives the communication between manager and employee, says Barbara Magusin, director of training development for Ceridian's human resources group.

At this point, the system is divorced from either ratings or compensation. "Our old system was a traditional process—an annual appraisal tied closely to salary action; you were told how you were doing at the same time you were told whether you got a raise or not," she explains. "There was also a numerical rating tied to some verbiage." It was helpful to some degree, she acknowledges. "Certain people like to know what grade they got. Unfortunately, it was not very helpful in terms of what, specifically, you were doing right. We needed something better."

The result is a performance management tool that guides the conversation between employee and manager. "It's used at least quarterly, so an employee can assume four meetings per year at a minimum," Magusin says. "Employees own the process—the tool actually resides on their own PC. They add data to it, set the meeting with their manager, and lead the conversation."

Employees use the system to write a performance plan that includes work objectives, dates reviewed, the resources required, and actions necessary to achieve those objectives. Quarterly meetings allow employees and managers to assess objectives against the goals of the business and to tweak those that might be out of step with current needs.

The system imposes discipline on busy managers, says Magusin. And since managers clear their calendars two days a quarter for perfomance management meetings with subordinates, even shy or reluctant employees are ensured access. "I send out my objectives and [my employees] see my objectives as I give them to my manager. That's a signal to employees: It's time to do this. But because employees own this process, and it benefits them so much, they're happy to keep managers honest, so to speak."

Allowing employees to take responsibility for their own performance defuses the adversarial nature of the appraisal, says Jerry Sterner, a consultant with Kepner-Tregoe Incorporated in Princeton, NJ. "The focus should be on creating a performance plan that allows people to know exactly what's expected of them. How are we going to measure results? What will success look like? Then, at the end of the quarter, there's no disagreement about where we stand. We ironed out all those things up front."

Too often, he says, employees have had no input into the process and don't know what results they're expected to produce. "Timely input that guides performance in the future—that's the catalyst that gets people to want to take on responsibility. Clear expectations, measurement, consequences, and feedback allow people to take accountability for their own performance."

Sterner, a former plant manager, confesses he used to hate the yearly appraisal cycle. He considered the process mandated by his company so demotivating, in fact, that he substituted his own. "We laid out plans so people saw the appraisal system as an opportunity to review their progress throughout the year. I laid out objectives and sat down with the people who reported to me. I asked them, 'What part of this can you sign up for?' We'd determine what was important about those things. We'd also lay out measurements around those important goals: What do we mean by improved quality? Increased compliance to specification? What are we talking about? We all had the same understanding of expectations and actual performance. At the end of the year," he says, "there was little difference of opinion between how I assessed their performance and how they did."

Yes, joint objective-setting, negotiation, explaining and coaching take more time on the supervisor's part, he admits. But the process gets more ownership and commitment from people than if they're handed objectives and expected to comply. "It's 'pay me now or pay me later'," says consultant Sterner. "You can put effort into laying out clear expectations, measurements, feedback and consequences, or nurse everyone along and put out fires all year long, and then start it all over again the next year."

LINE OF SIGHT

One of the objectives of a coherent performance management system is to focus employees' "line of sight"; the system should enable them to see how their own objectives tie to the business objectives of the organization. A common way to do that is to formalize the method Sterner intuitively devised as a plant manager: Desirable objectives, goals, results—call them what you will—cascade down from top to bottom.

International Thomsen Publishing is a 4,000-employee collection of some 30 publishing companies that range in size from 20 to 600 employees, each of which had its own performance-appraisal system. ITP recently introduced a process throughout the organization that consists of performance-planning, ongoing review and coaching, and a performance review at the end of the process. Part of the goal was to strengthen the connection between company objectives and performance criteria.

"We wanted to tie the process into the actual business cycle of the organization," says Ron Frederick, vice president of human resources and organizational development at ITP's Stamford, CT, headquarters. Business planning for the next year begins in late fall throughout the organization, he explains. Managers and employees then translate those corporate goals into goals and objectives for every individual. Performance reviews are held company-wide in January and February.

Frederick characterizes the system as a top-down, bottom-up collaboration that helps employees feel as if they're part of the process rather than its victims. "There's nothing particularly earthshaking about [this system]," he says, "but the way we'd been doing it hadn't accomplished those goals."

More and more frequently, organizations want "line of sight" to mean more than the ability to connect your individual objectives to this year's sales or profit goals. They also want the behaviors you use to accomplish your goals to align with the corporate culture and values. That means employees are evaluated not only on results they achieve, but how they achieve them.

Edward Ridolfi, vice president of education, development, and training for The McGraw-Hill Companies, a New York publishing operation with 17,000 employees, explains how such a dual-purpose system applies to his job. One of his goals is to have McGraw-Hill University, a new "corporate college," operating by a specific date. His boss will evaluate the ways in which he goes about doing that and the dimensions or specific behaviors he uses to achieve his goal, as well as whether or not he meets it. The site will not only be operating, for example, but he must have collaborated effectively with others within and outside the organization to get it up and running.

In other words, Ridolfi explains, "I'm rated not only on accomplishing my goals, but on accomplishing them with specific behaviors." Those behaviors are measured by observations from peers and his subordinates. "I or my manager contact people I work with to see if I've involved them or if I've just been directing them." The system is designed to encourage leaders to collaborate with their people, he says, to encourage them to put forth their best efforts.

It's a different process from the company's previous appraisal system, which was by-the-book, management-by-objectives. "We modified it because of discontent with the mechanical aspects of goal-setting," he says. "In this age of cooperation and team-building, managers are not directing but managing through relationships. There was no way [in our old system] to include those behaviors we thought were important. [Our current program] has the best of the MBO stuff, but also a series of dimensions or behaviors."

LINKING UP SYSTEMS

A strict MBO evaluation system generated similar dissatisfaction at Sprint Corporation in Westwood, KS. "The kind of action-planning, MBO meetings supervisors used to have with their folks were not only not effective, but sometimes detrimental," says Karen Mailliard, vice president of human resources development for the telecommunications giant. "People could get good ratings if they met their numbers, even if they left bodies in their wake."

In 1991, Sprint began to define its core dimensions—leadership, communication, management, personal effectiveness, professional knowledge, customer focus and team approach—and the behaviors that described them. The CEO considered the exercise so important that he wordsmithed sections of the first draft with Mailliard's staff. The dimensions became the foundation for Sprint's "Link" approach to performance management. Each of the company's human resources systems—performance review, training and development, succession planning and compensation decisions—are linked to the same set of behaviors.

The emphasis on dimensions, explains Mailliard, "says that it's important to us that people made their customer service numbers, for example, but it's equally important how they did the job. In other words, is there evidence that they used leadership and communication [behaviors] to accomplish the job? Or maybe they didn't meet their numbers, but if they performed these behaviors, they should get credit for that."

A 360-degree feedback process links to the same dimensions and behaviors. Four subordinates, four peers, the boss, and the individual complete a 55-item questionnaire—recording their answers with a telephone voice-prompt system, naturally enough—that provides a composite rating, and a picture of strengths and developmental needs. This information is used to craft an individual development plan that boss and subordinate create together. Sprint's Development Guide, a catalog of activities, books, and training courses, is also keyed to the same seven dimensions.

The Link performance management system piloted in 1994; 75 percent of Sprint's salaried employees will be using it by the end of 1996. Mailliard characterizes it as a vast improvement over the old MBO process. "The improvement in understanding how the company's business objectives tie to department goals and individual goals is out of sight," she says. The benefits were obvious to her when employees attended training on the Link system. "The feedback we got was, 'This is the first time in my life I understood how what I do supports my vice president.' It helps them focus on what is really important."

But it wasn't an easy change for all—like some engineers. "They never thought about *how* they accomplish a project. The concept was foreign to them," says Mailliard. "Or a sales guy, who'd say, 'Who cares how I meet my revenue goals?' So we had to say, 'Let's talk about this.' It's a real mind shift for folks to understand they're paid and rated on *how* they do the job."

THE TAR PIT OF PAY

You knew we had to bring it up, didn't you? When it comes to connecting performance evaluations with merit pay, most experts advise against it—unless your organization has a well-defined, pay-for-performance compensation structure.

A performance management system that requires several reviews throughout the year is one way to make sure that employees' focus is on the feedback rather than on translating their "exceeds expectations" rating into dollars. Mini-reviews that check an individual's progress against goals can disconnect money from development issues. Other techniques include removing ratings from the appraisal process so that merit increases are a separate managerial decision or separating the due dates for reviews and salary decisions by several months.

Then there's the straightforward approach. "In the best performance review I ever had," says Forum consultant Reiss, "my boss said, 'Here's your increase. Here's why. Now here's your review.' I paid attention. Otherwise, you're sitting there thinking, 'Let's get to the dollars.'"

Part of the goal in reinventing the performance-appraisal process at ITP, says Frederick, was to disconnect annual reviews from compensation discussions by as much as three months. The new review system eliminated ratings and substituted narrative in their place.

Under the new system, managers rank employees to decide how to distribute the salary pool available for the work group. The objective of this exercise, says Frederick, is to give managers a better sense of the overall strengths and weaknesses of their staffs. "The ranking is not shared with the employee," he says. "If an employee is getting no increase or a small increase, the manager will explain the reason why. It may not be solely performance, but other factors such as level of pay and pay scale."

PAPER TRAILS

Regardless of the system an organization uses, the simple fact is it will only be as good or forthright or helpful as the managers who use it. And no matter how rigidly structured, tightly controlled and multifaceted your performance management system, it can't remove the "curse" altogether. Employees, being human, are still going to dread receiving evaluations. And managers, being human, are still going to dislike giving them. So why not drop evaluations and concentrate on teaching managers to communicate regularly and honestly with employees?

"You might be able to get away with that if you had a development culture," says Jeff Stoner, a senior consultant with Personnel Decisions International. That means a solid, ongoing feedback and development process for employees, "But you'd still need to support salary and promotion decisions," he says.

And then there are termination decisions. Accurate evaluations of poor performers who end up getting fired offer documentation in case employees later bring wrongful-termination lawsuits. "If you abolish performance appraisals, you are going to give a summer home to every plaintiff's lawyer," says Jonathan Segal, an attorney with the Philadelphia law firm of Wolf, Block, Schorr and Solis-Cohn.

Segal, a management attorney who speaks to human resources audiences about performance-appraisal issues, contends that even when lay-offs are made for economic reasons, performance often forms the basis for decisions about who goes and who stays. "You didn't eliminate jobs," he says. "You restructured. Why did you give Jean's responsibilities to John and not vice versa? It comes down to the fact that you thought John was a better performer."

And how do you demonstrate who is the better performer without documentation? asks Segal. "If those in management positions merely say they're going on merit, it will get you into court in a minute." Former employees will contend they were laid off because they are female, young, old, Jewish, Catholic, disabled—fill in the blank. "The burden is on the employer to prove it wasn't discrimination," says Segal. "Without a performance appraisal, I have nothing concrete."

Many organizations consider protection against litigation one of the top priorities of their performance-appraisal systems, says Segal. "But because managers don't like to give bad news, they overevaluate substantially. The practical effect is that performance appraisals are done so poorly, they are used against the company in litigation."

He describes how inaccurate appraisals backfire in court: You fire an employee because of poor performance. However, your last evaluation of that person is "excellent" because you rated everyone "excellent." The company ends up in court, defending itself against a wrongful-termination suit. The plaintiff's lawyer says, "Why did you let this person go?" You say: "For poor performance." The plaintiff's lawyer points to exhibit A, the last performance appraisal, and asks, "Were you lying then or are you lying now?" Says Segal: "You're dead."

ACCOUNTABILITY

When it comes to honestly reviewing performance, McGraw-Hill's Ridolfi acknowledges, "Managers don't want to do this. They don't want to tell anyone, 'You're a two.' But that's your job. Step up to the plate or go sit in the dugout."

Ridolfi sees performance appraisal in terms of accountability. In corporate America, he points out, companies are accountable to their stockholders, just as managers are accountable for their employees, and employees are accountable for their performance. Without some kind of performance-review system, Ridolfi asks, "How will you know where you're going or whether you got there?"

That said, he thinks McGraw-Hill's current system is a transitional solution. "I think the rating system will go away," he says. "[Performance review] will become a dialogue between manager and associates, a goal-setting process that is summarized by a narrative. It won't be a formalized or specific evaluation of performance by the so-called boss or supervisor, but by all who are involved in a significant way in accomplishing the objectives."

ITP's Frederick echoes Ridolfi. Of his company's new performance management system, he says, "We don't pretend we have the answer here. But we'll try it for a couple of years and fine-tune it as we go. Then we'll look at it again and see how it's working for us."

He acknowledges that "the best appraisal system would be no appraisal system, but one in which people got good, honest feedback and knew what they needed to do to improve. It ain't that simple."

Indeed not. "I don't think the corporation is ready for that yet," says Ridolfi. "Employees are ready for it, but corporate America isn't."

FUTURE VISION

by Michael A. Verespej

Kathleen Cote isn't your typical CEO. Indeed, her first job in the business world in 1971 was as a $100-a-week clerk for CTI Cryogenics in Waltham, Mass. And she took that job only after she couldn't find a teaching job to her liking. But it is more than just her background and her climb to the top from the bottom that makes Kathleen Cote different from most other CEOs. From the instant you meet her, you sense a directness and openness that many CEOs lack. There's no preoccupation with any other task or eyes that dart off in another direction. This is the time that the newly appointed CEO of Computervision Corporation has set aside for you, and she even apologizes—even though it is clearly unnecessary—when she stops to take a very short call from the company chairman.

It's also clear that Cote was driving the company toward a new future even before she became CEO in November. She headed the operating committee that developed the strategy that turned around the fortunes of the once high-flying CAD/CAM hardware and software giant after losses of nearly $1.3 billion from 1991 through 1993. That led to Cote becoming president and chief operating officer in December 1995 and the decision six months later to name her as CEO.

Still, her rise to CEO wasn't only because of her business savvy. She has a reputation for delivering projects on time as well as an ability to focus on the task at hand and explain it to others. And she does all that with a people-management style that Computervision needed.

But above all Cote knows how she wants to run a company.

She clearly explains her vision of what the $300 million dollar company must do to succeed and what she must do as the CEO to make that happen. There is no hint of a personal agenda, only an unwavering focus and a commitment to making Computervision—and its employees—successful.

"The most important thing for any organization is to have everyone focused on the same objectives and to have the objectives clearly defined," insists Cote. "The expectations we set for ourselves are geared toward achieving those objectives, and then all individual performance objectives are aligned to those corporate objectives. The top three things I am working on have to be the top three things everyone is working on. We are only going to be successful together."

With that in mind, Cote had managers identify where Computervision was winning business and losing business, shifted the focus of its business to providing product-development solutions through software and services, and clearly defined for all employees the objectives of the company.

As a result, the Bedford, Mass., company posted a net income of $9.8 million in 1994, turned a $22.8 million profit in 1995, and made a slight earnings improvement in 1996 to $26 million.

However, Computervision lost $5.9 million in the fourth quarter of 1996, abruptly ending a string of 11 consecutive profitable quarters. That caused earnings per share—which some analysts had predicted might reach as high as 74 cents per share for the full year—to dip to 40 cents per share for 1996 compared to 43 cents the year before. What's more, Computervision's earnings per share from continuing software business operations in the fourth quarter of 1996 was just nine cents per share before a restructuring charge of $11.5 million and another $3 million charge associated with the purchase of an English technology firm. With the charge, Computervision lost 13 cents per share from continuing software business operations in the fourth quarter.

But, despite the unexpected fourth quarter loss, analysts still see solid earnings for Computervision in 1997.

Indeed, Thomas Galloway, a senior vice president with Kadick Inc., a Charlottesville, Va., investment firm, is predicting a 33% annual increase in net income both this year and next, pushing net income to $84.8 million by 1998. Along the way, he expects the stock price to double. "I don't think the stock is getting any respect. I expect a price as high as $19 by the end of the year. There is considerable upside potential with limited downside risk."

In addition to the game plan, analysts like Cote's open and direct management style that has turned the once-isolated ivory towers at Computervision inside-out.

"On my first day on the job," says Cote, "everyone got an e-mail, telling them that I had moved into the ivory tower. I told them: 'It's lonely. Stop by and see me.'"

What's more, Cote frequently uses e-mail to ask employees for their thoughts and has coffee in the building's atrium each Friday morning. "I chat with everyone, and everyone can chat with me about whatever they want. And I encourage them to come by and see me."

"You never know what other people will say about my management style," says the Computervision CEO. "But I would say that I am very open. I believe that I am accessible. I see myself as someone that people can talk to and believe they will be listened to. But you will also hear back from me a direct, honest viewpoint."

It's a management style that seems to work well for Computervision employees and please Wall Street as well.

"People now feel that they can provide input and have their voice heard," says one manager. "There is more excitement among employees because there is now a defined strategy. Having an overall strategy makes it more satisfying for individuals. It is easier to contribute because you know what needs to be done."

With the entire workforce involved, Computervision products are "gaining significant momentum" in the market, says Sheila Ennis, senior technology analyst with Hambrecht & Quist LLC, a San Francisco investment bank.

A case in point: contracts to use Computervision's Electronic Product Definition (EPD) approach to product development were signed in the second half of 1996 by Rolls Royce Aerospace Group, Boeing Commercial Airline Group, Lockheed Martin Astronautics, Volvo GM Heavy Trucks, and BMW Rolls Royce. Their interest in EPD? Its family of software products "represents a significant advantage over the competition's offerings," says Ennis. The products allow everyone in an organization and even its customers and suppliers to store data and designs so everyone involved can electronically create, manage, develop, test, share data, and participate in the ongoing product-development process.

"The bottom line is that Computervision has battled back to become, once again, the industry leader it was for many years," says Dave Weisberg, publisher of the "Engineering Automation Report," an Englewood, Colorado-based newsletter. "Computervision has a better grasp than other software vendors of what it takes [for users of its products] to be successful. [Computervision realizes] the solution to their customers' problems is an understanding of how the entire product life cycle can benefit from using today's design and data-management tools."

That credit again goes to Cote, say analysts, for defining the objectives of the company and for defining them within the context of the EPD approach.

"Every company must start by asking itself, 'What businesses are we in; what are the values and benefits we can bring to the market?' and how that maps out in relation to our customers, our competitors, industry needs, and individual markets," says Cote. "Then you have to make sure that you have a sustainable advantage and deliver and execute against a business plan that is a financial plan for profitability."

"Our marketing, our product development, our financial method, and our rewards are all aligned to the same strategy and tied to EPD," she asserts. "I sit down with the heads of marketing and go through their plans program by program and ask whether it has a direct link to the operating plan and our strategy."

A dictatorial approach? Hardly. Rather, Cote is convinced such face-to-face meetings are integral to reminding managers of the need to stick to the objectives. "I'm a firm believer that if you stay on course and never get off, you will have great success. There really is no surprise if you have a plan in place. When you have a plan, the challenge is to continue to cycle through that process to identify threats and opportunities and to redirect as necessary to make sure that you stay on course.

"I have high expectations on results, on meeting objectives, and on people doing what they say they are going to do," says Cote. "I don't like surprises. If something is not going right, let me know what you can do about it to work through the issues and the problem. I try to be direct and honest with my people and tell them what is on my mind, and I expect [them] to do the same."

Part of that directness certainly comes from the road Cote took to the top. Even though she displayed an innate grasp of the computer industry during a seven-year stint early in her business career as director of manufacturing at Wang Laboratories Inc., Lowell, Massachusetts, she hasn't forgotten where she started.

"I know what it is like to be down in an organization and wondering how—or if—you are contributing to the overall success of the company," she says. As a result, she insists on "involving people at every level of the organization."

"If we are going to succeed as a company," says Cote, "everyone has to understand and know the objectives of the company. When everyone is aligned behind the same goals and is accountable to those goals, you can achieve more."

With the sale of its Open Service Solutions business expected to be completed this quarter, a slimmed-down Computervision will be in position to build on its strengths and grow revenues and profits. The sale will also help reduce long-term debt at Computervision by nearly 65% to $50 million.

Because of the changes, Kadick's Galloway conservatively predicts that Computervision will increase earnings from 43 cents per share in 1995 to $1.24 per share in 1998. Hambrecht & Quist's Ennis is even more optimistic. She anticipates earnings per share of $1.16 in 1997. But, speculates Galloway, "It may take two or more quarters for investors to regain confidence in Computervision's ability to consistently grow software revenues and earnings."

Clearly, though, Cote is intent on growth in both of those areas.

"In 1996 we demonstrated that we could bring our customers value, win new customers, and be seen as a growth company," says Cote. "Now that we have been through some level of a successful transition, we are poised to grow. We have a single strategy, our EPD strategy. We will align behind it and focus on implementing that strategy. We want to be the first company on the list when customers think of who can best help them to be successful in implementing and improving their product-development process."

Indeed, that is what Weisberg of "Engineering Automation Report" considers a real strength of Computervision. "When you talk to the top people at Computervision, their focus is inevitably on their users and what these [customer] organizations are accomplishing" with the EPD products.

Cote, however, won't be content with just a few short-term successes. "We need to grow the top line between 10% and 20% every year," says Cote. "That is our objective, along with profits that increase by 25% annually at the operating income levels. That is the kind of growth we need."

To achieve those objectives, everyone must be "going in the same direction so that each person understands where he or she fits into the overall strategy, is fully engaged, and feels that he or she is part of making the strategy happen and helping the company to grow.

"I want Computervision to be a place where people derive personal growth, success, and satisfaction by being part of a company that values their contribution and encourages their participation and leadership," says Cote. "It is my job to knock down the barriers so that people can work together and contribute fully and to make sure that the opportunities exist for personal growth. I have to make sure employees can focus their behavior behind a strategy and that they can play a role in its implementation and see its results."

She says, an "end of the day" yardstick sometimes is the best measure of whether the company is on track and succeeding. "As a company," asserts Cote, "at the end of the day we need to have improved shareholder value, and that is driven by how you bring your customers value, and all that is driven from employees understanding what we are trying to do."

Just as important, she says, "At the end of the day, each worker has to feel that he or she is continuing to help the company achieve its objectives, each worker has be satisfied with his or her contributions toward that, and each worker has to feel that he or she has learned something that contributed to their personal growth.

"If at the end of the day, the people in the company are satisfied that they are contributing, then we are moving forward."

PARABLES OF LEADERSHIP

by W. Chan Kim and Renée A. Mauborgne

Students of management have sought for years to understand why the very same activities lead to renewal in one company and to more-of-the-same performance in another. Almost always, the answer that is given is leadership, the ability to inspire confidence and support among the men and women on whose competence and commitment performance depends. Yet while we intuitively recognize leaders whenever we meet them, it has never been easy to answer the question: What is leadership? The essence of leadership cannot be reduced to a series of personal attributes nor confined to a set of particular roles and activities. It is like the challenge of describing a bowl: we can describe a bowl in terms of the clay from which it is made. But a true picture must include the hollow that is carved into the clay—the unseen space that defines the bowl's shape and capacity.

We have searched for ways to capture the unseen space of leadership. The longer this search went on, the more we found ourselves talking about lessons which one of us first heard as a youth in the temples of Kyung Nam province of Korea. These lessons came from Oriental masters who taught the wisdom of life through parables, and they gave us a fresh understanding of the essence of leadership. They provided us with the inspiration and insights we needed to create parables that could capture the unseen space of leadership.

The parables that follow show the essential qualities of leadership and the acts that define a leader: the ability to hear what is left unspoken, humility, commitment, the value of looking at reality from many vantage points, the ability to create an organization that draws out the unique strengths of every member. These parables provide an occasion for reflecting on the essence of leadership as well as on one's own work and life.

THE SOUND OF THE FOREST

Back in the third century A.D., the King Ts'ao sent his son, Prince T'ai, to the temple to study under the great master Pan Ku. Because Prince T'ai was to succeed his father as king, Pan Ku was to teach the boy the basics of being a good ruler. When the prince arrived at the temple, the master sent him alone to the Ming-Li Forest. After one year, the prince was to return to the temple to describe the sound of the forest.

When Prince T'ai returned, Pan Ku asked the boy to describe all that he could hear. "Master," replied the prince, "I could hear the cuckoos sing, the leaves rustle, the hummingbirds hum, the crickets chirp, the grass blow, the bees buzz, and the wind whisper and holler." When the prince had finished, the master told him to go back to the forest to listen to what more he could hear. The prince was puzzled by the master's request. Had he not discerned every sound already?

For days and nights on end, the young prince sat alone in the forest listening. But he heard no sounds other than those he had already heard. Then one morning, as the prince sat silently beneath the trees, he started to discern faint sounds unlike those he had ever heard before. The more acutely he listened, the clearer the sounds became. The feeling of enlightenment enveloped the boy. "These must be the sounds the master wished me to discern," he reflected.

When Prince T'ai returned to the temple, the master asked him what more he had heard. "Master," responded the prince reverently, "when I listened most closely, I could hear the unheard—the sound of flowers opening, the sound of the sun warming the earth, and the sound of the grass drinking the morning dew." The master nodded approvingly. "To hear the unheard," remarked Pan Ku, "is a necessary discipline to be a good ruler. For only when a ruler has learned to listen closely to the people's hearts, hearing their feelings uncommunicated, pains unexpressed, and complaints not spoken of, can he hope to inspire confidence in his people, understand when something is wrong, and meet the true needs of his citizens. The demise of states comes when leaders listen only to superficial words and do not penetrate deeply into the souls of the people to hear their true opinions, feelings, and desires."

FIRE AND WATER

In the fourth century B.C., hidden within the state of Lu, lay the district over which Duke Chuang governed. The district, though small, had prospered exceedingly well under Chuang's predecessor. But since Chuang's appointment to the post, its affairs had deteriorated markedly. Taken aback by the sad turn of events, Chuang set out to the Han mountain to seek the wisdom of the great master Mu-sun.

When the duke arrived at the mountain, he found the great master sitting peacefully on a small rock looking out at the adjoining valley. After the duke had explained his situation to Mu-sun, he waited with bated breath for the great master to speak. Contrary to Chuang's expectation, however, the master whispered not a word. Rather, he smiled softly and gestured to the duke to follow him.

Silently they walked until before them lay the Tan Fu River, whose end could not be seen, it was so long and broad. After meditating on the river, Mu-sun set out to build a fire. When at last it was lit and the flames were aglow, the master had Chuang sit by his side. There they sat for hours on end as the fire burned brilliantly into the night.

With the coming of dawn, when the flames no longer danced, Mu-sun pointed to the river. Then, for the first time since the duke's arrival, the great master spoke, "Now do you understand why you are unable to do as your predecessor did—to sustain the greatness of your district?"

Chuang looked perplexed; he understood now no better than before. Slowly shame enveloped the duke. "Great master," he said, "forgive my ignorance, for the wisdom you impart I cannot comprehend." Mu-sun then spoke for the second time. "Reflect, Chuang, on the nature of the fire as it burned before us last night. It was strong and powerful. Its flames leapt upward as they danced and cried in vainglorious pride. No strong trees nor wild beasts could have matched its mighty force. With ease it could have conquered all that lay in its path.

"In contrast, Chuang, consider the river. It starts as but a small stream in the distant mountains. Sometimes it flows slowly, sometimes quickly, but always it sails downward, taking the low ground as its course. It willingly permeates every crack in the earth and willingly embraces every crevice in the land, so humble is its nature. When we listen to the water, it can scarcely be heard. When we touch it, it can scarcely be felt, so gentle is its nature.

"Yet in the end, what is left of the once mighty fire? Only a handful of ashes. For the fire is so strong, Chuang, that it not only destroys all that lies in its path but eventually falls prey to its own strength and is consumed. It is not so with the calm and quiet river. For as it was, so it is, so it will always be: forever flowing, growing deeper, broader, ever more powerful as it journeys down to the unfathomable ocean, providing life and sustenance to all."

After a moment of silence, Mu-sun turned to the duke. "As it is with nature, Chuang, so it is with rulers. For as it is not fire but water that envelops all and is the well of life, so it is not mighty and authoritative rulers but rulers with humbleness and deep-reaching inner strength who capture the people's hearts and are springs of prosperity to their states. Reflect, Chuang," continued the master, "on what type of ruler you are. Perhaps the answer that you seek will lie there."

Like a flash of lightning, the truth seized the duke's heart. No longer proud but embarrassud and uncertain, he looked up with his enlightened eye. Chuang was now blind to all but the sun rising over the river.

THE LESSON OF THE BABBLING BROOK

The time was the fourth century B.C., the period of the Warring States in China. The grand general of the Chin State was seated in his chamber in the king's palace with Meung, the soon-to-be-appointed general of the Third Division, at his side. A messenger, Lieutenant Yu, had just arrived with a report on the logistics of the upcoming battle between General Li's First Division and the Second Division of the Wei State, led by General Su.

"Grand General," said Lieutenant Yu, "I bring good news. The First Division enjoys a significant advantage—our troops outnumber the Second Division's four to one, weaponry is in abundant supply, and the regiment remains well fed. General Li bids me assure you that victory will be ours, the Chin flag will fly forever." As the grand general glanced at the report, a look of anguish came over his face. He clenched his fists and ordered Lieutenant Yu to dispatch reinforcements and return to the battlefield at once.

After the lieutenant had fled, the grand general walked over to the balcony and looked out to the horizon. "Alas," he said to Meung, "yet another division of our state will fall."

Meung was perplexed. "Grand General," he said, "forgive my impudence, but I fail to understand your conviction. General Li's division has many times the manpower and weaponry of General Su's division, and yet you are convinced victory will not be ours. How can this be?"

The grand general looked somberly at Meung but did not answer. Instead, he brought Meung to a large lake behind the palace. When the grand general and Meung were seated on a rock, the general threw a small piece of paper into the water. It did not move but simply floated on one spot. After observing the still piece of paper for some time; Meung became restless and inquired again: "Grand General, what does this mean? I have meditated on the paper for more than one hour and your lesson has not enlightened me nor provided the answer to my question."

Once again, the general did not respond but had Meung follow him. They walked until they came to a very narrow, babbling brook. Again the grand general threw a small piece of paper onto the water. This time it did not stand still but sailed swiftly along and vanished. The grand general turned to Meung, "Now do you understand why General Su's regiment will carry the day and not ours?"

Meung, still perplexed, asked the grand general to explain further. "Meung," said the general, "the first regiment is like the lake, large with much weaponry. But note General Li's position. He so arrogantly assumes victory that he does not fight. He has stationed himself behind the back line. It is not so with General Su. He is in the front line, side by side with his troops, and he has placed the rear of his regiment next to the river. His commitment to die in order to win will beget the troops' commitment in turn. Just as the babbling brook, which rushes in one direction, carries the paper easily while the large lake cannot, so it is that a regiment small in size but unified in commitment will win. Remember, weaponry and manpower are important, but it is the general's commitment that determines victory."

Four days later, Lieutenant Yu and his reinforcements arrived at the site of the battle. The Wei, not the Chin, flag graced the sky. The First Division had been defeated.

THE WISDOM OF THE MOUNTAIN

In ancient China, on top of Mount Ping stood a temple where the enlightened one, Hwan, dwelled. Of his many disciples, only one is known to us, Lao-li. For more than 20 years, Lao-li studied and meditated under the great master, Hwan. Although Lao-li was one of the brightest and most determined of disciples, he had yet to reach enlightenment. The wisdom of life was not his.

Lao-li struggled with his lot for days, nights, months, even years until one morning, the sight of a falling cherry blossom spoke to his heart. "I can no longer fight my destiny," he reflected. "Like the cherry blossom, I must gracefully resign myself to my lot." From that moment forth, Lao-li determined to retreat down the mountain, giving up his hope of enlightenment.

Lao-li searched for Hwan to tell him of his decision. The master sat before a white wall, deep in meditation. Reverently, Lao-li approached him. "Enlightened one," he said. But before he could continue, the master spoke, "Tomorrow I will join you on your journey down the mountain." No more needed to be said. The great master understood.

The next morning, before their descent, the master looked out into the vastness surrounding the mountain peak. "Tell me, Lao-li," he said, "what do you see?" "Master, I see the sun beginning to wake just below the horizon, meandering hills and mountains that go on for miles, and couched in the valley below, a lake and an old town." The master listened to Lao-li's response. He smiled, and then they took the first steps of their long descent.

Hour after hour, as the sun crossed the sky, they pursued their journey, stopping only once as they approached the foot of the mountain. Again Hwan asked Lao-li to tell him what he saw. "Great wise one, in the distance I see roosters as they run around barns, cows asleep in sprouting meadows, old ones basking in the late afternoon sun, and children romping by a brook." The master, remaining silent, continued to walk until they reached the gate to the town. There the master gestured to Lao-li, and together they sat under an old tree. "What did you learn today, Lao-li?" asked the master. "Perhaps this is the last wisdom I will impart to you." Silence was Lao-li's response.

At last, after long silence, the master continued. "The road to enlightenment is like the journey down the mountain. It comes only to those who realize that what one sees at the top of the mountain is not what one sees at the bottom. Without this wisdom, we close our minds to all that we cannot view from our position and so limit our capacity to grow and improve. But with this wisdom, Lao-li, there comes an awakening. We recognize that alone one sees only so much—which, in truth, is not much at all. This is the wisdom that opens our minds to improvement, knocks down prejudices, and teaches us to respect what at first we cannot view. Never forget this last lesson, Lao-li: what you cannot see can be seen from a different part of the mountains."

When the master stopped speaking, Lao-li looked out to the horizon, and as the sun set before him, it seemed to rise in his heart. Lao-li turned to the master, but the great one was gone. So the old Chinese tale ends. But it has been said that Lao-li returned to the mountain to live out his life. He became a great enlightened one.

THE WHEEL AND THE LIGHT

Back in the third century B.C., the outbreak of fighting following the collapse of the Qin Dynasty had just ended. In its place now stood the Han Dynasty, whose emperor, Liu Bang, had consolidated China into a unified empire for the first time. To commemorate the event, Liu Bang had invited high-ranking military and political officials, poets, and teachers to a grand celebration. Among them was Chen Cen, the master to whom Liu Bang had often gone for enlightenment during his campaign to unite China.

The celebration was in full swing. A banquet grander than any ever seen was being held. At the center table sat Liu Bang with his three heads of staff: Xiao He, who administered the logistics or unification; Han Xin, who organized and led the fighting activity; and Chang Yang, who formulated the diplomatic and political strategies. At another table sat Chan Cen and his three disciples.

While food was served, speeches given, honors presented, and entertainment performed, all looked on with pride and exhilaration—all except Chen Cen's three disciples, who sat awestruck. Only midway through the festivities did they utter their first words. "Master," they remarked, "all is grand, all is befitting, but at the heart of the celebration lies one enigma." Sensing his disciples' hesitation, the master gently encouraged them to continue.

"At the central table sits Xiao He," they proceeded. "Xiao He's knowledge of logistics cannot be refuted. Under his administration, the soldiers have always been well fed and properly armed, whatever the terrain. Next to him is Han Xin. Han Xin's military tactics are beyond reproach. He understands exactly where to ambush the enemy, when to advance, and when to retreat. He has won every battle he has led. Last is Chang Yang. Chang Yang sees the dynamics of political and diplomatic relations in his palm. He knows which states to form alliances with, how to gain political favors, and how to corner heads of states into surrendering without battle. This we understand well. What we cannot comprehend is the centerpiece of the table, the emperor himself. Liu Bang cannot claim noble birth, and his knowledge of logistics, fighting, and diplomacy does not equal that of his heads of staff. How is it, then, that he is emperor?"

The master smiled and asked his disciples to imagine the wheel of a chariot. "What determines the strength of a wheel in carrying a chariot forward?" he asked. After a moment of reflection, his disciples responded, "Is it not the sturdiness of the spokes, Master?" "But then, why is it," he rejoined, "that two wheels made of identical spokes differ in strength?" After a moment, the master continued, "See beyond what is seen. Never forget that a wheel is made not only of spokes but also of the space between the spokes. Sturdy spokes poorly placed make a weak wheel. Whether their full potential is realized depends on the harmony between them. The essence of wheelmaking lies in the craftsman's ability to conceive and create the space that holds and balances the spokes within the wheel. Think now, who is the craftsman here?"

A glimmer of moonlight was visible behind the door. Silence reigned until one disciple said, "But master, how does a craftsman secure the harmony between the spokes?" "Think of sunlight," replied the master. "The sun nurtures and vitalizes the trees and flowers. It does so by giving away its light. But in the end, in which direction do they all grow? So it is with a master craftsman like Liu Bang. After placing individuals in positions that fully realize their potential, he secures harmony among them by giving them all credit for their distinctive achievements. And in the end, as the trees and flowers grow toward the giver, the sun, individuals grow toward Liu Bang with devotion."

INDEX OF KEY TERMS